D1325931

CONTENTS

4 1991: A YEAR TO SAVOUR

5 GOLF COURSES OF GREAT BRITAIN AND IRELAND

FOREWORD

José-Maria Olazabal

I am delighted to provide the Foreword to the second edition of the *Benson and Hedges Golf Year*. This most colourful book is a review of the past season and a preview of 1991.

When I arrived at St Mellion for the Benson and Hedges International, one thing I did not want to look at was the European Order of Merit table. I had played reasonably well in the US Masters at Augusta, but in Europe I had registered very few pesetas against my name; it was already May, and the season was two and a half months old. Winning at St Mellion completely turned my year around. It was a very close finish between myself and Ian Woosnam, and whilst I would dearly love to retain my title in 1991, I pray that I will not have to hole a tricky downhill five-footer in front of all those watching ducks on the 18th green!

As well as being the watershed to my year, the win at St Mellion was especially pleasing because it was my first win in Britain since turning professional. I suppose it is ironic that it should have happened on a course designed by the American Jack Nicklaus.

Fortunately, for much of the year I was able to retain my St Mellion form. At Portmarnock in July I won my first tournament in Ireland,

and in September I had my first French victory, in the Lancôme Trophy near Paris.

The most frustrating times for me in 1990 were in the Open at St Andrews and at Medinah at the US Open. On both occasions I felt I played well from tee to green but ruined my chances through poor putting. If only I am able to putt as well in next year's Majors as I did at Firestone in the World Series last August! As that was my first win on American soil, I guess I will look back at 1990 as a year of firsts. The year ended well for me with a second red blazer for retaining my Japanese Masters title.

In 1991, it would be marvellous if I could add a different colour blazer to my wardrobe, although I'm sure that one English person in particular will be out to stop me! Nick's magnificent triumphs at Augusta and St Andrews are explored thoroughly in the *Benson and Hedges Golf Year*, as indeed are all of golf's important events worldwide. I am confident that you will find this book makes a highly entertaining and informative read . . . And if you study it carefully, you might discover how Europe is going to retain the Ryder Cup in September!

José-Maria Olazabal

BENSON and HEDGES
INTERNATIONAL OPEN

Lancôme Trophy (France)   *Carrolls Irish Open (Ireland)*   *NEC World Series (United States)*

THE CONQUISTADOR

Taiheiyo Masters (Japan)

Benson and Hedges International (England)

SPONSOR'S MESSAGE

We are very proud to welcome you to the second edition of the *Benson and Hedges Golf Year*.

A lot has happened in the world of golf over the past year, not least the continuing rise in the fortunes of European golf. Comment and analysis of this and much more can be found in this second edition. Editor Nick Edmund has once again produced a book of superb quality – built on the success of the highly acclaimed first edition. Over 150 of the best golf photographs have been included to ensure that in every respect this *Benson and Hedges Golf Year* is the best year-book on the market.

We are delighted that one of the world's top golfers and the current Benson and Hedges International Champion, José-Maria Olazabal, has generously given his time to write the foreword to the second edition. We wish him continued success in 1991.

Our long association with the Royal and Ancient game is therefore set to continue into the 1990s, not only through this magnificent year-book but also through the Benson and Hedges International at St Mellion in Cornwall.

Barry Jenner
Marketing Manager
Benson and Hedges

INTRODUCTION

We are confident that this second *Benson and Hedges Golf Year* is an improvement on the well-received first edition; hopefully it is as informative and readable as it is undoubtedly colourful. We have of course been greatly assisted by the fact that 1990 was an especially memorable year: a year dominated in many respects by the towering presence of an Englishman, Nick Faldo, and the continued rise in international stature of a young Spaniard, José-Maria Olazabal, who it may not have escaped your notice has provided the foreword to this edition – and unashamedly proud we are of it too!

From January to December, and from Europe to America, Japan to Australia, it was a riveting opening to the golfing decade – on and off the fairways. The *Benson and Hedges Golf Year* charts in detail all the major happenings and the leading personalities who made headlines around the world, the leading men and women, professionals and amateurs. In addition to looking back, the book looks forward to 1991 – to the Major championships, the Ryder and Walker Cups, and all the important national and international events on the golfing calendar.

For easy reference the 256 pages have been divided into five sections. Section One, '1990: A Year to Remember', is an editorial review summarizing and commenting on the major talking points of the past season. This is followed by an in-depth look at how the Masters at Augusta, the US Open at Medinah, the Open at St Andrews, and the USPGA at Shoal Creek were won and lost. A plethora of spectacular pictures accompanies detailed text which includes lively commentaries from four of golf's leading writers, Tim Glover, Derek Lawrenson, John Hopkins and David Davies.

The third section, 'Global Golf', draws together results from all over the world; again, for handy reference there are seven subsections: Europe, the United States, Australia, Japan, the Rest of the World, Seniors and Amateurs. In addition to comprehensive analyses there are numerous supporting photos.

This coming season, 1991, promises a great deal. In Section Four, with the help of two more of golf's renowned scribes, Dave Hamilton and Alistair Tait, we look ahead to the year's Major championships and the eagerly awaited Ryder Cup encounter at Kiawah Island as well as Great Britain and Ireland's defence of the Walker Cup at Portmarnock. Last year Nick Faldo won two of golf's grand slam events; at Augusta this year he attempts to achieve an unprecedented hat trick of Masters victories, and at Royal Birkdale he will be hoping to win his third Open Championship. These venues, together with the US Open at Hazeltine and the USPGA at Crooked Stick, are investigated. Finally those not content to merely read about golf will find Section Five particularly helpful, as it is a directory listing all golf clubs in Great Britain and Ireland, giving telephone numbers, addresses and course yardages.

As editor of the *Benson and Hedges Golf Year* I would like to take this opportunity to thank a few people without whom this second edition would not have made it to the first tee. At Partridge Press, Debbie Beckerman, Bipin Patel, Alison Tulett and Judith Wardman have been extremely supportive, as has Bob Brand, the book's Associate Editor. I'm sure you will agree that the photographs in this book, a great majority of which have been provided by Allsport, are outstanding. For help in selecting appropriate pictures I would like to thank two of Britain's top golf photographers, Dave Cannon and Matthew Harris.

Nick Edmund, 1 January 1991

I

1990
A YEAR TO REMEMBER

1990: A YEAR TO REMEMBER

Halcyon days

More than one golf magazine has suggested that 1990 was something less than a vintage year for golf. My, we have become spoilt of late! It was an outstanding year in so many respects; not all that happened was necessarily beneficial to golf's future well-being, but an unprecedented level of interest was generated nonetheless. The first year of the decade frequently saw history being created on the fairways and just off the fairways – in the rough, so to speak, there was plenty of accompanying 'rough' talking.

Each of the four Major championships was extraordinary. At Augusta, Nick Faldo emulated Jack Nicklaus's hitherto unique achievement of winning successive Masters titles and he not only did it in thrilling style, birdieing three of the last six holes to catch Ray Floyd before going on to beat him in a play-off, but he did it in the company of Jack Nicklaus him-

self, whom he partnered in the final round. It was a magical moment.

Many recent US Opens have been dour affairs – not so the one in 1990 at Medinah. For one thing Nick Faldo kept alive his grand slam hopes right up until his last tantalizing putt on the final green. Then we saluted the Championship's oldest ever winner, Hale Irwin, who celebrated his 72nd-hole birdie in a way few who witnessed it are likely to forget!

An Open Championship at St Andrews could never be dull, and again if you happen to be British this one was particularly special! Faldo became the first 'home winner' at the Home of Golf for 51 years; he also became the first player since Tom Watson in 1982 to win two Majors in a year. If the final day at St Andrews was a little anti-climactic (because of Nick's total domination), the second day's

The Final Act: Nick Faldo holes out on the 18th green at St Andrews

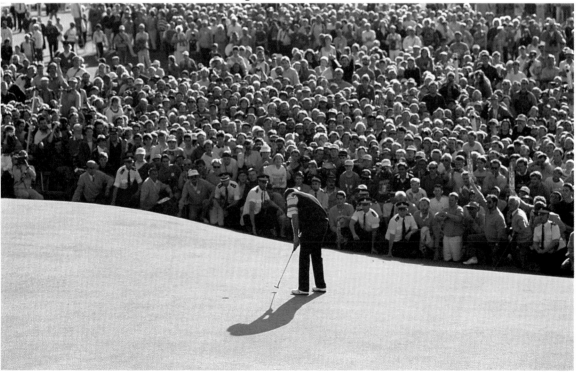

action more than compensated. Finally there was the USPGA at Shoal Creek, which for a variety of reasons attracted more international attention and caused more spilling of ink than probably any previous 'PGA Championship.

With Faldo easily heading the table of aggregate performances in the year's Major championships (Olazabal incidentally finished second) and with European players occupying three of the top four places in the Sony World Rankings come December, 1990 confirmed that these are halcyon days for European golf.

What was so new about 1990 was the realization that there could be halcyon days even without the charismatic presence on centre stage of Seve Ballesteros. Seve's relative decline, which everyone on this side of the Atlantic at least must hope is only temporary, can be placed in the debit column of 1990. Other debits include the almost year-long squabbling over the future of the Ryder Cup, hardly helped, it is submitted, by the unfortunate decision to return to The Belfry in 1993. As Spanish eyes saw red, so Irish eyes must have glimpsed a 41st shade of green.

Ballesteros was deeply involved during the Ryder Cup wrangle and, as always, harboured strong opinions. He also spoke up at the English Open, where he made a plea for something to be done to curb the effect of recent technological advances in golf equipment manufacture which he feels have reduced the element of skill in the game.

Seve surely has a point, and he is supported in his contention by Jack Nicklaus and Gary Player. An associated worry is that golf balls are flying much further than they did twenty years ago; if the trend continues, classic courses like Sunningdale and Gleneagles will soon be considered too short to stage important championships, and that would be tragic. Not long ago people marvelled at Gary Player's talent for playing bunker shots; nowadays one often hears of players who, facing a tricky approach, deliberately aim at traps, so confident are they of getting up and down from sand.

But let's forget the grousing for the time being. There was plenty to marvel at in 1990 – in all four corners of the globe. In Europe Ian Woosnam played some phenomenal golf, and in America the colourful personalities of Greg Norman and Lee Trevino regularly commanded star billing. Both Britain's Faldo and Spain's Olazabal won on three continents, and 1990 saw the highly successful birth of the women's Solheim Cup.

This coming year we have the Ryder and Walker Cups to look forward to, in addition, of course, to the Major championships, which in 1991 take us to the fairways of Augusta, Hazeltine (scene of Tony Jacklin's US Open triumph in 1970), Royal Birkdale and the wonderfully named Crooked Stick in Indiana. These are marvellous times to be playing and watching golf, and we should enjoy them whilst they last – long may we be spoilt!

Cutting a dash in gold, green and red

We all grow up to be suspicious of men in white coats, but what of those sporting gold, green or red jackets? Who are these outlandish dressers? I am referring of course to Messrs Norman, Faldo and Olazabal, respectively ranked numbers one, two and three in the world at the end of 1990. Their flamboyant taste in clothing is simply a result of their having had a monopoly of winning the Australian, US and Japanese (Taiheiyo) Masters tournaments in 1989 and 1990. So jealous are they of their jackets that they haven't even divided the spoils of victory amongst themselves.

Greg Norman is the man with an impressive collection of gold jackets – six in all – but he would doubtless swop his entire Australian Masters wardrobe for just one of Nick Faldo's Augusta winning green jackets. José-Maria? The young Spaniard is being widely tipped as a future US Masters champion, and little wonder too, given the way he almost nonchalantly retained his Taiheiyo Masters title last November, winning beneath the shadows of Mount Fuji by an impressive five strokes from Jumbo Ozaki and Bernhard Langer.

Golf's dashing trio were rarely out of the news in 1990. Norman had an extraordinary up-and-down type of year. He eventually held on to his number-one world-ranking position by the skin of his teeth, much to the dismay – even disgust – of the jingoistic British press. In his first tournament of the year, in California he finished fifth, then a week later at Palm Meadows in Australia, he opened his account with rounds of 66-63 but then had to disqualify himself; he won his sixth Australian Masters title at Huntingdale in February after a thrilling head-to-head last-round battle with Faldo, yet then failed to make the cut at Augusta in April. He won two titles on the US PGA Tour, one of them, the prestigious Doral Ryder Open, thanks to a sensational ten-under-par final-round 62, which he followed up with an extra-hole eagle for good measure; he would have won two more American tournaments but for players holing full 7-iron shots (Robert Gamez) and 30-yard bunker shots (David Frost) at the final hole to defeat him by a single stroke. However, he finished the year as leading moneywinner for the second time, and, as in 1989, he recorded the lowest scoring average.

For two days Norman led the Open Championship at St Andrews with brilliant rounds of 66-66 before falling apart at the seams on the third day; in the World Matchplay at Wentworth he hit a miraculous shot while standing partly out of bounds to the final green during his quarter-final match with Wayne Grady, which he went on to win; but then lost in the semi-finals to Mark McNulty. Late in the year, bidding for a fourth Australian Open title, he held a two-stroke halfway lead at the Australian GC, near Sydney, after scoring an albatross and an eagle on the second day, but again he couldn't keep the momentum going and slipped back to finish equal third. Off the course he was chastized for catching a great white shark off the South Australian coast – some saw it as a tasteless publicity stunt – but was widely lauded for the way he continues to accept bitter setbacks so graciously.

For all Norman's latent brilliance and undeniable charisma, there can be little doubt as

The Power but not the Glory – what happened in the Open at St Andrews typified Greg Norman's roller-coaster year

to who at present is the real 'King of Clubs'. You never really know whether Norman is going to blaze a 65 or bumble his way to a 75 (paradoxically that adds to his appeal), but with Nick Faldo, if it is a big event, you just know he is going to produce the goods and be there or thereabouts at the finish. This is what presently sets him apart from his contemporaries. In stark contrast to Norman, he arrived at Augusta in 1990 having done precious little of note in the first three months of the year, but as Greg crept away quietly on Friday evening so Nick went on to rewrite the history books.

Two months later at Medinah, in the US Open, Faldo, despite not being completely happy with his game, launched a final-day challenge and came within a hair's breadth of tying Irwin and Donald to get into the play-off. Not many doubt that he would have emerged victorious on the Monday. Then of

Me and My Girl: Nick Faldo with faithful caddie Sunneson at Augusta (above) and St Andrews (below)

José-Maria Olazabal celebrates a crushing victory in America's World Series last August

course there was the Open Championship and the third-round showdown with Norman, which he won by a massive 9-stroke margin. Prior to St Andrews, it had been suggested that Nick had been extremely fortunate in each of his Major successes, in that on all three occasions Faldo would not have won if his chief rival had managed to par his last two holes. Such a line of argument, however, ignores the fact that these same rivals probably only dropped strokes because of the immense pressure Faldo had put them under. In any event, by the time the last putt had been holed in the 119th Open Championship, no one was calling Faldo lucky. The whole golfing world was in awe of him.

When he was not dominating the Major championships in 1990, Faldo seemed to be constantly fighting against a troublesome wrist injury; however, his year ended on a high note with victory in the inaugural Johnnie Walker Asian Classic in December, where a third-round course-record 62 set up a handsome four-shot win over Ian Woosnam.

If an Englishman presently sits on the golfing throne it may not be too long before we witness a Spanish succession. The further we got into 1990 the better Olazabal seemed to get. Four fairly frustrating months at the beginning of the year were ended when he triumphed at the 72nd hole at St Mellion in the Benson and Hedges International. If his victories at Portmarnock in the Irish Open and at Paris in the Lancôme Trophy were impressive in as much as they illustrated his great versatility, they were completely overshadowed by his extraordinary performance in the World Series tournament at Firestone in America. That week José-Maria defeated the cream of the US PGA Tour by no fewer than 12 strokes, the biggest winning margin in a US Tour event for sixteen years. The way he completely crushed the field with rounds of 61-67-67-67 was reminiscent of Ballesteros in the 1980 US Masters. Seve was twenty-three then; Olazabal was twenty-four at Firestone. Never one to play down momentous achievements, Gary Player described Olazabal's performance as 'comparable to winning two Majors in a week'. For

a long time it was certainly the talk of golf.

Consolation for losing out to Woosnam in the battle to head the European Order of Merit table came to Olazabal with the successful Taiheiyo Masters defence in Japan, then in his last tournament of the year he came desperately close to winning the $1 million first prize at Sun City in Bophuthatswana; teeing off in the final round 3 strokes behind his playing partner, South African David Frost, he eagled the 9th and headed the field after 16 holes, but was denied victory when Frost birdied the 17th and 18th. It was a truly electrifying finish, as both players hit shots to within 8 feet of the flag at the last; but only Frost holed his putt. A first Major title for Olazabal in 1991? Only a fool would bet heavily against it.

So Norman, Faldo and Olazabal, the men with the gold, green and red jackets, had become the Big Three by the end of the year, but they were by no means the only ones to hit the headlines in 1990.

No wonder David Frost looks pleased with himself, he's just won a million dollars!

Fire-breathing dragons and growling bears

1990 was the year when the Welsh dragon breathed fire, the Golden Bear growled and the Mexican laughed all the way to the bank. It was also the year when Germany won golf's World Cup, Japan was robbed in the Dunhill Cup, and Hale Irwin brought the house down at Medinah.

Woosnam could not win outside Europe in 1990, but what he did inside more than compensated. Compensated! There's an understatement. Woosnam ran amok for much of the season, burning up golf courses left, right and centre – here a 62, there a 62 . . . By the end of his 1990 campaign, five titles had been captured by the rampant Welshman, including a second World Matchplay Championship. From tee to green Woosnam's play is second to none, and when he starts rolling in the putts he is virtually unstoppable. Like Olazabal he must surely be due for a Major win soon.

Twenty Major championships is the career record of Jack Nicklaus, the Golden Bear, as he is affectionately known. Nicklaus has never relished the idea of playing seniors golf, and although he reached 50 in January of last year he entered only a handful of senior events. When he did play, however, he won as often as not, collecting two wins from four starts. In June he won the Mazda TPC Seniors title with an astonishing four-round total of 261, 27 under par. He also featured prominently on the leader boards at Augusta and Medinah; indeed but for a poor final nine holes in the Masters he would have finished third behind Faldo and Floyd.

Unlike Nicklaus, Lee Trevino got fully stuck into life on the US Seniors Tour in 1990. He seemed to enjoy every minute of his rookie year, and no wonder: 'Super Mex' won seven events and over $1 million! Like Nicklaus he won one of the four Senior Majors, the most prized of them all, the US Seniors Open, where he overcame 'the Bear' in a tight finish. The other two Senior Majors were claimed by Gary Player, whose win at stormy Turnberry in the Volvo Seniors British Open could not have had a more nail-biting finish.

Nick Faldo's valiant attempt to capture the US Open and so keep alive his Grand Slam dreams has been mentioned. Greg Norman also made a characteristically late bid during the final round at Medinah, scoring five birdies and eight pars in his first 13 holes before taking 6 at the 14th; but it was Greg's playing partner, 45-year-old Hale Irwin, who surprised everyone with his inspired inward nine of 31 on the Sunday. A string of birdies at the 11th, 12th, 13th and 14th was followed by an amazing three at the last, where he sunk a putt of fully 50 feet. When the ball vanished into the cup Irwin didn't just leap into the air but set off on an emotion-charged lap of honour, dancing around the green a-hooping and a-hollering. It was as if he had just scored the winning touchdown with three seconds to go in the Super Bowl final.

There was no stopping 'Super Mex' in 1990

Hale Irwin, the 'Medinah Express'

Walter Hagen declared on winning his second US Open title, 'Any player can win one US Open, but it takes a helluva a player to win two.' Hale Irwin has now won three, and though his first two wins no doubt meant an awful lot to him, one suspects that it is this one he will cherish the most. It was impossible to avoid feeling sorry for Mike Donald, who led for so long, not just during the final two rounds of the Championship but also in the play-off, where he looked a certain winner with four holes to play.

If Donald regards the 1990 US Open as 'the one that got away', how must Patty Sheehan describe her US Women's Open performance at Atlanta? At one time she led by no fewer than 9 strokes but still allowed Betsy King to overtake her and so to retain the trophy.

Australia didn't make a successful defence of the World Cup that they won at flooded Las Brisas in 1989, but they did win the Four Tours Championship at flooded Yomiuri. As for December's World Cup in Florida, it was won for the first time by Germany. Bernhard Langer was given magnificent support by a golfer named Torsten Giedeon, who most at Grand Cypress had never even heard of before. It was undoubtedly one of the shocks of 1990.

In the other big international team championship, the Dunhill Cup, Ireland defeated England in an exciting final at St Andrews, but most people felt that England were exceedingly lucky to be in the final at all, after losing one and halving two of their three matches against Japan in the semi-final. Unfortunately for the Japanese, the competition's rules decreed that if more than one game ended all square, those halved games had to be decided by extra holes, and as a result of the subsequent play-offs England went through. Rough justice, or what?

Germany's world! Langer and Giedeon pulled off a shock win in the World Cup of Golf at Grand Cypress

Japan's unlucky Dunhill Cup team

Flying sparks, rising stars and fallen heroes

The 1990 USPGA Championship at Shoal Creek will probably be best remembered for things other than Australian Wayne Grady's popular three-stroke win. Golf racism reared its ugly head down in Alabama. It started when the Chairman of Shoal Creek was asked by a journalist why it was that the club had no black members. In an answer that was a throwback to the days when civil rights were America's biggest domestic issue, he explained, 'That's not how we do things in Birmingham.'

Sparks started to fly, and it was soon revealed that of the 39 private clubs staging US Tour events in 1990, seventeen didn't have any black members. The power of the media: within a few days of the story breaking, Shoal Creek admitted its first black member, and before the end of the year so too had Augusta. So all's not well in America's Deep South? Oh, but it must be, for just weeks after the Shoal Creek storm the city of Atlanta, 'capital of the Deep South', was awarded the 1996 Olympic Games . . . the power of the dollar.

There was discord and disharmony of a different nature in Europe during 1990. The major griping was over the decision to stage the 1993 Ryder Cup at The Belfry. Before the decision was made Ballesteros was reputed to have said, 'If Spain is not selected for the 1993 match then I will lose some heart for the Ryder Cup'; and after his plea was ignored, he said 'My motivation will not be the same.' Apparently Spain has been earmarked for 1997, but what about Ireland? Not only has the country been providing Ryder Cup players

Robert Gamez

for much longer than continental Europe – players such as Christy O'Connor Senior, who played in more matches than anyone else, and Eamonn Darcy and Christy O'Connor Junior whose last-day heroics are part of Ryder Cup folklore – but it also offered in Portmarnock an outstanding golfcourse. Portmarnock has proved itself capable of staging big events; the Irish crowd would get behind the home team like no other, and moreover top Europeans, Ballesteros, Langer and Olazabal have all won on the famous links. The power of . . . .

Returning to Shoal Creek, one other worrying statistic for American golf was the fact that when Grady had got the better of Couples, Morgan and Stewart on the final day, it meant that three of the four Major championships had been won by 'overseas' players. Thank heavens for Hale! At 45, Irwin could hardly be said to be America's great hope for the future. Twenty-one-year-old Robert Gamez would seem to be the best candidate. Brilliant in the 1989 Walker Cup, Gamez turned professional at the end of that year and entered his first professional tournament last January, the Tucson Open. Not only did he win it, he did so by four strokes. Proof that this wasn't a one-off came in March, when he produced arguably the stroke of the year to eclipse Greg Norman in the Bay Hill Classic. With his Mexican looks Gamez is not surprisingly being hailed as the 'new Trevino', and after what he did at Bay Hill we can assume that he has at least inherited Super Mex's legendary luck.

Many of the brightest young stars in Europe are to be found parading their talents on the Women's Tour (WPGET). Florence Descampe from Belgium, just 21, won three events in 1990 and only missed out on a place in the eight-strong Solheim Cup side because she ran into top form right at the end of season. Her third and best win of the year was in the Woolmark Matchplay tournament, where she came from behind to defeat Dale Reid.

Florence Descampe, a triple winner on the Women's European tour in 1990

Another player who really made her presence felt in 1990 on the Women's European circuit was Sweden's Helen Alfredsson. Without a win and in only her second year on tour she captured the biggest prize of all, the Weetabix British Open at Woburn. Like Descampe she has a flamboyant personality, which to an extent masks an extremely competitive instinct. Alfredsson and Descampe may emerge as the Continent's leading players, but we tend to forget that Laura Davies is only in her twenties, and many feel that she has barely tapped her full potential.

Laura is capable of destroying a quality field the way Olazabal did in the World Series. It has been remarked how the young Spaniard's performance resembled his countryman Ballesteros's spectacular win in the 1980 US Masters. But what of Seve in 1990? There is precious little of his year that he would want us to recount. A solitary victory in March – and that in his own event, the Majorcan Open, which one of his companies promotes – was hardly what we have come to expect from arguably the world's most gifted golfer. No one seems to have discovered what the problem is; the fact that he became a father in the summer should not have had a detrimental effect on his game – Bernhard Langer also became a dad in 1990, and he ended the year playing his best golf since 1987.

A few uncharitable souls have suggested that Seve is over the top, that he has lost the desire to win, and that at 33 his best years are behind him. Their fuel for the desire argument was provided by Seve missing the cut in the last two Majors of the year. Missing out at St Andrews was especially saddening and hard to believe after his memorable triumph there in 1984 – the image of him punching the air with boyish enthusiasm on the 18th green, after holing his winning birdie putt, is still fresh in the memory.

Apart from his extraordinary natural talent Seve has one other thing going for him which suggests that he will regain his commanding form, and this is his immense pride. Being number two in the world is enough to make Seve scowl, but being only the second-best golfer in Spain, that hurts!

Sweden's Helen Alfredsson

Sandy Lyle and Curtis Strange were two other big names who disappointed in 1990; in fact neither won a 72-hole tournament all year. In Sandy's case it was for the second year running. Golf is a funny game; if you had asked 100 knowledgeable golfers at the end of 1988 to name the top five players in the world, you can bet that Ballesteros, Lyle and Strange would have appeared in every one of their lists. Two seasons ago they shared seventeen tournament victories including three of the four Major championships; in 1990 their combined talents could procure nothing more than the Majorcan Open – extraordinario!

Yesterday's Man? No way, José! Expect Seve to bounce back in 1991

A Major place in history

It may be a little premature to consider how great a golfer Nick Faldo has become – not that this ever stopped anyone from wanting to speculate! The one fact we can confidently quote is that between July 1987 and August 1990 Faldo won four of the fourteen Major Championships staged and had four further top-five finishes. To put such a record into perspective one could add that during the same period Greg Norman and Seve Ballesteros managed to win only one Major title between them.

Faldo's recent domination of the Big Four events has assured him of a significant mention in any book about 'golfing greats', for we are now living in 'the Faldo Years'; how long this era will last only time will tell. Nick knows that at the end of the day he will be judged primarily – some would say exclusively – on his performances in the Major Championships; that is why his entire life is presently structured around sixteen days of each year.

If one's most enduring memory of the 1990 season is of Faldo walking on to the 18th green at St Andrews, arms raised, saluting the crowd after having annihilated the field in the Open Championship, then the most symbolic moment was when he partnered Jack Nicklaus in the final round at Augusta and emulated the Great Man's achievement (until then unique achievement) of winning back-to-back Masters titles.

You sense with Faldo that he has drawn up a mental list of the top twenty or so players of all time and is now starting to tick off those whose achievements he has surpassed. If this is so, then he won't be able to put his metaphorical pen down until he has reached the names Bobby Jones and Jack Nicklaus; and if he has set himself that ultimate task it must feel like setting off to climb Everest on

a mountain bike – but then David Leadbetter, his faithful coach and guru, will already have ordered the oxygen equipment.

In last year's *Benson and Hedges Golf Year* we mapped out our 'Magical-Mystery World Tour'; this time we have made an attempt to draw up an All-time Top Twenty Golfers list – minus, of course, Nick Faldo. In a shameful cop-out, we considered it impossible to separate Nicklaus and Jones, whose Major Championship records stand alone and are worthy of a brief résumé:

Nicklaus has won six US Masters (a record), five USPGAs (a joint record), four US Opens (a joint record), three Open Championships and two US Amateurs. In addition to those twenty Major wins, he has finished runner-up on seventeen occasions. In the Open Championship he finished second seven times and was never out of the top six in the fifteen-year period between 1966 and 1980.

Bobby Jones's career was much shorter, as he retired from competitive golf in 1930 aged just twenty-eight, having achieved golf's original grand slam of winning the US Open, US Amateur, Open Championship and British Amateur all in the same year. In the thirty-one Major Championships he entered, he won thirteen and was first or second nineteen times. Between 1922 and 1930 his record in the US Open reads: 2nd, 1st, 2nd, 2nd, 1st, 11th, 2nd, 1st, 1st. Of the last three Open Championships he played in, he won them all. Perhaps the most remarkable fact is that, in the last eight years of his career, Walter Hagen and Gene Sarazen (both in our Top Twenty) only once finished ahead of him in championships.

Mount Everest? Better make that Jacob's Ladder!

GOLF'S ALL-TIME TOP TWENTY (post-1914)

1	Jack Nicklaus	(20 Major wins)
1	Bobby Jones	(13)
3	Ben Hogan	(9)
4	Tom Watson	(8)
5	Arnold Palmer	(8)
6	Walter Hagen	(11)
7	Gary Player	(9)
8	Sam Snead	(7)
9	Seve Ballesteros	(5)
10	Byron Nelson	(5)
11	Lee Trevino	(6)
12	Gene Sarazen	(7)
13	Greg Norman	(1)
14	Henry Cotton	(3)
15	Peter Thomson	(5)
16	Johnny Miller	(2)
17	Bobby Locke	(4)
18	Billy Casper	(3)
19	Curtis Strange	(2)
20	Ray Floyd	(4)
?	Faldo	(4)

Nicklaus and Faldo at Augusta

Ian Woosnam, one of the three Europeans in the top four of the Sony World Rankings

THE SONY WORLD RANKINGS

31 December 1990

Greg Norman and Nick Faldo

Pos.	Player	Circuit	Points average
1	Greg Norman	ANZ	18.95
2	Nick Faldo	Eur	18.54
3	José-Maria Olazabal	Eur	17.22
4	Ian Woosnam	Eur	15.47
5	Payne Stewart	USA	12.75
6	Paul Azinger	USA	11.63
7	Seve Ballesteros	Eur	10.15
8	Tom Kite	USA	10.10
9	Mark McNulty	Afr	10.06
10	Mark Calcavecchia	USA	9.96
11	Fred Couples	USA	9.69
12	Curtis Strange	USA	9.58
13	Larry Mize	USA	8.86
14	Bernhard Langer	Eur	8.78
15	Chip Beck	USA	8.58
16	Hale Irwin	USA	8.36
17	Masashi Ozaki	Jap	8.16
18	Tim Simpson	USA	7.78
19	Ronan Rafferty	Eur	7.71
20	Wayne Levi	USA	7.69
21	Lanny Wadkins	USA	7.49
22	Mark O'Meara	USA	7.39
23	Rodger Davis	ANZ	7.08
24	David Frost	Afr	7.01
25	Jodie Mudd	USA	6.64
26	Gil Morgan	USA	6.35
27	Wayne Grady	ANZ	6.32
28	Ben Crenshaw	USA	6.32
29	Peter Jacobsen	USA	6.27
30	Steve Jones	USA	6.18
31	Mark James	Eur	6.05
32	Mike Harwood	ANZ	5.88
33	Mike Reid	USA	5.81
34	Craig Stadler	USA	5.74
35	Eduardo Romero	SAM	5.71
36	Ian Baker-Finch	ANZ	5.65
37	Craig Parry	ANZ	5.30
38	Nick Price	Afr	5.28
39	Scott Hoch	USA	5.24
40	Mark McCumber	USA	5.18
41	Sandy Lyle	Eur	5.12
42	Bruce Lietzke	USA	5.05
43	Tom Watson	USA	5.03
44	Davis Love III	USA	4.91
45	Peter Senior	ANZ	4.67
46	David Feherty	Eur	4.65
47	Larry Nelson	USA	4.61
48	Ray Floyd	USA	4.56
49	Steve Pate	USA	4.53
50	Sam Torrance	Eur	4.41
51	Bob Tway	USA	4.33
52	Brett Ogle	ANZ	4.27
53	Robert Gamez	USA	4.22
54	Scott Simpson	USA	4.07
55	John Bland	Afr	4.06
56	Corey Pavin	USA	4.06
57	Ken Green	USA	4.04
58	Naomichi Ozaki	Jpn	3.99
59	Loren Roberts	USA	3.95
60	Peter Fowler	ANZ	3.91

Nick Faldo

2

THE MAJORS

THE US MASTERS
THE US OPEN
THE OPEN
THE USPGA

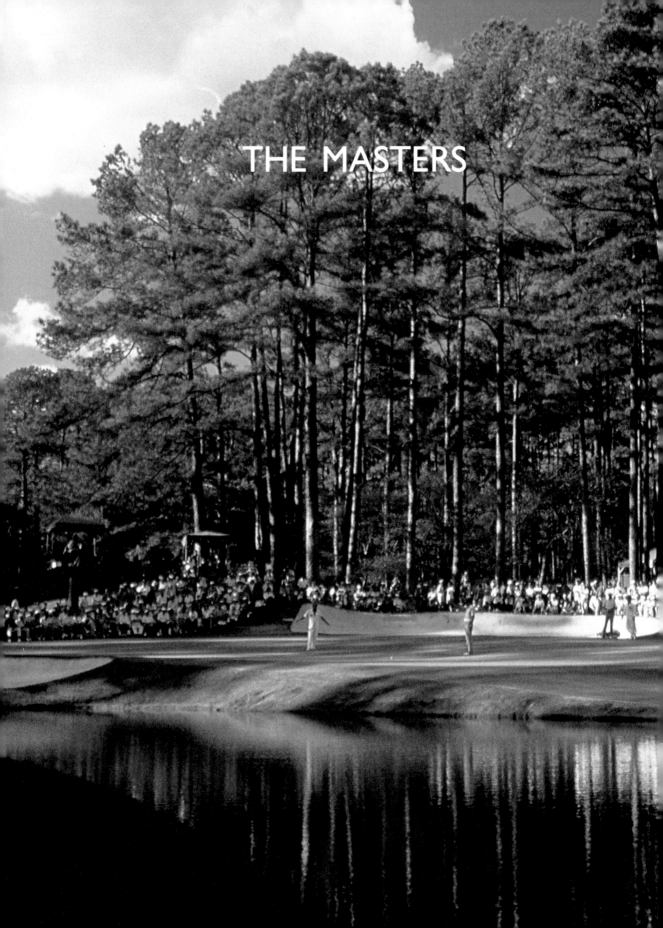

THE MASTERS

THE US MASTERS
ROLL OF CHAMPIONS

1934   Horton Smith
1935   *Gene Sarazen
1936   Horton Smith
1937   Byron Nelson
1938   Henry Picard
1939   Ralph Guldahl
1940   Jimmy Demaret
1941   Craig Wood
1942   *Byron Nelson
1943-5   No Tournaments played
1946   Herman Keiser
1947   Jimmy Demaret
1948   Claude Harmon
1949   Sam Snead
1950   Jimmy Demaret
1951   Ben Hogan
1952   Sam Snead
1953   Ben Hogan
1954   *Sam Snead
1955   Cary Middlecoff
1956   Jack Burke, Jr
1957   Doug Ford
1958   Arnold Palmer
1959   Art Wall, Jr
1960   Arnold Palmer
1961   Gary Player
1962   *Arnold Palmer
1963   Jack Nicklaus
1964   Arnold Palmer
1965   Jack Nicklaus
1966   *Jack Nicklaus
1967   Gay Brewer, Jr
1968   Bob Goalby
1969   George Archer
1970   *Billy Casper
1971   Charles Coody
1972   Jack Nicklaus
1973   Tommy Aaron
1974   Gary Player
1975   Jack Nicklaus
1976   Ray Floyd
1977   Tom Watson
1978   Gary Player
1979   *Fuzzy Zoeller
1980   Seve Ballesteros
1981   Tom Watson
1982   *Craig Stadler
1983   Seve Ballesteros
1984   Ben Crenshaw
1985   Bernhard Langer
1986   Jack Nicklaus
1987   *Larry Mize
1988   Sandy Lyle
1989   *Nick Faldo
1990   *Nick Faldo

* Winner in play-off.

(Previous page) The 16th at Augusta

Lyle, Langer, Ballesteros and Faldo – the 'European Masters'

THE US MASTERS

The 'European Masters'

Isn't Augusta amazing; and what a decade the 1980s were for European golf!

There were 44 US Masters tournaments between 1934, the year the first event was staged, and 1979, and European golfers won precisely none of them. In all that time, not a single green jacket crossed the Atlantic (although admittedly three were exported to South Africa). A pot of gold waited at the end of the Augusta rainbow for a European champion, but there seemed more hope of their finding the Lost Ark of the Covenant. Somehow the idea of a European Masters champion seemed incongruous, nothing more than a fanciful dream. That was how it was.

Then something extraordinary happened. In 1979 a 22-year-old Spaniard won the Open Championship at Lytham, despite spending precious little of the final day on the golf course proper. Seve's spectacular triumph took the Americans by surprise, but his victory at Augusta in April 1980 shook them rigid. At one stage on the Sunday afternoon that year Ballesteros led the field

by no fewer than ten strokes and eventually won by four. American pride had barely been restored when whirlwind Seve struck for a second time in 1983. In 1985 it was Bernhard Langer's turn, as Ballesteros finished joint second and American hopes floundered in Rae's Creek. Now there had been three European victories in the space of six years. With Ballesteros narrowly missing out in 1986 and again in 1987, and with Langer losing his Midas touch on the greens, it looked as if Europe's great run in the Masters might be drawing to a close. Sandy Lyle, of course, had other ideas and in 1988 became the first ever British winner. 'The greatest bunker shot in the history of the game' was how American golf historian Herbert Warren Wind described Lyle's 7-iron stroke from out of the sand at the 72nd hole of the tournament. Twelve months later the same kilt-clad Scotsman was helping Nick Faldo into the coveted green jacket. The Spaniard, the German, the Scotsman and now the Englishman – for the Americans it was no joke. Roll on the new decade.

THE 1990 US MASTERS

In April 1990 Nick Faldo came to Augusta acutely aware that only one man had ever successfully defended the Masters title. That was 24 years ago and the man was Jack Nicklaus, a golfer whose record in major championships dwarfs any other and one whose exploits at Augusta in the early seventies had encouraged the bewitched young Faldo to take up the game.

Nicklaus was now 50 years old but still a force to be reckoned with. It was only four years since his unforgettable last triumph at Augusta, Jack's sixth Masters victory; moreover only a week before coming to Augusta he had won the Tradition tournament on his US Seniors Tour debut. Clearly The Bear was still hungry.

Not for the first time the pre-tournament favourite was Greg Norman. Three times in the last four years the Australian had come tantalizingly close to winning the Masters. In 1986 Nicklaus had edged him out by a single stroke, though Norman had only himself to blame, for he dropped a shot at the final hole; in 1987 Larry Mize produced a stroke in a million to defeat Norman in a sudden-death play-off; and in 1989 Norman repeated his last-hole bogey to finish a stroke behind Faldo and Hoch. At the end of 1989 Norman commented: 'The way I see it, the 1980s were my front nine and the 1990s are going to be my back nine. I feel that I shot something like a 33 coming out but I want to come back in 31 or better.' Early in the year he looked intent

The Clubhouse at Augusta

On the tee, Seve Ballesteros

on being true to his word. By spring 1990 Norman had already won twice. In February he clinched his sixth Australian Masters title at Huntingdale (where he overcame Faldo in a head-to-head confrontation), and this was followed in March by a staggering performance in the Doral Ryder Open, where he shot a final-round 62 (10 under par) to get into a play-off then promptly eagled the first sudden-death hole. But Huntingdale isn't Augusta, and the Doral Ryder Open is not the Masters, and when it came to the crunch in April, Norman's form sadly deserted him.

On Masters Thursday, The Bear and The Shark went out together. Whereas Nicklaus had a steady 72, Norman shot 78, and come Friday evening Greg was out of the tournament, having missed the halfway cut for the first time in nine Masters appearances.

After first-day fireworks from Mike Donald, who scored a 64 but followed it with a disastrous 82, the tournament leader after 36 holes was Ray Floyd on 138 (70-68).

Floyd, the winner in 1976, was at 47 bidding to become the oldest ever Masters champion. Not withstanding his advancing years and the fact that Floyd had not won a regular Tour event for four years, and even that he had committed the major *faux pas* of winning the pre-tournament par-3 event, Floyd's prospects looked promising. Scott Hoch, he of the tweeked tiddler in '89, was only one behind, little-known John Huston was on 140, and Japan's Jumbo Ozaki was on 141, but many of the fancied challengers were some way off the pace.

Norman wasn't the only top player out of sorts with his game. After a relatively disappointing season in 1989, much had been expected of Ballesteros but after opening rounds of 74-73 he was never likely to be in contention. Also on 147 at the halfway stage was Ian Woosnam, while on 148, and only just scraping through to the weekend, was America's major hope, Open champion Mark Calcavecchia. Slightly better

Ray Floyd was attempting to become the oldest ever Masters champion

a 68, a score matched by Olazabal; Langer and Rafferty (playing in his first Masters) scored 69s, and Woosnam had a 70. Some former champions also advanced on Floyd. Fifty-four-year-old Gary Player revived old memories with a 68, Nicklaus stayed very much in contention with a 69, and Tom Watson fired 7 birdies in a round of 67. But both Floyd and, somewhat surprisingly, Huston didn't yield. Thanks to a tremendous back nine of 31, courtesy of sinking several long putts, Floyd added another 68. Huston did likewise.

So after three days the leader board looked like this: 206 Floyd; 208 Huston; 209 Faldo; 211 Nicklaus; 212 Langer and Hoch. It didn't need an Einstein to deduce that Faldo had an excellent chance of joining Nicklaus in the record books as only the second back-to-back champion. And who should Faldo be paired with on Sunday?

It was wonderfully, almost absurdly, ironic. Here was Faldo at Augusta out to emulate the great Nicklaus, the man who on this very course and in this very tournament had inspired him to take up the game in the first place – and now he was playing beside him as he defended the title. Not that Jack was there just to mark Nick's card! Nicklaus was after his seventh green jacket, and no golfer had ever won a Major seven times, nor for that matter had a 50-year-old won any of golf's Grand Slam prizes. Nicklaus and Faldo were playing for high stakes. So too were the one pair teeing off behind them. What a remarkable double Floyd was out to achieve: oldest winner of both the Masters and the US Open (the latter he became in 1986 at the age of 43). As for young Huston, all he had ever won was the Honda Classic.

Usually on the Sunday of the Masters at least one player launches a dramatic charge through the field, but it didn't happen in 1990; in fact a 68 by Lanny Wadkins was the best score on a day when only five players broke 70. Standing on the first tee Faldo felt confident but knew that if he was going to put Floyd under any pressure he required a sound start. As it happened he played the opening hole horribly, taking a 6 to immediately fall

placed on 143 were Fred Couples, Bernhard Langer, Curtis Strange and Faldo. Nicklaus had consolidated his opening 72 with a tidy 70.

Faldo was far from happy with his 71-72 start. He knew he could play a lot better. Significantly he was still very much in touch and it had not escaped his notice that many of the big names were struggling.

Faldo isn't the sort of golfer who relinquishes a title without a fight, and on Saturday he made his move with a superb 66. Like his boyhood idol Nicklaus, Faldo, it seems, has developed the knack of saving his best golf for when it matters most. It is this ability that separates him from Norman and the others at present. Saturday was Europeans' day at the Masters. As well as Faldo's 66, Ballesteros at last found some form with

5 shots behind – a major setback perhaps, but not cataclysmic; after all he had begun his final round in 1989 5 strokes adrift. A birdie at the 2nd was more encouraging. After 9 holes the gap between Floyd and Faldo had narrowed to just 2. Nicklaus was still 5 behind but Huston had fallen completely out of contention after taking 40 to the turn.

Golf's biggest cliché is that a major championship doesn't really start until the final 9 holes on Sunday. But this was a Masters full of irony, cliché and later *déjà vu*. Floyd started back 4-4-2 against Faldo's 5-4-3, and his lead was restored to 4 with just 6 holes to play. By now only Faldo had a hope of catching Floyd. It was asking too much of Nicklaus to repeat his back-nine heroics of 1986, but he had nonetheless covered himself in glory in achieving his 21st top ten finish in the Masters. No one else's record even comes close.

The 12th was a crucial hole as it dictated everything that followed. By salvaging a par against all the odds – his tee shot had plugged in a bunker – Faldo began to believe that fate was on his side. When Floyd immediately followed Faldo's 3 with a 2, the American mistakenly came to the conclusion that there was no way he could lose the tournament; as a result Floyd started to play defensively as Faldo proceeded to attack.

How many times has a US Masters been decided by a golfer coming to grief on Sunday at one or other of Augusta's short par-5s, the 13th and 15th? Curtis Strange in 1985 and Seve Ballesteros in 1986 are two celebrated examples, but there have been many others. Very aware of Augusta's history, Floyd played the 13th and 15th conservatively, electing to lay up safe short of Rae's Creek. Faldo had no option but to 'go for it', and so went for the green with his second on both holes. Both times he made it, and the net result was a two-shot swing to the defending champion. Two ahead with 3 to play, the odds still favoured Floyd. Then at the short 16th Faldo for the second year running holed a difficult putt for a 2. History seemed to be repeating itself; confirmation came when Floyd dropped a shot at the 17th, just as Hoch had done in 1989. Floyd's lead had suddenly gone, and on the 18th he nearly dropped another stroke

Nicklaus plays to his adoring audience

after visiting two bunkers. He was probably relieved to make it into the play-off.

So once again Faldo, carrying the hopes of all England, headed off down the 10th fairway against an American. Once again Faldo looked likely to lose the hole, although this time it was his skill rather than his opponent's lapse that prolonged the issue. *Déjà vu* became complete on the 11th when the Englishman triumphed, Floyd hitting his approach into the lake guarding the front of the green. It was Floyd's first taste of water all week.

For the first time since 1966 there was nobody to dress the champion. Faldo later said that he wished Nicklaus had been asked to perform the traditional honours – symbolically it would have been totally appropriate. Can Faldo possibly win it three times in succession? Of course there is more chance of finding the Lost Ark of the Covenant – but then don't they say that Nick Faldo bears an uncanny resemblance to a young Harrison Ford?

Faldo seals it at the second extra hole

1990 US MASTERS

FINAL SCORES

N. Faldo	71	72	66	69	278	$225,000
R. Floyd	70	68	68	72	278	135,000
(Faldo won play-off at second extra hole)						
J. Huston	66	74	68	75	283	72,500
L. Wadkins	72	73	70	68	283	72,500
F. Couples	74	69	72	69	284	50,000
J. Nicklaus	72	70	69	74	285	45,000
T. Watson	77	71	67	71	286	35,150
C. Strange	70	73	71	72	286	35,150
B. Langer	70	73	69	74	286	35,150
S. Ballesteros	74	73	68	71	286	35,150
S. Simpson	74	71	68	73	286	35,150
B. Britton	68	74	71	73	286	35,150
J.-M. Olazabal	72	73	68	74	287	26,300
S. Hoch	71	68	73	76	288	20,650
R. Rafferty	72	74	69	73	288	20,650
L. Mize	70	76	71	71	288	20,650
T. Kite	75	73	66	74	288	20,650
C. Stadler	72	70	74	72	288	20,650
B. Crenshaw	72	74	73	69	288	20,650
S. Jones	77	69	72	71	289	15,100
F. Zoeller	72	74	73	70	289	15,100
M. Calcavecchia	74	73	73	69	289	15,100
M. Ozaki	70	71	77	72	290	13,000
L. Trevino	78	69	72	72	291	11,000
G. Player	73	74	68	76	291	11,000
D. Hammond	71	74	75	71	291	11,000
A. North	71	73	77	71	292	9,267
J. Sluman	78	68	75	71	292	9,267
W. Grady	72	75	72	73	292	9,267
P. Jacobsen	67	75	76	75	293	8,133
J. Mudd	74	70	73	76	293	8,133
I. Woosnam	72	75	70	76	293	8,133
A. Bean	76	72	74	72	294	7,100
B. Glasson	70	75	76	73	294	7,100
N. Ozaki	75	73	74	72	294	7,100
B. Tway	72	76	73	74	295	6,133
M. McCumber	74	74	76	71	295	6,133
P. Stewart	71	73	77	74	295	6,133
C. Beck	72	74	75	75	296	5,500
C. Patton	71	73	74	78	296	(Am.)
M. Lye	75	73	73	75	296	5,500
D. Pooley	73	73	72	79	297	4,867
J. Mahaffey	72	74	75	76	297	4,867
P. Senior	72	75	73	77	297	4,867
T. Purtzer	71	77	76	74	298	4,250
M. Hulbert	71	71	77	79	298	4,250
M. Donald	64	82	77	76	299	3,900
L. Nelson	74	73	79	74	300	3,600
G. Archer	70	74	82	75	301	3,400

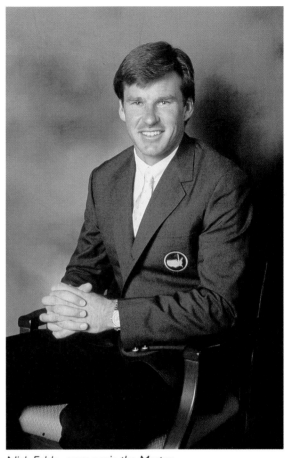

Nick Faldo, once again the Master

THE 1990 US MASTERS: COMMENTARY

Tim Glover, *The Independent*

The Americans are a parochial lot, but given the size and the racial mix of the country perhaps that is understandable. They are only just beginning to get to grips with Ian Woosnam's name, while Nick Faldo is still a professional golfer from Surrey, England.

The week after Faldo had reminded American golf, again, that it was vulnerable, even at a place as sacrosanct as Augusta National, he was not given the Hollywood treatment. He drove from Georgia to Hilton Head Island in South Carolina for the Heritage Classic, a championship he had won in 1984, his first victory in the United States. At the opening ceremony – the defending champion, Payne Stewart, drove a ball from the Harbor Town Golf Links into Calibogue Sound – it was proudly announced that the Heritage Classic had a world-class field: Greg Norman, Tom Kite, Ray Floyd etc. There was no mention of the double Masters champion.

When Faldo teed off in the first round, the locals again failed to recognize in any degree of style, the presence of the hottest player in the world. Not that it particularly concerned Faldo. He commandeered a French yacht and took to the Sound with his family. He looked at home behind the wheel, a Masters mariner shooting the breeze and reflecting on another astonishing week in Augusta.

To win one Masters at the second extra hole of a play-off against an opponent who misses a 2-foot putt for victory could be said to show an element of fortune. To do so again twelve months later on the same hole . . .

Scott Hoch, the first victim, was badly bruised after missing that putt and when he bumped into Faldo a few days later he was not impressed with the Englishman's bedside manner. The conversation had gone something like this:

Faldo: 'How are you doing?'

Hoch: 'All right, considering, but I haven't been able to sleep.'

Faldo: 'I know exactly what you mean. With all the interviews I've been giving I haven't been able to sleep either.'

It was not what Hoch wanted to hear. 'It wasn't the right thing to say. He tried to be friendly but it didn't come out right. I had to bite my tongue.'

Craig Stadler consoled Hoch and told him that Faldo's intention had not been to gloat. Stadler had found himself in a similar situation after beating Dan Pohl in a play-off for the Masters in 1982.

When Ray Floyd fell under Faldo's spell at the Masters, Hoch got to thinking. At Hilton Head, while Faldo was demonstrating on the practice ground the swing that is filling his wardrobe with green jackets, Hoch approached him, offered his congratulations and warmly shook his hand.

'I was not a fan of Faldo's. He wasn't my favourite person,' Hoch said, 'but I have to admit I was really impressed by what he did. He's gone up greatly in my estimation. I still think he was lucky against me but what he did against Floyd was no fluke. You don't get lucky twice.'

Jack Nicklaus, in 1965 and 1966, had been the only man to win the Masters in successive years and he was partly responsible for the Faldo phenomenon.

It is an oft told story, but it can't be repeated often enough. If, two decades ago, in Welwyn Garden City, a 13-year-old boy, probably self-centred, probably spoilt, sees, and seizes upon, a vision on a small television set of a golden-haired man striding across a green carpet, and decides at that moment that this would be his life, what excuses are left for the intrinsic cast of the world stage?

Faldo's obsession took him from Hertfordshire to the heights, but not high enough. A metamorphosis with David Leadbetter, and a few years later the imposing tadpole in a smallish pool becomes a frog that leaps the world.

It is no coincidence that Faldo's single-mindedness saw off Paul Azinger in the Open Championship at Muirfield and Hoch and Floyd in successive Masters. Perish the thought if Faldo had finished the wrong side of those hairline climaxes. Perish the thought is what he did.

When Hoch hovered, for what was an inordinately long time, over that short putt at the 10th in the 1989 Masters, Faldo said to himself: 'I'm still in this.' A year later at the same hole Faldo was in the same bunker and Floyd, apparently, was in charge. Faldo played a better shot from the sand than Floyd did from green velvet.

No matter. The 47-year-old Floyd would do to Faldo what Faldo did to Hoch. Floyd, a renowned frontrunner, would not choke on the trigger. He would draw first and the townsfolk could emerge safely from behind the shutters. Once again they were confounded by the tall stranger. Floyd let rip down the White Dogwood, the 11th, with a dogleg left, but Faldo outdrove him.

The pressure was back on Floyd. Before playing his second shot he disappeared left of the fairway: a call of nature, and the world's watching. Floyd spent a penny and lost a fortune.

Faldo noticed that when his opponent, no lightweight, returned, he was out of breath. And hurried. Floyd, from 176 yards, pulled a 7-iron and his ball flew progressively more left, from the green, green grass of home to the blue, blue water beyond the pale.

Faldo, iron will fortified, grasped an 8-iron and faded the ball into the heart of America. Floyd's putter stayed in its holster.

Floyd began the day at 10 under par and was 15 years and 3 strokes in front of Faldo. Of those in contention only Faldo, who was paired with and who outplayed Nicklaus, got the better of the course in the final round: a 69, following a 66.

He had been in only two bunkers in three rounds but when he drove into sand at the first hole of the fourth round and emerged with a double-bogey 6, he was 5 strokes behind. With 6 holes to play he was still 4 adrift of Floyd.

But while Floyd laid up, laid low, and waited for the jug, Faldo went for the jugular. No sudden-death play-off in the Masters has gone beyond the 11th, the first leg of Amen Corner. Mrs Thatcher called from No. 10 to congratulate him. However, it is the key to the Exchequer, No. 11, that Faldo has locked away in his memory.

Although four players, Ben Hogan, Jack Nicklaus, Gene Sarazen and Gary Player, have won all four Major championships, nobody has achieved what many people consider to be impossible in modern-day golf, a season's Grand Slam.

Faldo with one down and three to go prompted sufficient interest for the bookmakers to quote a price. There were already silver linings in the Green Jacket by the time Faldo got to Medinah for the US Open.

On the driving range Nicklaus went up to him and asked if he would like to play a two-ball. In 1971, sitting in front of the gogglebox, Faldo would have asked the Golden Bear the same question. Now even Faldo was prepared to entertain questions on the grandest slam of all.

Despite having little or no confidence in his driver, he remained on the leader board at Medinah and would have gone into another play-off but for a putt on the 72nd hole which missed by the thickness of a leaf.

If it had dropped, if . . .

Faldo awoke from the improbable dream, dried his eyes and focused his mind on St Andrews. 'After I missed that putt something happened inside,' he said. 'I told myself I was going to win the Open.'

THE US OPEN

THE US OPEN
ROLL OF CHAMPIONS

1895	Horace Rawlins	1942-5	No championships played
1896	James Foulis	1946	*Lloyd Mangrum
1897	Joe Lloyd	1947	*Lew Worsham
1898	Fred Herd	1948	Ben Hogan
1899	Willie Smith	1949	Cary Middlecoff
1900	Harry Vardon	1950	*Ben Hogan
1901	*Willie Anderson	1951	Ben Hogan
1902	Laurie Auchterlonie	1952	Julius Boros
1903	*Willie Anderson	1953	Ben Hogan
1904	Willie Anderson	1954	Ed Furgol
1905	Willie Anderson	1955	*Jack Fleck
1906	Alex Smith	1956	Cary Middlecoff
1907	Alex Ross	1957	*Dick Mayer
1908	*Fred McLeod	1958	Tommy Bolt
1909	George Sargent	1959	Billy Casper
1910	*Alex Smith	1960	Arnold Palmer
1911	*John McDermott	1961	Gene Littler
1912	John McDermott	1962	*Jack Nicklaus
1913	*Francis Ouimet	1963	*Julius Boros
1914	Walter Hagen	1964	Ken Venturi
1915	Jerome Travers	1965	*Gary Player
1916	Charles Evans, Jr	1966	*Billy Casper
1917-18	No championships played	1967	Jack Nicklaus
1919	*Walter Hagen	1968	Lee Trevino
1920	Edward Ray	1969	Orville Moody
1921	James M. Barnes	1970	Tony Jacklin
1922	Gene Sarazen	1971	*Lee Trevino
1923	*Robert T. Jones	1972	Jack Nicklaus
1924	Cyril Walker	1973	Johnny Miller
1925	*W. MacFarlane	1974	Hale Irwin
1926	Robert T. Jones	1975	*Lou Graham
1927	*Tommy Armour	1976	Jerry Pate
1928	*Johnny Farrell	1977	Hubert Green
1929	Robert T. Jones	1978	Andy North
1930	Robert T. Jones	1979	Hale Irwin
1931	*Billy Burke	1980	Jack Nicklaus
1932	Gene Sarazen	1981	David Graham
1933	Johnny Goodman	1982	Tom Watson
1934	Olin Dutra	1983	Larry Nelson
1935	Sam Parks, Jr	1984	*Fuzzy Zoeller
1936	Tony Manero	1985	Andy North
1937	Ralph Guldahl	1986	Ray Floyd
1938	Ralph Guldahl	1987	Scott Simpson
1939	*Byron Nelson	1988	*Curtis Strange
1940	*Lawson Little	1989	Curtis Strange
1941	Craig Wood	1990	*Hale Irwin

* Winner in play-off.

(Previous page) Medinah, 1990

THE 1990 US OPEN

Apparently we owe the bizarre setting of the 1990 US Open Championship to the Ancient Arabic Order of the Nobles of the Mystic Shrine of North America, although 'the Shriners' will suffice. Medinah, which they constructed in the 1920s, became their golfing Mecca, and the extraordinary clubhouse is testimony to the fact that they took their golf seriously. One wonders what the Honourable Company of Edinburgh Golfers would make of it all.

1990 wasn't the first time that Medinah had hosted the US Open. Cary Middlecoff won here in 1949, and in 1975 Lou Graham defeated John Mahaffey in a play-off. That was the Open that nobody seemed to want to win, as on the Sunday afternoon several players threw away clear chances of victory; among them was Jack Nicklaus, who bogied the last three holes to miss the play-off by two strokes, and two emerging talents, 25-year-old Tom Watson (whom they called the choker!) – he opened 67-68 but finished 78-77 – and 23-year-old Ben Crenshaw, who led after 70 holes but hit his tee shot at the 17th into Lake Kadijah (named incidentally after Mohammed's wife). Fifteen years on, Nicklaus, Watson and Crenshaw were back at Medinah. Jack was in a perky mood following his recent performance in the Seniors Tournament Players Championship, which he won with a record score of 27 under par. Also at Medinah, of course, were Curtis Strange, going for a US Open hat-trick, and Nick Faldo, going for the second leg of the Grand Slam. It is difficult to say who was under the greater pressure, as only one man has ever won three successive US Opens (Willie Anderson in the years 1903–1905) and only one player has won a Grand Slam (Bobby Jones in 1930). On form Nick Faldo had much the better chance of winning this championship, but Ballesteros, Norman, Woosnam, Olazabal and every American golfer worth his salt were out to stop him.

What about the golf course? Medinah had been christened 'The Monster', not because of any mythical Arabian beast lurking in the murky depths of Lake Kadijah, but largely because it was presented as the longest-ever US Open course, weighing in at a hefty 7,195 yards – and it was expected to play every inch of it. Medinah is situated on the outskirts of Chicago, Al Capone's Windy City, and it has long had a reputation for being a bit of a slog. Add to this the fact that a course isn't considered fit to stage America's premier championship unless its fairways have been narrowed to painful proportions, and the threat to golfing reputations was plain. But in June last year it seems that this monstrous gangster had forgotten to bring its violin case.

For three days there was barely a breath of wind while heavy rain on the eve of the championship had turned Medinah into something of a soggy dartboard. The US Open was meant to separate the men from the boys, but for the greater part of the championship the names hogging the top of the leader board were Messrs Simpson, Sluman, Simpson, Donald and Brown. On the first day no fewer than 39 players broke the par of 72 (in 1975 the winning score was 3 over) easily setting a new US Open record. The leaders on 66 were Scot Simpson, Jeff Sluman and Tim Simpson. Unable to break par were Faldo (72), Norman (72), Ballesteros (73), Strange (73) and Olazabal (73). The best-placed European was Woosnam, who had a 70; and also in 'red figures', bidding for a record fifth US Open, was Nicklaus on 71.

The scoring on Friday was less spectacular, but the leader board didn't look much different. Tim Simpson (69) and Jeff Sluman (70) stayed on top of the pile, on 135 and 136 respectively, and Mike Donald added a 70 to his first-round 67 to claim third spot. This was something of a triumph for Donald, as two months earlier at Augusta he had left

45

Curtis Strange chases an historic hat trick

The 17th at Medinah – Ian Woosnam's nemesis

the starting blocks like Ben Johnson, shooting a 64, only to feel dopish on day two after scoring an 82.

Much less pleased with himself was Ian Woosnam, who reached the 17th tee of the second round 7 under par for the championship but contrived to take a triple-bogey 6 at the penultimate hole, and this without being in the water: Woosnam fluffed a chip and took 3 putts from 4 feet. At least on 140 he was still very much in contention. Nick Faldo was also kicking himself on Friday evening after dropping shots at each of the last two holes. He was on 144 and now 9 strokes off the lead. Strange was only one ahead of him on 143 and Norman one behind on 145, as was Nicklaus, 10 off the pace. The Spanish pair, Ballesteros and Olazabal, were in slightly better shape after both scored 69s for a 142 total. In his back nine of 32, Seve hit arguably the shot of the week at the 10th, a 6-iron from under the trees which finished just inches from the flag. 'Not many 'foreigners'

have won the US Open, have they?' Seve was reminded in the press tent after his round. 'How many Americans have won the Spanish Open?' responded Seve. Notable players failing to make the halfway cut in the 90th US Open were Sandy Lyle, Bernhard Langer, Payne Stewart, Mark Calcavecchia and, from the class of '75, Watson and Crenshaw.

Saturday was a strange day at the US Open. Yes, Curtis forced himself very much into the frame and on course for that historic third win after a fine 68, which lifted him to 5 under par. What was particularly odd, however, was the way the players at the front of the field started tossing away strokes on the back nine. A number of players got themselves to 8 or 9 under par before committing golfing hari-kiri. Lake Kadijah seemed to develop magnetic powers on Saturday afternoon; it was a bit like watching a replay of the final day in 1975. As the leaders retreated towards the pack suddenly a number of the pre-tournament favourites who had hitherto been only on

Mike Donald

the fringe of things now found themselves right back in contention.

Faldo was shadowing Curtis Strange. Nick has a gift for timing his runs to perfection: in the Masters he had scored a third-round 66, now on US Open Saturday he matched Strange's 68 (later at St Andrews he would compose a 67 on day three). Faldo had moved to minus four which at the end of the day left him just 3 shots behind surprise leaders Mike Donald and Billy Ray Brown. Besides Faldo and Strange some 25 golfers were within 4 strokes of Donald and Brown; they included Larry Nelson (6 under), Olazabal, Zoeller and Mize (5 under), Ballesteros, Nicklaus and Irwin (3 under). Poor Woosnam once again fell foul of the 17th, this time making a double-bogey 5 after hitting into the water from the tee. He played the 18th with the look of a man who had lost all interest in the championship – indeed he admitted as much later – and another wasted shot at the last dropped him back to 2 under par. He was only 5 off the lead at the end of the day, but the 17th hole had effectively killed his challenge (ironically the same was to happen at St Andrews' 17th) and certainly destroyed his spirit. Can you imagine Faldo or Nicklaus losing interest when only 5 behind? Greg Norman was also 2 under par after a third-round 69, and everybody was aware of what he was capable of doing on Sunday afternoons. So thanks to the Simpsons and Slumans pressing their self-destruct buttons, the 1990 US Open Championship had come alive – and it was almost anyone's for the taking.

Few people would have put their overnight money on either Mike Donald or Billy Ray Brown. It cannot be easy sleeping on a US Open Championship lead, especially when more than twenty players of such a pedigree are breathing closely down your neck. Thirty-four-year-old Mike Donald had won only once on the US Tour in 13 years, and as for Billy Ray Brown, this was his first US Open. On Sunday Mike Donald birdied the first two holes and then played par golf all the way to the 16th. Curtis Strange would have been proud of such a performance, particularly as he himself couldn't muster any

serious challenge. The defending champion finished with a 75. Donald led practically all day, while Billy Ray Brown, his playing partner, remained doggedly in touch. Inevitably somebody had to launch a last-round assault. The challenge didn't materialize from the Spaniards (Seve faded, but Olazabal at least finished in the top ten for the second year running), nor did it come from the Welshman, whose fire had been extinguished by Lake Kadijah. When Donald and Brown looked over their shoulders it was at Greg Norman and Nick Faldo, the world's two leading players, and at 45-year-old former champion Hale Irwin.

Norman had 8 pars and 5 birdies in his first 13 holes. Now at 7 under par a good finish by the Australian might set a target that no one could catch. But sadly Greg lost it on the 14th, where he took 6, and he eventually finished 3 shots too many. Playing with Norman was Hale Irwin, twice a winner of the US Open, but not since 1979. He hadn't won on Tour for four years and in fact was only playing in the championship by way of a special invitation from the USGA (his ten-year winner's exemption having just expired). At 45, not too many people expected that he would be the one all others had to try to catch. Irwin took 36 to the turn but came home in a brilliant 31, collecting 4 straight birdies from the 11th before holing a mammoth, rollercoaster putt on the 18th green (it was all of 50 feet) for a 5th birdie. It was all too much for the normally sober Irwin, who danced around the green blowing kisses and shaking hands 'high fives' style with anyone and everyone. And why not? 'In my twenty-two years of professional golf I have never made a putt like that to win or come close to winning. It was easily four times longer than any putt I have made all week.' Irwin's 67 made him leader in the clubhouse on 8 under par.

While Irwin was performing his heroics Nick Faldo was putting together another of his marvellous Major performances. Despite some wretched driving Nick was still hitting his irons as straight as a die. He was rewarded with birdies at the 1st, 5th, 11th and 14th. The one at 14 put him 8 under and at that

Hale's comet goes into orbit at the 72nd hole

So near and yet so far – Faldo sees his Grand Slam dreams slip away

He's off again . . . Irwin sinks the decisive putt at the 91st hole

moment he looked unstoppable. But Nick uncharacteristically three-putted the 16th and despite playing superb shots to the 17th and 18th couldn't quite get the shot back. His 12-foot putt on the final green to tie Irwin went desperately close; but it just wasn't to be. It wasn't to be for Billy Ray Brown either; after making a gallant 2 at the 17th he missed a shorter putt than Faldo, again to tie Irwin. And then finally there was Mike Donald. Like Faldo he dropped his first stroke of the day at the difficult 16th, but two pars were enough to get him into a play-off.

It was the year's second Major play-off, although this one was scheduled to be over 18 holes on the Monday. Ray Floyd will be able to sympathize with Mike Donald, for Irwin, like Faldo in the Masters, didn't get ahead until the winning putt. It actually came on the 19th extra hole – an 8-footer for a birdie – after Irwin had reminded Donald that 2 up with 5 to play never wins. Mike Donald's name just wasn't on the trophy. Hale Irwin's was . . . for the third time. Who said old champions never come back?

1990 US OPEN
FINAL SCORES

H. Irwin	69	70	74	67	280	$180,000
M. Donald	67	70	72	71	280	108,000

(Irwin won at first extra hole following tied 18-hole play-off)

N. Faldo	72	72	68	69	281	56,878
B.R. Brown	69	71	69	72	281	56,878
G. Norman	72	73	69	69	283	33,271
T. Simpson	66	69	75	73	283	33,271
M. Brooks	68	70	72	73	283	33,271
S. Jones	67	76	74	67	284	22,236
C. Stadler	71	70	72	71	284	22,236
S. Hoch	70	73	69	72	284	22,236
T. Sieckmann	70	74	68	72	284	22,236
J.-M. Olazabal	73	69	69	73	284	22,236
F. Zoeller	73	70	68	73	284	22,236
J. Benepe	72	70	73	70	285	15,712
J. Huston	68	72	73	72	285	15,712
J. Inman	72	71	70	72	285	15,712
S. Simpson	66	73	73	73	285	15,712
L. Mize	72	70	69	74	285	15,712
J. Sluman	66	70	74	75	285	15,712
L. Nelson	74	67	69	75	285	15,712
S. Elkington	73	71	73	69	286	12,843
I. Woosnam	70	70	74	72	286	12,843
C. Strange	73	70	68	75	286	12,843
M. Ozaki	73	72	74	68	287	11,308
W. Heintzelman	70	75	74	68	287	11,308
C. Pavin	74	70	73	70	287	11,308
B. Tuten	74	70	72	71	287	11,308
P. Azinger	72	72	69	74	287	11,308
P. Mickelson	74	71	71	72	288	(Am.)
C. Beck	71	71	73	73	288	10,022
M. Hulbert	76	66	71	75	288	10,022
B. Claar	70	71	71	76	288	10,022
T. Byrum	70	75	74	70	289	8,221
K. Triplett	72	70	75	72	289	8,221
B. Lohr	71	74	72	72	289	8,221
I. Aoki	73	69	74	73	289	8,221
D. Frost	72	72	72	73	289	8,221
B. Tway	69	72	74	74	289	8,221
S. Pate	75	68	72	74	289	8,221
B. Wadkins	71	73	71	74	289	8,221
S. Ballesteros	73	69	71	76	289	8,221
J. Nicklaus	71	74	68	76	289	8,221
J. Gallagher Jnr	71	69	72	77	289	8,221
T. Schulz	73	70	69	77	289	8,221
M. Reid	70	73	68	78	289	8,221
C. Parry	72	71	68	79	290	6,687
D. Barr	74	71	75	71	291	6,140
M. McCumber	76	68	74	73	291	6,140

Hale Irwin, US Open champion for the third time

R. Thompson	71	73	72	75	291	6,140
D. Rummells	73	71	70	77	291	6,140
R. Stewart	70	74	73	75	292	5,184
B. Glasson	71	73	72	76	292	5,184
A. North	74	71	71	76	292	5,184
G. Twiggs	72	70	73	77	292	5,184
L. Wadkins	72	72	70	78	292	5,184
T. Kite	75	70	74	74	293	4,694
B. McCallister	71	72	75	75	293	4,694
D. Duval	72	72	72	77	293	(Am.)
B. Gilder	71	70	74	78	293	4,694
G. Morgan	70	72	73	78	293	4,694
S. Verplank	72	69	77	76	294	4,529
R. Gamez	72	73	73	76	294	4,529
R. Rafferty	75	70	73	78	296	4,507
D. Graham	72	73	74	79	298	4,507
H. Twitty	73	72	77	77	299	4,507
B. Faxon	70	74	76	81	301	4,507
M.E. Smith	72	72	82	80	306	4,507
R. Wylie	70	75	81	82	308	4,507

THE 1990 US OPEN: COMMENTARY

Derek Lawrenson, *Birmingham Post and Mail*

'The slums of Chicago are full of the first-round leaders of major championships.'

That quote from Peter Jacobsen was my favourite of 1990, even if in literal terms it makes no sense at all, since the golfer in 500th place on the money list still makes more than the trashman living in a Windy City housing project. But in addition to their evocative powers the words carried a lovely symmetry, for the first-round leader of the Masters did indeed end up in Chicago just two months later. Then again, Chicago, fun, earthy and with a big heart, really was his kind of town.

Forgotten about Mike Donald already? Such is the fate of a man who followed up a 64 at Augusta with a round exactly a shot a hole worse 24 hours later. Such is the fate of one of life's runners-up. Asked who he thought would win the US Open, Jim Murray from the *Los Angeles Times* had a mischievous glint in his eye as he cast his mind back to the Masters. While the names of Strange, Ballesteros, Norman and Faldo dominated nomination papers, his choice stood out a mile. He had written down Mike Donald. People laughed, and Murray laughed with them. Donald win a Major? About as likely as Donald Duck. But in a stirring rendition of an American dream, Donald almost made it happen.

They say the US Tour is full of faceless players, and they probably look at the likes of Donald when they say it. But Donald is different. This is a man with class. This is a man who, when asked why he had not accepted an offer to endorse the products of a clothing company, replied: 'Would you accept money to look like a jerk?' Oh, Mike, never look around at your colleagues.

Donald is a blue-collar player on a stuffed-shirt circuit. After the Houston Open, he hung around as a rock group, Duck Soup, entertained pundits behind the 18th green. And in the final moments of the US Open, when Billy Ray Brown had a 10-footer to head for the play-off, Donald looked at him and said: 'Go ahead. Make it.'

His rationale was simple, although in a sport that is perhaps the most selfish of them all it was not so simple that virtually everyone else would have overlooked it. The best he could do with his own putt was join Irwin in the play-off. But the bottom line was: 'Winning the US Open was Billy Ray's dream too.'

Well, Billy Ray's dream was extinguished when the putt stayed out, but Donald kept his alive. What memories he took away from the year! As with many golfers, his first leanings towards the professional game came after watching pictures of the Masters. For years there was never a chance of playing in it. Between 1981 and 1988 he finished between 73rd and 100th in the money list every year save one, when he rose to 46th. His single moment of grace came in the US's mixed team championship in the December of 1984. He partnered Vicki Alvarez of the LPGA Tour to victory, but generally it was a time not so much of mixed foursomes as mixed fortunes. Donald had no interest in the sport when he was growing up. His summer game was America's summer game, and his parents only gave him a set of clubs because, well, what do you give the guy who has every baseball thing?

But the catcher's mitt was soon replaced by a rather smaller glove. By the middle of his teens Donald had given up baseball for golf and went to Georgia College with, among others, Jay Haas and Chip Beck. A row with the coach meant a trip home to Michigan. He sold flowers and umpired baseball matches for a year. Then the coach left, and Donald returned. The close proximity of Augusta was his field of dreams. But as recently as 1989, at round about the time Scott Hoch was missing the shortest putt that ever lost a Masters, Donald was losing a play-off too. That was for the Guaranty Classic or the second-rate salver, since the field comprises those who don't make the starting line-up for Augusta.

But Donald did rise above the classic journeyman's status that year. He finished 22nd on the money list and won his first tournament. And how appropriate that a player who likes to have a drink with his friends after events should end his sequence without a win in the Anheuser-Busch Classic.

That victory gained Donald his exemption into the Masters. After all these years, and he had caught sight of his 35th birthday, he had made it.

He made it count too. He had seven birdies in nine holes. We looked his name up in the tour book and saw that the rising star was from Hollywood. The second day, as he limped home with an 82, was an appropriate moment to learn that this was Hollywood, Florida, not California.

Donald ended both rounds in tears. He went into the press room after the first day and the first question, that his round must have felt like a dream, was enough. A dream! That was not the half of it.

Choked with emotion one day, simply choking the next. By the time the day's play ended, Donald was gone, and, after the obituaries the following morning, totally forgotten . . . Only to be resurrected in June at a club formed by the Ancient Arabic Order of Nobles of the Mystic Shrine of North America. They are known as Shriners for short, and they took a shine to Donald at Medinah.

Not that anyone took much notice when Donald's name was once more prominent on the first-day leader board. They remembered Jacobsen's quote. A few shook Murray's hand, but even he was smiling as they did so. But Donald refused to be trumped. He was back in the interview area after the second round and again after the third. He was a contender.

He was not alone. All told, just three shots separated the first 19 players going into the scheduled last day. Donald led 17 of them and was tied with the other, Billy Ray.

All day, Donald kept his nerve. There was Strange, there was Faldo, there was Norman, there was Nicklaus. But not once did any of them get their nose in front of Donald. And it needed a freak of a putt on the final hole, one that broke three ways, and one that the protagonist could have tried to repeat all day without holing (perhaps it was because Norman was his playing partner that it went in), for Hale Irwin to set a target that only Donald could meet.

'I did everything you are supposed to do at the US Open. I parred the course to death,' Donald said. While Irwin recalled his football days with a high-fiving lap of honour round the home green, Donald quietly embraced his mother. They would all be back in the morning.

It was a play-off Donald would dominate until it really mattered. Three shots ahead on the home stretch, he and Irwin would be level once more after 18 and when the Open finally decided to close after 91 holes it was Donald who was left on the outside looking in. There were more tears. There were warm congratulations for the victor, and Irwin had no need to indulge in insincere remarks at the end. With genuine feeling, he commented: 'God bless Mike. He is such a nice guy I almost wanted him to win. If it had not been me, I definitely would have wanted him to win.'

But there is only one winner, and it was Donald who drowned his sorrows in beer.

After Murray's prediction had appeared in the national newspaper *US Today*, Donald was asked about it. There was no ego tantrum. He said he had taken it in exactly the spirit it was intended. 'I thought it was kind of comical,' he said, and as he was leaving the press room he made straight for Murray, smiling broadly as he shook him by the hand. Murray replied: 'Go on. Go out there and make us both look good.' Well, the spoils went to Irwin, but there is no doubt that Donald looked good, no doubt at all.

THE OPEN

THE OPEN
ROLL OF CHAMPIONS

1860	Willie Park	1896	*Harry Vardon
1861	Tom Morris, Sr	1897	Harold H. Hilton
1862	Tom Morris, Sr	1898	Harry Vardon
1863	Willie Park	1899	Harry Vardon
1864	Tom Morris, Sr	1900	John H. Taylor
1865	Andrew Strath	1901	James Braid
1866	Willie Park	1902	Alexander Herd
1867	Tom Morris, Sr	1903	Harry Vardon
1868	Tom Morris, Jr	1904	Jack White
1869	Tom Morris, Jr	1905	James Braid
1870	Tom Morris, Jr	1906	James Braid
1871	No Championship Played	1907	Arnaud Massy
1872	Tom Morris, Jr	1908	James Braid
1873	Tom Kidd	1909	John H. Taylor
1874	Mungo Park	1910	James Braid
1875	Willie Park	1911	Harry Vardon
1876	Bob Martin	1912	Edward Ray
1877	Jamie Anderson	1913	John H. Taylor
1878	Jamie Anderson	1914	Harry Vardon
1879	Jamie Anderson	1915-19	No Championships Played
1880	Robert Ferguson	1920	George Duncan
1881	Robert Ferguson	1921	*Jock Hutchison
1882	Robert Ferguson	1922	Walter Hagen
1883	*Willie Fernie	1923	Arthur G. Havers
1884	Jack Simpson	1924	Walter Hagen
1885	Bob Martin	1925	James M. Barnes
1886	David Brown	1926	Robert T. Jones
1887	Willie Park, Jr	1927	Robert T. Jones
1888	Jack Burns	1928	Walter Hagen
1889	*Willie Park, Jr	1929	Walter Hagen
1890	John Ball	1930	Robert T. Jones
1891	Hugh Kirkaldy	1931	Tommy D. Armour
1892	Harold H. Hilton	1932	Gene Sarazen
1893	William Auchterlonie	1933	*Denny Shute
1894	John H. Taylor	1934	Henry Cotton
1895	John H. Taylor	1935	Alfred Perry
		1936	Alfred Padgham
		1937	Henry Cotton
		1938	R.A. Whitcombe
		1939	Richard Burton
		1940-45	No Championships Played

(Previous page) St Andrews, 1990

1946	Sam Snead	1969	Tony Jacklin
1947	Fred Daly	1970	*Jack Nicklaus
1948	Henry Cotton	1971	Lee Trevino
1949	*Bobby Locke	1972	Lee Trevino
1950	Bobby Locke	1973	Tom Weiskopf
1951	Max Faulkner	1974	Gary Player
1952	Bobby Locke	1975	*Tom Watson
1953	Ben Hogan	1976	Johnny Miller
1954	Peter Thomson	1977	Tom Watson
1955	Peter Thomson	1978	Jack Nicklaus
1956	Peter Thomson	1979	Seve Ballesteros
1957	Bobby Locke	1980	Tom Watson
1958	*Peter Thomson	1981	Bill Rogers
1959	Gary Player	1982	Tom Watson
1960	Kel Nagle	1983	Tom Watson
1961	Arnold Palmer	1984	Seve Ballesteros
1962	Arnold Palmer	1985	Sandy Lyle
1963	*Bob Charles	1986	Greg Norman
1964	Tony Lema	1987	Nick Faldo
1965	Peter Thomson	1988	Seve Ballesteros
1966	Jack Nicklaus	1989	*Mark Calcavecchia
1967	Roberto DeVicenzo	1990	Nick Faldo
1968	Gary Player		

* Winner in play-off.

Past champions gather at St Andrews – who would rise above the crowd in 1990?

THE 1990 OPEN CHAMPIONSHIP

The temperatures climbed so high in London during the third week of July last year that a number of Old Bailey judges suggested that barristers might remove their wigs and gowns in Court. It must have been awfully hot. North of the border it was almost as warm – certainly in the ancient kingdom of Fife, where at St Andrews the world's oldest and most celebrated golf links was playing host to the game's greatest championship. More than 200,000 people (a sizeable jury by any standards – but all good men and true) came to view the evidence at first hand. Who, they were being asked, is the Champion Golfer? Who is the world's number-one player? After four heady, and sometimes scorching, days there was only one possible verdict they could deliver. At St Andrews, the very home of golf, the case was proven beyond reasonable doubt. Yet for two days it was anything but certain.

A great deal of pre-championship conversation centred on the final appearance in the event of Arnold Palmer. Not even Royal Birkdale, it seems, the scene of Palmer's first Open triumph, can tempt him back this year. Palmer is a living legend if ever there was one: the player more responsible than any other for revitalizing the Open and for establishing it as the supreme championship of golf. It had all started at St Andrews in 1960, when Palmer, then holder of both the US Open and Masters titles, came to play in the Centenary Open. He came to win the first three legs of the Grand Slam but failed to get into a play-off by just one stroke. By a cruel twist of fate, 30 years on a single stroke would again deny him a fitting climax to his Open career.

Talking of Grand Slams and single strokes, Nick Faldo arrived at St Andrews still rueing the 12-foot putt he had missed a month earlier at the 72nd hole of the US Open at Medinah. Had Faldo holed it, then he too might have been playing for golfing immortality.

And talking of twists of fate, the draw for the first two days of play in the championship raised many a disbelieving eyebrow. Not for the first time in recent years Palmer found himself in the same threesome as his great '60s rival Gary Player, while Faldo learned that he was to go out with Scott Hoch, the player he had defeated in the 1989 Masters (some jingoistically expressed regret that Ray Floyd wasn't the third group member). Faldo's Ryder Cup partner Ian Woosnam, strongly fancied to do well at St Andrews after brilliantly winning his previous two events, was paired with Curtis Strange, who beat the Welshman to tie the last Ryder Cup. Australian Greg Norman was mischievously placed with Bob Tway and Robert Gamez – two of that all too large group of players who had holed miraculous shots at the final hole to deny Norman of titles he thought were coming his way. Finally there was the trio of Ballesteros, Watson and Price. No fun for the latter two perhaps but a chance for Seve to relive his Open triumphs of 1984 (over Watson at St Andrews) and 1988 (over Price at Royal Lytham).

So then to the first tee, and where were the first-day rabbits? In the 1989 Open at Troon the early pace had been set by the practically unknown Channel Islander Wayne Stephens. That championship had been memorably concluded, or, rather, so nearly concluded, by a stunning course-record 64 from Greg Norman. This year the Australian seemed determined not to leave his championship bid until the Sunday afternoon. In fact Norman started where he left off (give or take a bunker or two), producing a marvellous 66. It wasn't quite as spectacular as the round at Troon, where he opened with 6 straight birdies, but he started with a 3, ended with a 3, and had 4 further birdies in between. Moreover he didn't drop a single stroke all day – a most 'un-Norman like' start.

Unfortunately for Greg it didn't exactly scatter the field. He was soon joined at the top of the leader board by American Michael

Allen, winner of the 1989 Scottish Open, who got lucky at the 13th holing a putt estimated to be the length of at least two cricket pitches (not that an American would understand what that meant). More significantly, only one behind Norman was Nick Faldo. Nick was three strokes behind his great rival as he crossed the Swilcan Bridge and walked up the 18th fairway. However, he must have been thinking of how to defeat Norman when he played a wonderfully deft pitch and run to the final green from 50 yards out. Sure enough, in it went for the only eagle at the 18th all week. But this was no fluke shot: it was a superbly measured stroke, and in any event the following day Norman would even the score, so to speak, at the 14th.

Several players returned first-round 68s. Among this group were Ian Woosnam and Scotland's Sam Torrance. It was a good day for Australia, with Craig Parry and Ian Baker-Finch both scoring 68s – a very satisfying start for Baker-Finch in particular, it being 11 strokes fewer than his last Open round at St Andrews in 1984. Leading the US challenge

were the bohemian figure of Payne Stewart (dressed in the colours of the Washington Redskins) and Peter Jacobsen, who took 6 at the infamous Road Hole 17th yet still considered it 'an honour to have been eaten alive by such a great hole'. Ballesteros got himself to 3 under par before he too succumbed to the 17th. Ballesteros's 71 was matched by defending champion Mark Calcavecchia. The outspoken Nebraskan described his performance as 'disgusting'. Also on 71 was Nicklaus, twice a champion at St Andrews, and the Golden Bear's playing partner Olazabal, who arguably played the best golf of the day hitting every green in regulation, but took 37 putts.

If Thursday was a good day for watching golf, then Friday was a classic. 'In my 20 years of covering the Open Championship I cannot think of a more riveting afternoon than this, other than at Turnberry in 1977,' wrote Michael Williams in the *Daily Telegraph*. Let's start, though, with the bad news. So exceptional was the scoring throughout the first two days that the halfway cut was made at a record low of 1 under par (143). As a

Bunkered Ballesteros – no repeat win for Seve at St Andrews

Nick Faldo eagles the 18th in round one

Greg Norman drives at the 2nd

result it was sadly farewell to Arnold Palmer (73-71) and to Gary Player (72-73). Other former champions who didn't stay for the weekend were Tom Weiskopf, Bob Charles and a trio whom few would have expected to bow out so early, Watson, Ballesteros and Calcavecchia. For Seve it just about summed up his year.

The biggest surprise on Friday morning was provided by 27-year-old Jamie Spence from Kent. Playing in the first group of the day and off at 7.15 a.m. he returned a magnificent 65. This was his first ever visit to St Andrews. His round contained 8 birdies, and he finished in dramatic style almost holing his approach to the infamous 17th then missing a short putt at the 18th for a 64. At midday on Friday Jamie Spence was leading the 119th Open Championship. First to overtake Spence was Payne Stewart (now representing the Green Bay Packers), who repeated his first-round score of 68. Stewart must have thought he

would be there or thereabouts at the end of the day, but Greg Norman and Nick Faldo had other ideas.

Teeing off within 30 minutes of one another the 'Big Two' started to trade birdies. It really was reminiscent of Nicklaus and Watson at Turnberry all those years ago. Faldo had the better start, opening 4-3 to Norman's 4-5. Greg birdied the 4th, Nick the 5th and 6th. Both players birdied the 7th and the Australian birdied the 8th and 9th. When each birdied the 10th and made their pars at the 11th, they were 10 under par and Norman had just gone 3-2-3-3-3. Remarkably, at this stage two other golfers were keeping in touch, namely Ian Woosnam and Craig Parry, both of whom recorded 6 birdies in their opening 10 holes. But the mighty little men couldn't keep pace with the mighty big men, and they fell away on the back nine. Neither could make any more birdies and the 17th once again bared its teeth, Parry taking 5, Woosnam a very costly 6.

The 13th proved a difficult hole all week, and here Norman dropped his second shot of the day. However, it was only a temporary setback, as on the 14th he regained the outright lead by hitting a magnificent 75-yard wedge shot which pitched 3 feet beyond the flag then spun back into the hole for an eagle 3. Take that, Mr Tway and Mr Gamez! Lesser golfers than Faldo might have crumbled, but the Englishman replied by striking two marvellous iron shots to the 15th and 16th; so good were they in fact that back-to-back birdies were a formality. Playing ahead of Faldo, Norman had also birdied the 16th. At 12 under par the world's two leading players came to the 18th requiring 3s to better Henry Cotton's 36-hole record score of 132. Both missed it by a whisker, and so, 56 years on, Henry's record still stands.

When the dust and dusk settled, Faldo and Norman stood shoulder to shoulder four strokes clear of the field; Faldo had scored 67-65, Norman 66-66. Together, in two days, they had taken St Andrews apart, recording 23 birdies and 2 eagles between them. They had mugged the Old Lady. Parry with a 69 and Stewart were their closest

Olazabal 'knocked down the flagsticks' but couldn't read the greens

pursuers, but they were now 4 shots adrift. Woosnam, Spence, Price and Reid were 5 strokes back, with Olazabal heading a group on 138, 6 behind. Nicklaus, who comfortably made his 28th Open Championship cut, commented that for two days Olazabal had been 'Knocking down flags all week' but that the young Spaniard had putted poorly. Faldo and Norman had also been 'knocking down flags', but they had also been holing the putts. Now the field was scattered.

Not surprisingly the Saturday morning headlines were full of the Faldo/Norman supershow and there was much talk of a weekend-long Turnberry-style confrontation; a head-to-head duel between the game's two brightest stars. We were only halfway through the championship, but all other challengers were already being discounted. Would Faldo, the supreme golfing machine, win his fourth major title in as many seasons, or could Greg Norman maintain his momentum and at last add to his solitary Open success of 1986?

David Miller wrote a particularly perceptive article in *The Times* headed 'Why Norman needs to win the title'. Exploring why glory and greatness had so often passed the dashing Australian by, he ventured: 'You sense that those clear blue eyes lack the inner steel of, say, a Palmer a Watson . . . or a Faldo', and he concluded 'a lot of major prizes have eluded Norman. This one is by no means his at this stage. As he says the weather could change. And when he says that you half wonder whether subconsciously he means that he could change.'

The weather didn't change on day three – nor did Nick Faldo – but sadly Greg Norman did. Norman in full cry is a wonderful sight, but Norman on a bad day is painful to watch. On Saturday he couldn't putt to save his life, let alone win the Open. The way the leading pair played the first two holes set the pattern for the day. On the first, Faldo was 16 feet from the pin in 2, Norman was a shade closer: Faldo holed, Norman missed. On the 2nd

Payne Stewart – who else!

It was star-spangled Stewart on Sunday

Faldo made a solid 4, Norman three-putted for a 5. Nick continued to pile on the pressure, playing flawless golf, and although Norman held it together for a few holes he collapsed on the back nine.

If Norman wasn't destined to chase Faldo, who might? Could anyone charge through the pack? There were two spectacular performances on Saturday. Very early in the day, Paul Broadhurst, who had only just qualified for the weekend, equalled the Open Championship record with a superb 63. Then Ian Baker-Finch, who started the day 8 behind Faldo and Norman, made up 6 of those strokes in his first 6 holes with 4 birdies and an eagle – and he hadn't finished either. With further birdies at the 9th, 10th and 12th he moved to 13 under par and was now a staggering 9 under for the 12 holes he had played. Baker-Finch was threatening to make Norman's fourth-round surge at Troon look almost ordinary. Fortunately for Faldo, the tall, bespectacled Queenslander at last ran out

of steam: there were no more birdies, instead 5 pars and a dropped shot at the 17th (where else). He eventually finished with a 64.

As Faldo continued to play so relentlessly, indeed so brilliantly – he turned in 33 to Norman's 36 and then birdied the 11th to go to 16 under par – the 63s and 64s needed to come from the likes of Olazabal, Woosnam or Stewart. Unfortunately for the young Spaniard he still couldn't hole a putt of more than 8 feet, and a frustrating week was crowned at the 17th when he putted from off the green into the Road Hole bunker – the cardinal sin. Woosnam for the second day in succession stormed to the turn in 32 only to throw away all his good work on the back nine. An interesting statistic is that during Open Championship week Woosnam played the first nine holes in a total of 13 under par but the back nine in 1 over. Faldo, on the other hand, played each nine in 9 under par. And what of Payne Stewart? He was playing for the Los Angeles Rams on Saturday, and they performed just as stylishly as the Washington Redskins and the Green Bay Packers had on Thursday and Friday. Payne's vital statistics looked impressive: 68-68-68. In every previous Open at St Andrews, and there had been 23 of them, he would now have been leading the championship. Instead he ended Saturday 5 behind, level with Baker-Finch. Faldo came home in 34 for a round of 67. His three-round total of 199 set a new championship record, and he achieved it in the grand manner with a glorious 3 at the 18th. As Faldo signed for his 67, so Norman signed for a catastrophic 76. 'His three-putting was absolutely killing him,' observed Nick, who added generously, 'He just didn't have the run of the ball'. Norman, not surprisingly, was speechless.

Faldo's Norman conquest effectively killed the tournament. Five ahead with 18 to play is hardly an impregnable lead in most situations, especially, one might think, in an Open

Championship at St Andrews. But when the player at the head of the field is a golfer of Nick Faldo's stature, a man, remember, with 'inner steel', it was essentially all over bar the shouting. Any overnight Doubting Thomases were given their answer on the first hole of the final round when Faldo hit his approach to within 2 feet of the pin. It was an outrageous stroke, the shot indeed of a champion elect.

After what had happened on Saturday, Greg Norman was never going to shoot a 62 on Sunday. Courageously he did manage a 69. Nor could Ian Baker-Finch, who went out last partnering Faldo, repeat his front-nine form of the day before. The only golfer who seriously mounted a challenge to Faldo was Payne Stewart. On Sunday he really was the all-American boy. Dressed from head to toe in the Stars and Stripes, 'fit for burial at sea', as Raymond Jacobs of the *Glasgow Herald*

After the Alamo – Greg and Nick shake hands after the third round, in which Faldo scored a 67, Norman a 76

Woosnam played like a Welsh tiger on the front nine and a Welsh rarebit on the back nine

Ian Baker-Finch couldn't produce Saturday's form (a 64) on Sunday and struggled to a closing 73

wryly remarked, he got at one stage to within 2 strokes of Faldo. That was when he made a 3 at the 12th, his 4th birdie of the day. Faldo, however, didn't flinch, and over the closing holes Stewart dropped 3 strokes, and this effectively buried his dreams. Turning in a steady 35, Faldo, playing as resolutely and faultlessly as he had at Muirfield in 1987, compiled a series of 9 straight pars from the 6th before producing a decisive birdie at the 15th, where he hit a glorious 6-iron to within 8 feet of the flag. Faldo finished with a 71 for a total of 270, 5 ahead of Stewart and the fast-finishing Mark McNulty, whose 65 was the best score of the day. Ian Woosnam (69) and Jodie Mudd (66) finished a further stroke behind, and sharing sixth place were Greg Norman and Ian Baker-Finch on 277.

Tom Watson's record four-round score of 268 was one of only a few records that Faldo hadn't overhauled, but of course, at Turnberry, Tom had been pursued to the very last putt by Jack Nicklaus, whereas Faldo's final round had been little more than a Sunday afternoon stroll in the park.

Until 1990 Sam Snead, Jack Nicklaus and Seve Ballesteros shared something special: they alone had experienced the thrill of winning a Masters title at Augusta and an Open Championship at St Andrews. Now Faldo has joined the select trio; in fact he has gone one better, for he has achieved the wondrous double in the same calendar year. I guess that must make him feel pretty good.

Faldo at the double – Nick salutes his second Open success and his second Major win of 1990

1990 OPEN CHAMPIONSHIP
FINAL SCORES

N. Faldo	67	65	67	71	270	£85,000
M. McNulty	74	68	68	65	275	60,000
P. Stewart	68	68	68	71	275	60,000
J. Mudd	72	66	72	66	276	40,000
I. Woosnam	68	69	70	69	276	40,000
G. Norman	66	66	76	69	277	28,500
I. Baker-Finch	68	72	64	73	277	28,500
D. Graham	72	71	70	66	279	22,000
S. Pate	70	68	72	69	279	22,000
D. Hammond	70	71	68	70	279	22,000
C. Pavin	71	69	68	71	279	22,000
V. Singh	70	69	72	69	280	16,375
R. Gamez	70	72	67	71	280	16,375
T. Simpson	70	69	69	72	280	16,375
P. Broadhurst	74	69	63	74	280	16,375
M. Roe	71	70	72	68	281	11,150
S. Jones	72	67	72	70	281	11,150
J.-M. Olazabal	71	67	71	72	281	11,150
S. Lyle	72	70	67	72	281	11,150
P. Jacobsen	68	70	70	73	281	11,150
F. Nobilo	72	67	68	74	281	11,150
E. Darcy	71	71	72	68	282	7,933
J. Spence	72	65	73	72	282	7,933
C. Parry	68	68	69	77	282	7,933
L. Trevino	69	70	73	71	283	6,383
J. Sluman	72	70	70	71	283	6,383
C. O'Connor Jr	68	72	71	72	273	6,383
F. Couples	71	70	70	72	283	6,383
J. Rivero	70	70	70	73	283	6,383
N. Price	70	67	71	75	283	6,383
R. Rafferty	70	71	73	70	284	5,125
L. Mize	71	72	70	71	284	5,125
M. James	73	69	70	72	284	5,125
M. McCumber	69	74	69	72	284	5,125
G. Powers	74	69	69	72	284	5,125
B. Crenshaw	74	69	68	73	284	5,125
B. Norton	71	72	68	73	284	5,125
V. Fernandez	72	67	69	76	284	5,125
N. Ozaki	71	71	74	69	285	4,216
A. North	71	71	72	71	285	4,216
R. Floyd	72	71	71	71	285	4,216
D. Pooley	70	73	71	71	285	4,216
S. Torrance	68	70	75	72	285	4,216
D. Cooper	72	71	69	73	285	4,216
S. Simpson	73	70	69	73	285	4,216
M. Reid	70	67	73	75	285	4,216
M. Hulbert	70	70	70	75	285	4,216
B. Langer	74	69	75	68	286	3,720
C. Montgomerie	72	69	74	71	286	3,720
M. O'Meara	70	69	73	74	286	3,720
P. Fowler	73	68	71	74	286	3,720
P. Azinger	73	68	68	77	286	3,720
H. Irwin	72	68	75	72	287	3,475
J. Bland	71	72	72	72	287	3,475
E. Romero	69	71	74	73	287	3,475
M. Allen	66	75	73	73	287	3,475
J. Rutledge	71	69	76	72	288	3,225
M. Clayton	72	71	72	73	288	3,225
B. McAllister	71	68	75	74	288	3,225
D. Mijovic	69	74	71	74	288	3,225
D. Ray	71	69	73	75	288	3,225
A. Sorenson	70	68	71	79	288	3,225
J. Nicklaus	71	70	77	71	289	2,950
P. Baker	73	68	75	73	289	2,950
R. Chapman	72	70	74	73	289	2,950
M. Poxon	68	72	74	75	289	2,950
D. Canipe	72	70	69	78	289	2,950
D. Feherty	74	69	71	76	290	2,775
J. Berendt	75	66	72	77	290	2,775
A. Saavedra	72	69	75	75	291	2,700
M. Mackenzie	70	71	76	75	292	2,700
J.M. Canizares	72	70	78	76	296	2,700

Nick Faldo, Open champion 1990

THE 1990 OPEN CHAMPIONSHIP: COMMENTARY

John Hopkins, *Sunday Times*

If any doubts existed as to Nick Faldo's standing in golf, then they were blown to the four points of the compass by one of his rounds in 1990. Which round? Have a guess.

The fourth at Augusta, a 69, despite starting with a two-over-par six? The second round in the Open, a 65? The fourth round in the Open, a 71, that brought him his fourth major title? All these rounds have individual merits, but none is the one in question.

The round of the year came on the Saturday of the Open, when Faldo looked into the eyes of the devils that torment British golfers and stared them all down. What's more, he faced up to Greg Norman, his close challenger and playing partner, the man ranked No. 1 golfer in the world, and destroyed him too. There was nothing Faldo was asked to do that sunny afternoon that proved to be beyond him, and that was the moment he became unquestionably the best golfer in the world. After defeating Norman by nine strokes and opening up a five-stroke lead, there was as much chance of Faldo failing to win the 119th Open as of the sun failing to come up the next morning.

What is it that drives Faldo more determinedly, more successfully than any other contemporary golfer? He has enormous belief in himself, for one thing. This has enabled him to take decisions in his career that have almost always been right even though they seemed wrong at the time. These range from returning home from university in America after less than three months – a wet decision, said his critics – to his decision to rebuild his swing – which was described as madness in some quarters; if it ain't bust, don't fix it, they said.

Thoughtful and quiet off the course, Faldo becomes highly articulate on it. He knows more about his golf swing than anyone other than David Leadbetter, his coach, and he knows more about the golf swing than any professional Leadbetter has ever talked to at length.

Allied to these attributes is a remarkable ability to conduct his life the way he wants to. When Faldo says he won't play in a five-billion-yen tournament in Japan, wild horses and thumbscrews won't get him to change his mind. His no is not a maybe, a perhaps or a might. It's a no and that's all there is to it.

It's easy to suggest that he has a burning ambition to succeed, which he has. But so do Ballesteros, whose enthusiasm in victory is generated by a measure of delight that he has stuck it to someone yet again, and Ian Woosnam, who seems determined to prove that his size can be an attribute because it makes him want things more.

At six foot three, Faldo isn't driven by the small man's mentality. Nor does he feel he has wrongs to right every time he steps on to a golf course. His desire is that of a mechanic who keeps working on a piece of machinery until every part meshes so smoothly with the others it's difficult to tell whether the machine is running or not.

Peter Alliss once remarked that Faldo would probably play just as well if he wasn't watched by a single spectator. It's not insignificant that Faldo is an only child and thus used to long hours spent in his own company. Faldo seeks perfection from his swing and he wants it for his own satisfaction more than anything else.

In his ability to drive himself on from within, Faldo resembles Jack Nicklaus. Nicklaus didn't need to feed off a crowd, though he could do so, as he demonstrated in winning the Masters at Augusta in 1986. He had no need to stick pins into a wax effigy of a rival. He knew that was what they were doing to him. He concentrated on himself and his own golf.

Faldo resembles Nicklaus in other ways, too – his attention to detail being just one. As Nicklaus developed the practice of doing yardages to measure distances, so Faldo's search for perfection is such that he will cut his fingernails at the beginning of the week lest the sensitivity of his hands on his putter is affected in a tournament.

It was watching Nicklaus at the 1971 Masters that gave Faldo the inspiration to take up the game himself, and nearly 20 years later the two of them played the fourth round of the Masters together. And when Faldo successfully defended his US Masters title in 1990 he became only the second man to do so. The other was Nicklaus.

Prior to the start of the USPGA Nicklaus acknowledged Faldo as the game's dominant player. 'If you feel you can dominate the world of golf, then you can,' said Nicklaus to Faldo, a generous statement, and one that meant a lot to Faldo. And while no one can suggest that Faldo's four major titles approach Nicklaus's record of overall dominance, to have won four of the 14 major championships, starting at the 1987 Open and continuing to the end of 1990, is a run of success worthy of Nicklaus at his best.

I suspect that Faldo comes nearest to Nicklaus in his awareness of his own strengths and limitations and his ability to maximize the strengths and minimize the weaknesses. Take risks, Faldo says to himself, but only when the danger is as small as it can be. Otherwise what is the point? You might as well settle for the safe approach, and if you drop a shot, well, there'll be later opportunities to get it back. In other words, taking a 5 on a par-4 hole is not disastrous, whereas risking everything on going for a 4 and ending with a 6 or a 7 probably is.

One example of this kind of thinking came at the Road Hole at St Andrews during the Open. Faldo knew that the 17th never gave up a par easily and decided therefore to regard it as a par-5 and be done with it. He bogied it three days out of four, but so what. He still finished 18 under par.

It would be hard to find two golfers of such eminence who like the challenges presented by the Old Course more than Nicklaus and Faldo – or have dealt with these challenges more successfully. Nicklaus has competed in five Opens at the home of golf and won two of them and finished second in a third, a better strike record than at any other Open course. Faldo's overall record in events at St Andrews would stand comparison with anyone's: one victory from three Opens, and only one defeat in the Dunhill Cup, 11 rounds at an average of 68.27.

In the autumn of 1987 Faldo told me that he hoped he wouldn't have to continue playing professional golf after he was 45. 'I hope by then I will have made so much I won't need to carry on,' he said. 'I don't want to lose my sanity. You dedicate your life to golf, sacrificing so much, living out of a suitcase, being away from home. It'll be nice in 15 years to sit back in a big house in the country and do a bit of business, some course architecture and that's it.

'Having children makes you think a hell of a lot. They're such wonderful things that you don't want to miss any of their growing up. And you hope that you become a good enough parent that they don't want to miss you. You want them to love you back as much as you love them.'

The way Faldo is going he may not last another ten years, never mind until he is 45. He has added three more major titles to his haul since then and they have brought him enormous riches and the concomitant pressures and exacted a considerable physical toll.

The time to quit may be sooner than he thinks, perhaps in 1997, when he will be 40. Neither Arnold Palmer nor Lee Trevino managed to stop at this age and nor did Nicklaus. Will Faldo?

THE USPGA

USPGA CHAMPIONSHIP
ROLL OF CHAMPIONS

1916	James M. Barnes	1957	Lionel Hebert
1917-18	No championships played	1958	Dow Finsterwald
1919	James M. Barnes	1959	Bob Rosburg
1920	Jock Hutchison	1960	Jay Hebert
1921	Walter Hagen	1961	*Jerry Barber
1922	Gene Sarazen	1962	Gary Player
1923	Gene Sarazen	1963	Jack Nicklaus
1924	Walter Hagen	1964	Bobby Nichols
1925	Walter Hagen	1965	Dave Marr
1926	Walter Hagen	1966	Al Geiberger
1927	Walter Hagen	1967	*Don January
1928	Leo Diegel	1968	Julius Boros
1929	Leo Diegel	1969	Ray Floyd
1930	Tommy Armour	1970	Dave Stockton
1931	Tom Creavy	1971	Jack Nicklaus
1932	Olin Dutra	1972	Gary Player
1933	Gene Sarazen	1973	Jack Nicklaus
1934	Paul Runyan	1974	Lee Trevino
1935	Johnny Revolta	1975	Jack Nicklaus
1936	Denny Shute	1976	Dave Stockton
1937	Denny Shute	1977	*Lanny Wadkins
1938	Paul Runyan	1978	*John Mahaffey
1939	Henry Picard	1979	*David Graham
1940	Byron Nelson	1980	Jack Nicklaus
1941	Vic Ghezzi	1981	Larry Nelson
1942	Sam Snead	1982	Ray Floyd
1943	No championship played	1983	Hal Sutton
1944	Bob Hamilton	1984	Lee Trevino
1945	Byron Nelson	1985	Hubert Green
1946	Ben Hogan	1986	Bob Tway
1947	Jim Ferrier	1987	*Larry Nelson
1948	Ben Hogan	1988	Jeff Sluman
1949	Sam Snead	1989	Payne Stewart
1950	Chandler Harper	1990	Wayne Grady
1951	Sam Snead		
1952	Jim Turnesa		
1953	Walter Burkemo		
1954	Chick Harbert	*** Winner in play-off.**	
1955	Doug Ford		
1956	Jack Burke		

(Previous page) Shoal Creek, 1990

THE 1990 USPGA CHAMPIONSHIP

Shoal Creek, Alabama – a wonderful-sounding name, don't you think? It conjures up lazy, hazy, images of the sleepy Deep South – Good Ol' Dixie. Good Ol' Dixie it may be but the atmosphere surrounding the venue for the 72nd Championship of the American Professional Golfers' Association (the USPGA) last August was anything but hazy and lazy.

Firstly on the eve of the tournament the host club was accused of having racist membership policies. Apparently only golfers who were whiter than white stood a chance of being admitted at Shoal Creek. Not that the problem of golf racism is exactly confined to Shoal Creek; as one American journalist nicely put it, discrimination is more widely practised than putting in numerous country clubs right across America. Several sponsors threatened to pull out when there was talk of mass picketing and for a while it looked as if the USPGA might switch venues at the eleventh hour. It didn't happen, but no sooner had a compromise been reached and calm restored than the players inspected the course and started shrieking with displeasure. 'What have you done to Jack's course?' they demanded. An early Nicklaus creation, Shoal Creek had originally been intended as nothing more than 'a course for fun and enjoyment', not a championship test at all. The decision to stage the 1984 USPGA at Shoal Creek had therefore been a surprising one, but it had proved an extremely popular choice. Almost to a man the competitors praised its subtle charms. Lee Trevino won the championship, his sixth, and presumably final, Major, breaking 70 in all four rounds. It became known as the year of the 'golden oldies', for Trevino was then 44, and finishing joint second was 48-year-old Gary Player, who returned a brilliant 63 on the second day.

So why all the fuss in 1990? Could Shoal Creek have changed so much? The powers at Shoal Creek were presumably a little miffed that somebody could shoot 69-68-67-69 (15 under par) in their championship debut and so they decided this time to let the rough grow . . . and grow. It was so thick that often a ball which came to rest just inches off the fairway had to be hacked out sideways with a sand iron. Nor were the fairways exactly wide. It was difficult enough hitting the ball on to the green, but sometimes it was even more difficult staying on the green having reached it. Most of Shoal Creek's putting surfaces were as hard as rock; balls were regularly pitching close to the flag only for them to bounce on through the green . . . and into that rough! This time it had been determined that Shoal Creek would be a test of endurance, a test of accuracy, and perhaps above all a test of patience.

It was a test which many of the game's big names failed on all three counts. Who would have thought it possible that the top ten golfers in the world (according to the Sony rankings at the time) would each return a score of 77 or higher? That is what happened at hazy, lazy Shoal Creek.

Given the degree of challenge that lay ahead and considering the kind of form he was in, there are no prizes for guessing who the favourite was at Shoal Creek. Before the season started, Faldo had declared that his ambition in golf was to achieve so much that long after he left the scene people would boast 'I saw Faldo play.' At Shoal Creek, more than 3,000 people were content just to watch him practise. After his performance at St Andrews there was no doubting that he had become 'The Man'. Jack Nicklaus sought him out at Shoal Creek and told him as much, adding 'I just wanted to tell you that it was a pleasure watching you play in the Open.' Gary Player was also widely quoted as saying that he thought Faldo would be the next player to win all four of golf's major prizes.

Nobody hits the ball straighter than Nick Faldo, but the Masters champion wasn't at all impressed with the way Shoal Creek had

Surprise first-round leader, Bobby Wadkins

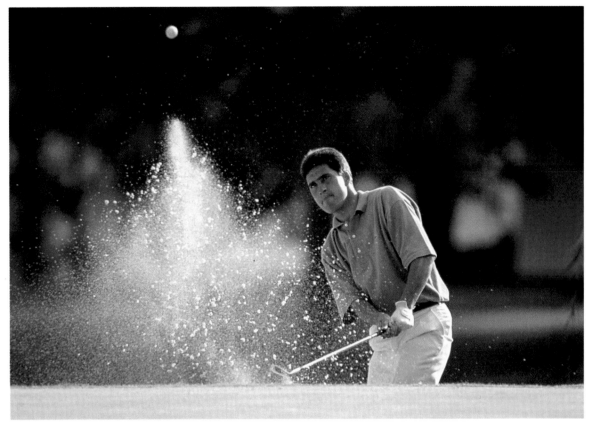

Chema chameleon – Olazabal blended nicely with the surroundings but the European challenge never really materialized

been set up for the championship. 'They might as well spray red paint down the edge of the fairways and call the rough a hazard,' he said. Poor Shoal Creek: even the defending champion, Payne Stewart, gave it the thumbs down!

Of course somebody had to win the 1990 USPGA Championship. Curtis Strange? Seve Ballesteros? or Bernhard Langer, perhaps? Or how about Nicklaus, Lanny Wadkins, Mark Calcavecchia or the evergreen Trevino, now cleaning up on the US Seniors Tour? Hardly. None of them made it through the weekend. The halfway cut fell at 151, 7 over par, the highest total since 1958. Ballesteros missed it by a mile, shooting 77-83; but there were still more than a dozen players behind him. On the first day only three players broke 70; Bobby Wadkins (brother of Lanny), who has never won a US Tour event, led on 68, followed by Fred Couples and Mark O'Meara on 69. Only two others bettered Faldo's opening 71. With Norman, Ballesteros and Calcavecchia taking 77, Nicklaus 78, Strange and Kite 79, it was a very promising start for the favourite. Payne Stewart, the one golfer who had given Nick something to worry about on the last day at St Andrews, also scored 71 to start a spirited defence of his title.

Nick started to go backwards on Friday. A lacklustre 75 dropped him down the field and left him 7 shots off the pace. Collecting one of the four sub-70 rounds on day two was Greg Norman, who in so doing edged one ahead of Faldo in their private battle. But it was that other Queenslander who was grabbing the headlines – the one everybody tends to forget to mention when recounting the thrilling finish to the Open at Troon in 1989 – Mr Perennial Runner-up himself, Wayne Grady. He achieved the best score of the day, a 5-under-par 67, to add to his first-round 72, and now led the tournament on 139. Just one behind Grady after 36 holes were Southerner Larry Mize (72-68) and a player few had expected to be in contention, given his reputation for waywardness off the tee, Seattle's Fred Couples (69-71). Freddy's nickname in America is 'Boom Boom', because he frequently hits a golf ball the way Roscoe Tanner used to hit a tennis ball. Shoal Creek hadn't been prepared for a player like Couples. It had been set up for unerringly straight players like Wayne Grady or Payne Stewart. The colourful '89 PGA champion remained very much in touch on 143 after a second day 72.

In the third round Messrs Grady (72), Couples (73), and Stewart (70) continued to set the pace. Whereas Grady and Stewart played precise, measured golf, Couples sprayed shots all over Shoal Creek, but scrambled like a demon; he could easily have scored an 80 on Saturday. Nick Faldo did.

Watching the world's number one splashing around in the mud on the 10th, en route to a triple-bogey 7, showed that he is human after all. News of Faldo's debacle shared the headlines with a sensational round from Gil Morgan. An eye doctor by profession and celebrated golfer by trade, Morgan scorched around Shoal Creek in 65 strokes on Saturday. It was two shots fewer than any other player could manage all week. 'That's a 60 anywhere else,' reckoned Stewart.

On Saturday evening Grady led by 2 strokes from Couples and Stewart and by 3 from Morgan and Loren Roberts. The European challenge never really materialized: Olazabal eventually returned the lowest four-round total (294), but it was a dozen too many and Faldo regained some pride by scoring a 69 on the final day (to finish 'all square' with Norman in joint 19th place). Ian Woosnam finished somewhere in the middle of the field but was so frustrated with the course that he vowed never to play in the PGA again.

Of the leading contenders Stewart held a slight psychological advantage in that only he had won a Major before. He was in a confident, even cocky mood that Saturday evening. Perhaps he slept better than the others, but after 10 holes on Sunday, the man wearing green plus-twos and yellow socks was completely out of contention. The good doctor Morgan stayed in contention for a little longer, but for most of the day the contest was a straight fight between the Australian Grady and the American Couples.

It is difficult to imagine two more contrasting styles. Grady (who partnered Stewart on the final day and thought his choice of green and yellow, Australia's national colours, must be a good omen) is a grinder, or, as he puts it, 'I may not dazzle you with great play but I will beat you to death with persistence.' At Shoal Creek nobody hit more greens in regulation than Grady. Couples, on the other hand, is a 'hot-and-cold' flair player. His swing is wonderful to watch and he hits the ball the proverbial country mile, but you wouldn't want your life resting on his short game; moreover, Fred has a reputation for cracking under pressure. After 12 holes, during which he compiled 8 pars and 4 birdies, Couples had overtaken Grady. He was playing like a man heading for his first Major title when suddenly the wheels came off and Fred dropped 4 strokes in succession between the 13th and 16th. Couples' capitulation opened the door for Grady. While the distressed American was busy shooting himself in the foot missing a series of short putts, the personable Australian was collecting par after par. It was sufficient for him to clinch the last Major of the year. Grady finished 7 under par, 3 ahead of Couples and 4 ahead of Morgan; nobody else ended below par. Grady had beaten Shoal Creek to death with his persistence.

Grady's first Major win was thoroughly deserved – 'fair dinkum', you could say. In 1989 the giant trophy had been won by Stewart playing in the colours of the Chicago Bears, one of America's top football teams; now at Shoal Creek it was the turn of Aussie Rules. And Good Ol' Wayne had most definitely made the Grade.

Wayne Grady shows perfect balance

*Dr Gil Morgan charged through the field on Saturday
with a third-round 65*

Wayne clinches things on the final green

Overnight favourite Payne Stewart played like a crab on Sunday

For a while Fred Couples looked to have it in the bag – then the wheels came off

1990 USPGA
FINAL SCORES

Player					Total	Prize
W. Grady	72	67	72	71	282	$225,000
F. Couples	69	71	73	72	285	135,000
G. Morgan	77	72	65	72	286	90,000
B. Britton	72	74	72	71	289	73,500
C. Beck	71	70	78	71	290	51,666
B. Mayfair	70	71	75	74	290	51,666
L. Roberts	73	71	70	76	290	51,666
M. McNulty	74	72	75	71	292	34,375
D. Pooley	75	74	71	72	292	34,375
T. Simpson	71	73	75	73	292	34,375
P. Stewart	71	72	70	79	292	34,375
H. Irwin	77	72	70	74	293	27,000
L. Mize	72	68	76	77	293	27,000
J.-M. Olazabal	73	77	72	72	294	20,600
M. Hatalsky	73	78	71	72	294	20,600
C. Pavin	73	75	72	74	294	20,600
F. Zoeller	72	71	76	75	294	20,600
B. Andrade	75	72	73	74	294	20,600
N. Faldo	71	75	80	69	295	14,000
M. O'Meara	69	76	79	71	295	14,000
T. Watson	74	71	77	73	295	14,000
G. Norman	77	69	76	73	295	14,000
M. Wiebe	74	73	75	73	295	14,000
B. McCallister	75	73	74	73	295	14,000
B. Boyd	74	74	71	76	296	14,000
M. Brooks	78	69	76	73	296	8,650
R. Stewart	73	73	75	75	296	8,650
C. Perry	75	74	72	75	296	8,650
P. Jacobsen	74	75	71	76	296	8,650
B. Tennyson	71	77	71	77	296	8,650
T. Purtzer	74	74	77	72	297	6,500
D. Rummells	73	73	77	74	297	6,500
B. Crenshaw	74	70	78	75	297	6,500
J. Sluman	74	74	73	76	297	6,500
P. Azinger	76	70	74	77	297	6,500
S. Verplank	70	76	73	78	297	6,500
I. Woosnam	74	75	70	78	297	6,500
D. Frost	76	74	69	78	297	6,500
S. Pate	71	75	71	80	297	6,500
I. Aoki	72	74	78	74	298	4,750
T. Kite	79	71	74	74	298	4,750
J. Mahaffey	75	72	76	75	298	4,750
D. Love III	72	72	77	77	298	4,750
C. Parry	74	72	75	77	298	4,750
M. Reid	71	78	78	72	299	3,750
S. Rachels	75	73	76	75	299	3,750
A. Magee	75	74	73	77	299	3,750
B. Tway	72	76	73	78	299	3,700
K. Perry	73	76	78	73	300	2,865
M. Hulbert	71	75	79	75	300	2,865

Wayne Grady, USPGA champion 1990

Player					Total	Prize
H. Sutton	72	74	78	76	300	2,865
R. Gamez	71	78	75	76	300	2,865
S. Utley	71	72	80	77	300	2,865
M. McCumber	73	76	74	77	300	2,865
R. Floyd	72	77	74	77	300	2,865
S. Hoch	78	73	72	77	300	2,865
D. Peoples	77	71	77	76	301	2,525
B. Gilder	73	78	73	77	301	2,525
I. Baker-Finch	74	71	78	78	301	2,525
C. Stadler	75	73	74	79	301	2,525
J. Huston	72	72	77	80	301	2,525
P. Senior	74	75	72	81	302	2,450
D. Hammond	77	70	80	76	303	2,400
N. Price	75	71	81	76	303	2,400
J. Delsing	75	73	73	82	303	2,400
D. Graham	75	75	75	79	304	2,325
B. Wadkins	68	75	80	81	304	2,325
S. Simpson	76	75	72	81	304	2,325
C. Hungate	72	77	79	77	305	2,225
E. Fiori	75	76	77	77	305	2,225
M. Ozaki	75	74	79	77	305	2,225
J. Blair III	73	76	76	80	305	2,225
R. Mediate	75	72	77	81	305	2,225
B. Ford	75	75	79	77	306	2,150

1990 USPGA: COMMENTARY

David Davies, *The Guardian*

You can almost hear the glee in the quizmaster's voice. 'It is called the Rodman Wanamaker Trophy and it is played for in August of every year. For two points, what is the sport and what is the event?'

It is the kind of poser that would send those great big, beery eyes of Ian Botham rolling up to his eyebrows on *A Question of Sport*, and yet the Rodman Wanamaker Trophy is given for one of the world's most prestigious sporting events: one that began in 1916 and has continued, with interruptions for World Wars only, to the present day.

It is, of course, the United States Professional Golfers' Association Championship trophy, the present holder of which is that amiable Aussie Wayne Grady. Mr Wanamaker was one of the founding fathers of the USPGA and indeed gave his trophy for an event which was specifically to be modelled on the lines of 'the British tournament, the News of the World'. That of course was matchplay; so too were all the early USPGAs, and the first winner was a Cornishman, who triumphed over a St Andrean in the final, Jim Barnes beating Jock Hutchinson by one hole.

Perhaps the biggest single change since their day was the switch from matchplay to stroke play which took place in 1958. The committeemen of the 1950s probably felt they had little option but to change, but what a shame it all looks from 30-odd years later. Matchplay is, as has often been said, the raw blood and guts of the game; it brings totally different emphases to the playing of it, and would it not now be wonderful to watch someone, say Severiano Ballesteros, compile the kind of Walter Hagenesque record of winning four championships, and 22 matches, consecutively?

There is, however, little chance of that. The present championship is firmly committed to stroke play and it has, in the years since the changeover, seen some historical moments.

There was the wonderful occasion, again at Shoal Creek, this time in 1984, when Lee Trevino, at the age of 44, took the title. He won in some style by holing a putt of at least 15 feet on the last green, and for a few moments he just stood there. It transpired later that he wasn't sure how to celebrate. 'At first I thought I'd jump in the air. But hell, I'm too old to jump. Anyways, I can jump as high as I used to, but I can't stay up there as long. Then I thought I'd throw my cap in the air, but I remembered that it wasn't mine. I'd forgotten mine that morning and had to borrow one from a guy in the clubhouse.' Finally Trevino just kissed the putter which had holed the final putt and which he had bought for £25 from the pro's shop at the Dutch Open three weeks before.

The PGA has hosted other highlights. There was Jack Nicklaus's win in 1973, which was his 14th Major championship and an emotional time for the Golden Bear. He had set himself the career task of beating the Majors haul of Bobby Jones, who won 13, and this was the moment of achievement. Nicklaus also won in 1971, which was not all that amazing, given that he was winning a great many things at that time, but the PGA is, of course, the last of the season's Majors and Nicklaus then opened up 1972 by winning the US Masters and the US Open.

That meant he had three in a row, and with the Open Championship at Muirfield, one of his favourite courses, there was an obvious chance of him winning and thus holding all four titles at one time. Whether such an achievement would be called the Grand Slam never got to be debated, because someone called Trevino got in the way. Muirfield '72 was the time that Supermex chipped in at the 17th, or 71st, when he had given up hope, and when Tony Jacklin finished 6,5 to finish third. Nicklaus, finishing bogey, par, par, came second, one behind Trevino, two shots short of an almost unthinkable feat.

He had to be content with holding three Major titles at once, equalling with Ben Hogan the most any man has done since Bobby Jones won the Open and Amateur Championships of Great Britain and America in the same year. It was that mark of three which Faldo, prior to the PGA winner of the US Masters and the Open, wanted to emulate when he came to Shoal Creek last year.

If Shoal Creek suited anyone that week it was Faldo: he would be the man to put the heavy money on, with a saver perhaps on José-Maria Olazabal. Both men had the kind of game that would agree perfectly with the conditions as laid down: thick, clinging, penal rough which would reward men who could hit the ball straight and, if they strayed, had the short game to save par. That might have been a job description of Faldo and Olazabal going into the 1990 USPGA, and, of course, as is the way with racing certainties, they not only never figured, they finished way down the track. None of the Europeans coped with the course, despite the fact that the Alabaman weather, confidently predicted to be very hot and exceedingly humid, was neither. It was nigh perfect for golf, but another European, Ian Woosnam, nevertheless departed in ill-humour with everything related to Shoal Creek. After a final-round 78, he said: 'This is the last time I play in this thing. I don't like the rough and I don't like the way they've set up the greens. I hear they may bring the US Open here and if they do I won't play in that either.'

Faldo concurred. 'I'm glad it's over,' he said. 'I've never known a week when so many pros' heads came off.' Fuzzy Zoeller lost another part of his anatomy. He said: 'The rough is just stupid. We work our butts off all year long to learn how to chip and then find that skill taken away from us. There's no talent to chipping in these conditions. You just hit it out and hope to hole your 30-footer.'

The PGA refused to cut back the rough, which certainly was overdone. Hit a ball into it and there was no option but to take a wedge and hack out sideways, which is profoundly unexciting for the spectator and extremely irritating to the player. But the PGA officials, and those of Shoal Creek, aware that the modern emphasis is on making life difficult, if not impossible, for the player, touched not a blade. They were aware, too, that officials of the United States Golf Association were present, making a judgement on whether the venue would be suitable for the staging of a US Open, and as officials of that organization had set the trends in penal grass-growing, it was always unlikely that Shoal would be shaved.

So the players just had to suffer, and suffer they did. After four rounds there were only three players under par: Grady, Couples and Morgan. Grady, to his immense credit, won from the front, playing the entire last round knowing that he was expected to win. He produced some rigorous play, par after par, and it was far too much for Couples, who has frequently folded under pressure. No sooner had Couples taken a one-shot lead, after 12 holes, than he bogied the next four holes, and we were able to experience the pure pleasure of a Grady press conference.

With one of the widest smiles in sport he told us how he still rated his country-man Greg Norman as the better player, even though they each have one Major champion-ship. 'Yeah,' said Grady, 'that's true, but he's got 55 other wins around the world. But he's a great bloke.' The great bloke in person had previously finished down the field, left in a private jet and, while heading for Florida, radioed back to the club. 'How's my mate Grades doin'?' he asked. Told he was lead-ing, Norman said: 'Tell him to stick right in there.'

'Grades' did so. The title meant that, in addition to $225,000, he received various other privileges. The press officer read some of them out. 'You are exempt from qualifying for the PGA for life, the US Tour for ten years, the US Masters for five years and the Open Championship for three years,' he said. Grady, in danger of being consumed by his grin, sat there and rubbed his hands. 'You beaut.,' he said, 'you bloody beauty.'

3

GLOBAL GOLF

EUROPE
THE UNITED STATES
AUSTRALIA
JAPAN
THE REST OF THE WORLD
SENIORS
AMATEURS

EUROPE

Ian Woosnam overshadows Mark McNulty

Helen Alfredsson overshadows Marie-Laure de Lorenzi

1990 EUROPEAN TOUR REVIEW

There is of course no such thing in golf as a world tour; however, there is one genuinely international tour, and it is to be found in Europe. The facts speak for themselves: in 1990 the 37 Volvo PGA European Tour events were staged in sixteen different countries, and the winners of those events represented no fewer than thirteen different nations and five continents.

In 1991 the tour will run from the middle of February to the beginning of November.

As the season gets longer and longer, so Ian Woosnam gets richer and richer. In 1990, he topped the European Order of Merit table for the second time, setting a new record winnings total of £574,166 and that figure does not include the £100,000 he collected for winning his second World Matchplay Championship. It was a year when both Ballesteros and Woosnam passed the £2 million earnings barrier; Seve was first to get there, but by the end of the year 'little Woosie' had edged his nose in front.

Just as it was Faldo's year in the Majors, so it was the Welshman's year on tour: five times he mounted the winners' rostrum and four times he finished runner-up. Ian Woosnam neither looks, acts nor swings a club remotely like Johnny Miller, but there were times in 1990 when his scoring was reminiscent of the mercurial American's purple patch in the mid-1970s. At Monte Carlo in July he recorded a 60, at Gleneagles just a week later he had a 62 and at the beginning of October he set yet another course record with a ten-under-par 62 in the German Masters. No other player won tournaments back-to-back on the Volvo tour – Woosnam did it twice. Against such brilliance it is to the immense credit of Mark McNulty and José-Maria Olazabal that they chased Woosnam all the way to the finishing line. In fact McNulty, who won in France and in Germany and finished second three times to Woosnam (as well as runner-up to Faldo at St Andrews), came within two strokes of tieing Mike Harwood in the season's final event at Valderrama. Had he actually done so, and then gone on to win the play-off, he and not Woosnam would have finished the year as leading moneywinner.

Again to emphasize the tour's internationalism, Zimbabwean McNulty's two wins were matched by Bernhard Langer of Germany, Ronan Rafferty of Northern Ireland, Mark James of England, Stephen McAllister of Scotland and Australians Mike Harwood and Rodger Davis. The one triple winner was the Spaniard Olazabal. In the mid-1980's the best three golfers in Europe were undoubtedly Ballesteros, Langer and Lyle. On 1990s form it would be difficult to argue against Faldo, Woosnam and Olazabal; at the end of the year they occupied three of the top four places in the Sony World Rankings. But if those world rankings are likely to stir anyone more than the Americans, then it is Messrs Ballesteros, Langer and Lyle. If 1990 had been a Ryder Cup year, Ireland's David Feherty, who led his country to a thrilling Dunhill Cup success over England, and Scotland's Colin Montgomerie would have achieved automatic selection; it will be interesting to see how they

and the likes of Howard Clark and Gordon Brand Jnr, both of whom had disappointing years, fare in 1991.

The Ryder Cup must have seemed light-years away when the tour teed off last February and the players battled not so much against each other as against the elements and the prospect of being blown out to sea. So much for sunny Portugal! This was the inaugural Atlantic Open at Estela, eventually won by Stephen McAllister following an extraordinary six-man play-off. It was extraordinary not just because of the number of players involved (a tour record) but because, of the six, only McAllister could manage to par the first extra hole. It was then a case of from the ridiculous to the sublime. There can be few more dramatic settings in golf than the Emirates Club in Dubai. The second event on the European tour was staged at this golfing oasis in the desert, victory going to Eamonn Darcy, who led all the way following an opening 64. After the Scotsman and the Irishman, it was the turn of the Welshman.

Given how much money Woosnam was about to win in the ensuing months it was rather ironic that his first success of 1990 should come in the American Express-sponsored Mediterranean Open. The venue for this new event was Las Brisas in southern Spain, scene of the 1989 World Cup which witnessed some atrocious weather. Whoever said that 'the rain in Spain falls mainly on the plain' had never visited Las Brisas; once again the heavens opened. Saturday's play was rained off, but on the Sunday, as nearby Gibraltar Airport stayed closed, it was Woosnam who held his game together best in the swirling March winds.

The Majorcan Open is only a little older than the Atlantic and Mediterranean Opens. In its first three years it has been dominated by those two Spanish Masters, Ballesteros and Olazabal. In 1988 Seve outgunned his young rival on the last day; in 1989 it was the young pretender who triumphed, but in 1990 Ballesteros regained the title. He did it in some style too, coming back from 5 behind in the final round. Sweden's Magnus Persson was the unfortunate victim, going down in a play-off. It was the 60th victory of Ballesteros's illustrious career, but few at the time could have imagined that it would be his solitary success in 1990.

In the middle of March the tour did a bit of island-hopping, moving from the Balearics to the Canaries. The Tenerife Open was played at Amerilla in the shadows of a massive volcano, Mount Teidi, and amid some extraordinary vegetation. Olazabal was the favourite to win the event, but he played from the wrong side of a cactus and managed to disqualify himself. Eventually 43-year-old Argentinian Vicente Fernandez landed the first prize after a sudden-death play-off. It was the tour's third play-off in only five weeks.

The players then returned to the mainland, but the Argentinian flag was still flying when Eduardo Romero finished ahead of the field in the Volvo Open. The scoring that week was as spectacular as the Florentine backdrop. In the first two rounds the big Argentinian shot 68-66 but still found himself 5 behind the big Scot, Colin Montgomerie. Whereas Montgomerie couldn't quite keep it going, Romero added rounds of 64-67 for a winning 23-under-par total. Finishing joint second with Montgomerie in Florence was tour rookie Russell Claydon.

In the last week of March the 'circus' moved to the south of France. This time it was the Australians who impressed. Tall, thin Brett Ogle, arguably the longest hitter on tour, won the AGF Open, and his compatriot Wayne Riley won a £20,000 Volvo estate car for a hole-in-one. Riley's only problem was that in March last year he was in the midst of a drink-driving ban.

Into April, and while Nick Faldo was retaining his Masters crown in America, Fijian Vijay Singh was collecting the El Bosque Open in Valencia. Seven days later Mark McNulty, who it would seem has something of a penchant for the Côte d'Azur, won the Cannes Open. In 1989 McNulty had won at Monaco. A very strong field assembled for the Madrid Open, and a worthy champion was produced in Bernhard Langer. The locals had no doubt hoped for a Ballesteros *v.* Olazabal contest,

Stephen McAllister won the year's opening event at Estela in Portugal after a six-man play-off

but unfortunately 'the king' missed the cut and 'the crown prince' finished outside the top fifty. Rodger Davis finished second to Langer, and in third place, after a magnificent final-day 61, was Australia's walking one-iron Brett Ogle.

Around this time Rodger Davis revealed that he had wagered £1,000 on himself at 33-1 to finish in the top three in the Order of Merit. It was looking a good bet when, a week after his second-place finish in the Madrid Open, he went one better at Club de Campo to win the Spanish Open. In a reversal of roles, Langer finished second, tied with the fast-finishing Nick Faldo and Peter Fowler. Langer actually missed a six-footer to tie the Australian, but his consolation was to win a Peugeot car for having the week's best five-round total, including the pre-tournament pro-am; it was a good two weeks' work for Langer, as in the Madrid Open he had been presented with the keys to a new Volvo for precisely the same reason.

I have to say that my money was on Langer (each way) at St Mellion in the first week of May. The 19th Benson & Hedges International boasted a formidable line-up: Nick Faldo was making his first appearance in Britain since his historic triumph at Augusta; Ballesteros, Olazabal, Woosnam, Rafferty, Davis and McNulty were all out to beat him ... and then, of course, there was my man Langer. It was the kiss of death; at his first hole Langer bagged an 8 and dropped four strokes. I threw away my betting slip. But Bernhard wasn't the only one suffering over the picturesque but extremely testing Jack Nicklaus layout: Nick Faldo took 78 in the first round, his worst score of the year apart from the 80 he recorded at Shoal Creek; and in the second round Ballesteros, who had opened with a promising 68, shot a 77. But, as one might expect in Cornwall, the cream eventually rose to the top: Faldo made the halfway cut and eventually finished in joint 12th place, and the top four places were occupied by Olazabal, Woosnam, Langer (he must have found my betting slip), and McNulty. The same four players, admittedly in different positions, finished 1-2-3-4 in the final Volvo Order of Merit table. Olazabal's exciting one-stroke win over Woosnam was his first on British soil since turning professional. As an amateur he had won the triple crown of British Boys, British Youths and British Amateur titles; now victory at St Mellion set him up for the greatest year of his career ... so far!

Ian Woosnam missed a three-foot putt on the 71st hole at St Mellion, and he was left to rue several missed opportunities a week later in Belgium, when he again finished second, this time to Ove Sellberg. There was only one possible winner in the next tournament, the Italian Open, as Richard Boxall ran away from the field shooting 24 birdies and one eagle. In the first round Boxall set a course-record 65; the following day he scored a 64. Olazabal finished a distant second, 5 behind the man from Surrey.

One of the European tour's most prestigious events is undoubtedly the Volvo PGA Championship, staged at Wentworth, the tour's HQ. In late 1990 Wentworth was as dry as the proverbial tinderbox. In the previous two years, victory had gone first to Woosnam then to Faldo, and they of course played a kind of decider in the World Matchplay late in 1989. This time for most of PGA week it looked as if Olazabal would gain his second win of the year, despite suffering from a touch of flu. However, on the fourth day, as the Spaniard weakened, Australian Mike Harwood battled through to snatch a surprise victory. Faldo didn't give up the trophy without a fight, mind you. In front of a large Bank Holiday crowd the Wentworth Club member produced a marvellous back-nine onslaught, firing seven birdies in an inward 30; at the end of the day it proved just one too many.

As May changed into June – and still it refused to rain in southern England – Mark James won the British Masters at Woburn. As Dunhill sponsor this tournament, it was paradoxical to see numerous 'no smoking' signs on the course. In the event it was James who caught fire at the weekend with a brilliant 66 on Saturday followed by an outward half of 30 on Sunday. Not surprisingly, no one could catch him, and he cemented his reputation as arguably Europe's best front-runner. The defending champion Faldo couldn't find any inspiration at all, or as he put it, 'I played lousy, putted lousy and the weather's lousy'. Only an Englishman could detest continuous sunshine.

One golfer who usually looks as if he's feeling lousy is American Craig Stadler, US Masters champion of 1982. Universally known as 'The Walrus', Stadler can often be found at about this time of year basking in Scandinavia. 1990 unfortunately saw the last Scandinavian Open, because in 1991 the event merges with the PLM Open to become the Scandinavian Masters. Stadler, however, had clearly decided to give the tournament a send-off to remember, as in the final round he produced a stunning eleven-under-par 61. It broke the course record by three strokes and

Eamonn Darcy plays towards the magnificent clubhouse of the Emirates Golf Club, Dubai

landed him the handsome first prize. Rumour has it that for one fleeting moment Craig's moustache curled up at the ends ... And from one celebrated moustache to another ... that £1,000 bet was looking good again in the middle of June when Rodger Davis won a four-way play-off at Moor Park in the Wang National Pro-Celebrity. Jolly Rodger became the first double winner of 1990. One week later there was another.

St Mellion and Portmarnock are as different as chalk and cheese, and the weather for the Irish Open was decidedly less friendly than it had been for the B&H International in Cornwall. But Olazabal demonstrated that he is a man for all seasons as well as a master on all surfaces by holding off the spirited challenge of Open champion Mark Calcavecchia.

For a time it looked as if a Frenchman, Marc Farry, might win the Irish Open, but he unfortunately collapsed under the final-day pressure. The following week an Irishman did

win the French Open. Philip Walton holed a 20-foot putt on the final green to tie Langer and then defeated the German in extra time to gain his first tour success. It was an unforgettable week for Walton, as he also scored a hole-in-one on the second day. At Monte Carlo seven days later there was another ace, as Ballesteros recorded his first-ever tournament hole-in-one. Might this spur him on to victory in his adopted home? Well, any such thoughts he might have been harbouring were shattered on the final day, as Woosnam charged around the Mount Angel course in 60 strokes to win by 5. A pitch and a single putt at the last (his final drive left him just 75 yards from the flag) and Woosnam could have claimed the tour's first ever sub-60 score.

The fired-up Welshman made a pretty good attempt at it too, in the Scottish Open at Gleneagles. This time his birdie blitz came in a second-round 62. Gordon Brand Jnr and

Mark McNulty gave Woosnam a run for his money, but in this kind of form no one was likely to stop him. It was the tournament before the Open and Woosnam's heroics must have sent shivers down the spines of almost every other competitor. One player, though, who wouldn't have left Gleneagles feeling too perturbed was Nick Faldo; in the final round he at last found his touch, scoring a best-of-the-day 65 – precisely as he had done on the eve of the US Masters in April. Nick only made the halfway cut at Gleneagles thanks to a birdie-birdie finish to his second round; without those birdies there would have been no competitive weekend golf for Nick – no 65 – and ... well, who knows what might or might not have happened at St Andrews. (The Open Championship is reviewed fully in section two.)

The next two tournaments saw British players leading from start to finish. Stephen McAllister proved that his Atlantic Open win was no fluke by taking the Dutch Open title at Kennemer – the Scot clearly relishes links golf – and then Ronan Rafferty opened his 1990 account by spreadeagling the field in the PLM Open in Sweden.

Regrettably nobody had the luck of the Irish to hole in one at the 14th at Fulford during the Murphy's Cup in August – had anyone so managed they could have walked away (!) with 13,750 pints of Murphy's Irish stout. Tony Johnstone must have felt like getting pretty inebriated after his second-day 61, which contained eight successive birdies. This being the tour's one stableford event, Johnstone's score was actually recorded as 23 points; still it set him firmly on the road to a well-earned victory. After Fulford came The Belfry and the English Open. It was a tournament that Seve appeared to have within his grasp until he three-putted himself out of contention. David Feherty eagled the 71st hole and waited behind the final green knowing that only the defending champion, Mark James, and Sam Torrance could catch him, and both needed to par the notorious 18th to do so. In fact against all the odds both birdied the hole, and James eventually emerged the winner following a sudden-death play-off

against Torrance. It was the Englishman's second win of the year, but spare a thought for poor old Sam – earlier in the week he had been penalized a stroke for waiting more than ten seconds to allow his ball to drop into the hole at the 10th.

After uncharacteristically missing the cut at The Belfry, his first for many a month, McNulty bounced back with a vengeance to grab the German Open title. A superb last-round 65 lifted the amiable Zimbabwean back to the top of the Order of Merit. In the week when McNulty was winning at Hubbelrath, Olazabal was compiling the performance of the year in America's World Series (see the US Tour review). At the end of August, that other young lion, Rafferty, won the European Masters at Crans-sur-Sierre, helped immeasurably by a front nine of 28 on the second day. There is no pleasing some people, however, as Ronan reckoned he didn't play particularly well all week – and that includes that 28!

A less welcome Irish accent was bothering the players and organizers at Sunningdale soon after the European Open got under way. It was a bomb scare. 'My name is O'Connor,' said the voice (probably giving the first Irish golfing name that entered his head). 'There is a bomb planted under the grandstand by the 18th green.' Of course there wasn't, but play was disrupted for three and a half hours all the same. Fortunately it didn't sour proceedings, and American import Tim Simpson was quoted as saying later in the week, 'I only wish our tour would play at places like Sunningdale instead of a whole lot of boring courses where the genius of guys like Seve Ballesteros counts for very little.' Simpson himself might have won the tournament but for twice tangling with the trees at the 17th. Going into the final round Faldo was the favourite after a superb 64 on day three. He played the first three holes on Sunday in 4 under par but then, surprisingly, could make no further headway and eventually finished equal fourth, tied with Simpson and Olazabal. Ahead of him were Canizares, Woosnam and the man none of them could quite catch, Australian Peter Senior. It was

Woosnam, number one in Europe for the second time

something of an unexpected win – Senior's pedigree has never been doubted, but only a few months earlier his form had deserted him to such an extent that he was reputedly unable to string two good shots together.

Stringing two good shots together has never been a problem for Olazabal. Having gained his first British win in May and his first Irish win in June, in September he left his rivals trailing behind with a final-round 65 in Paris to capture his first French victory in the prestigious Lancôme tournament.

As Ian Woosnam set about winning his second World Matchplay crown at Wentworth (see below), David Feherty and Paul Azinger were turning the BMW Open into a head-to-head affair after opening with scores of 62 and 63 respectively. Feherty led just about all the way but was caught at the death by his American opponent, who won in a play-off. It was a brilliant defence of his title by the Ulsterman, who at least gained some consolation a month later at St Andrews in the Dunhill Cup.

Dressed in a dragon-red sweater, Ian Woosnam won the Epson Grand Prix in front of his home crowd at St Pierre near Chepstow. Joint runners-up at wet and windy Chepstow were the familiar figures of McNulty and Olazabal. 'Woosie' now roared ahead of the Zimbabwean and the Spaniard in the race to head the Order of Merit table and kept his nose nicely in front courtesy of a brilliant last-day 62 in the German Masters at Stuttgart. It wasn't good enough, though, to overhaul Sam Torrance, whose two middle rounds were 65 and 64. It was 'slamming Sam's' first tour win since 1987. In second place was Bernhard Langer, at last seemingly discovering the form that made him such a formidable world force in the mid-1980s.

Langer emphasized the point in the Austrian Open a week later at Gut Altentann, a Jack Nicklaus-designed course near Salzburg. The Golden Bear played in the event, his first ever on the Volvo tour, and finished joint 11th. Rather like the BMW Open the tournament was essentially a head-to-head confrontation from the outset. This time it was the European player who triumphed as Langer defeated his old Ryder Cup adversary, Lanny Wadkins, in one of the year's tightest finishes.

As the season drew to a close, some extremely generous three-putting by Mike Harwood and Gordon Brand Jnr at Quinta do Lago enabled Mike McLean to emerge as an unexpected but extremely popular winner of the Portuguese Open-TPC; and then finally it was off to the end-of-season jamboree at Valderrama in southern Spain. McNulty's valiant attempt to overhaul Ian Woosnam at the top of the Merit table has already been commented upon. He will doubtless have another go next year; so surely will Olazabal, who might have won at Valderrama but for taking a triple-bogey seven at the 18th in the second round. In the end it was the six-foot-four Harwood who best weathered the trying conditions and the desperately difficult course to secure a marvellous Volvo PGA–Volvo Masters double. But the more significant Volvo double belonged to the five-foot-four Ian Woosnam.

Mike Harwood explores Wentworth's undergrowth en route to winning the Volvo PGA Championship

Ian Woosnam almost vanished without trace at St Mellion, but still finished second to Olazabal in the Benson and Hedges International

Great Scot! Torrance celebrates on his favourite green – the 18th at The Belfry

Olazabal, Spain's limbo dancing champion

Ballesteros tries some body Spanish

Agony or ecstasy? Philip Walton at the French Open

1990 VOLVO TOUR RESULTS

15-18 February
VINHO VERDE ATLANTIC OPEN *Campo Golfe, Estela, Oporto, Portugal*

*Stephen McAllister	71	71	72	74	288	£33,330
Ronan Rafferty	72	70	74	72	288	12,038
David Williams	70	71	73	74	288	12,038
Stephen Hamill	71	67	74	76	288	12,038
Richard Boxall	71	73	73	71	288	12,038
Anders Sorenson	68	73	70	77	288	12,038
Steven Bowman	71	73	73	72	289	4,632
Ronald Stelten	70	69	70	80	289	4,632
Steven Richardson	72	70	71	76	289	4,632
Ross Drummond	70	73	70	76	289	4,632
Miguel Angel Jimenez	73	68	72	76	289	4,632

22-25 February
EMIRATES AIRLINE DESERT CLASSIC *Emirates Golf Club, Dubai*

Eamonn Darcy	64	68	75	69	276	£45,825
David Feherty	73	69	70	68	280	30,530
Severiano Ballesteros	72	69	71	70	282	15,482
Des Smyth	68	71	74	69	282	15,482
David Gilford	70	73	69	72	284	11,655
Peter Fowler	72	70	73	70	285	8,250
Steven Richardson	72	70	72	71	285	8,250
Denis Durnian	72	67	73	73	285	8,250
Brett Ogle	71	73	75	67	286	5,175
Nick Faldo	72	73	72	69	286	5,175
Mark McNulty	69	74	71	72	286	5,175
Peter O'Malley	68	70	77	71	286	5,175
Bill Longmuir	70	69	74	73	286	5,175

1-4 March
AMERICAN EXPRESS MEDITERRANEAN OPEN *Las Brisas, Marbella, Spain*

Ian Woosnam	68	68	74	210	£66,660
Eduardo Romero	70	71	71	212	34,720
Miguel Angel Martin	69	69	74	212	34,720
Christy O'Connor Jnr	71	71	71	213	20,000
Mark James	67	71	76	214	16,940
Peter Smith	72	72	72	216	13,000
Andrew Murray	74	70	72	216	13,000
John Morgan	74	75	68	217	8,580
Peter Fowler	71	72	74	217	8,580
Mark McNulty	72	69	76	217	8,580
Mats Lanner	70	71	76	217	8,580

8-11 March
OPEN RENAULT DE BALEARES *Son Vida, Palma de Mallorca*

*Severiano Ballesteros	66	65	70	68	269	£45,825
Magnus Persson	65	65	66	73	269	30,530
Juan Quiros	68	64	71	68	271	17,215
Mark McNulty	67	70	69	66	272	13,750
Jean Van de Velde	71	66	69	67	273	10,640
Rodger Davis	70	64	70	69	273	10,640
Armando Saavedra	67	68	70	70	275	8,250
Bernhard Langer	66	70	70	70	276	6,875
Christy O'Connor Jnr	68	68	70	71	277	6,160

15-18 March
TENERIFE OPEN *Amarilla, Tenerife*

*Vicente Fernandez	67	74	72	69	282	£33,330
Mark Mouland	70	73	71	68	282	22,200
Christy O'Connor Jnr	74	71	66	73	284	10,330
Emmanuel Dussart	71	74	69	70	284	10,330
Tony Charnley	71	74	66	73	284	10,330
Miguel Angel Jimenez	68	72	75	70	285	7,000
Grant Turner	70	76	69	71	286	5,160
Manuel Pinero	68	73	73	72	286	5,160
Bradley Hughes	71	71	74	70	286	5,160

22-25 March
VOLVO OPEN DI FIRENZE *Ugolino, Italy*

Eduardo Romero	68	66	64	67	265	£33,330
Colin Montgomerie	65	64	67	70	266	17,360
Russell Claydon	63	68	66	69	266	17,360
Rodger Davis	69	63	71	66	269	9,235
Mats Hallberg	71	63	67	68	269	9,235
Peter O'Malley	67	64	68	71	270	7,000
Roger Chapman	65	66	70	71	272	5,160
Peter Senior	69	67	68	68	272	5,160
Jim Rutledge	72	65	64	71	272	5,160

* Winner after play-off

29 March-1 April
AGF OPEN *La Grande Motte, Montpelier*

Brett Ogle	72	66	70	70	278	£33,330
Paul Curry	70	71	69	71	281	17,360
Bill Longmuir	71	72	69	69	281	17,360
Denis Durnian	71	71	71	69	282	9,235
Mark McNulty	72	71	68	71	282	9,235
Mark James	77	68	67	71	283	7,000
Peter McWhinney	73	69	70	72	284	6,000
Miguel Angel Martin	68	74	72	71	285	4,493
Russell Claydon	73	71	70	71	285	4,493
Michael McLean	69	73	71	72	285	4,493

5-8 April
EL BOSQUE OPEN, VALENCIA, *El Bosque G&CC, Valencia*

Vijay Singh	66	69	74	69	278	£33,330
Chris Williams	68	71	70	71	280	17,360
Richard Boxall	70	69	70	71	280	17,360
Johan Rystrom	72	72	69	68	281	9,235
Brian Marchbank	69	69	75	68	281	9,235
Philip Parkin	68	72	71	71	282	5,620
Tony Charnley	72	72	67	71	282	5,620
Miguel Angel Jimenez	74	70	66	72	282	5,620
John Hawksworth	73	72	68	69	282	5,620

13-16 April
CREDIT LYONNAIS CANNES OPEN *Cannes Mougins Country Club*

Mark McNulty	69	71	69	71	280	£50,000
Ronan Rafferty	73	67	72	69	281	33,300
Mark Roe	72	71	66	73	282	18,780
Vijay Singh	69	72	74	69	284	11,800
Mark O'Meara	70	70	75	69	284	11,800
Jesper Parnevik	69	68	73	74	284	11,800
Anders Sorensen	68	68	75	73	284	11,800
Magnus Persson	70	74	68	73	285	6,740
Ian Woosnam	69	72	67	77	285	6,740
Howard Clark	72	68	73	72	285	6,740

19-22 April
CEPSA MADRID OPEN *Puerta de Hierro, Madrid*

Bernhard Langer	70	67	66	67	270	£45,825
Rodger Davis	67	70	68	66	271	30,530
Brett Ogle	72	66	73	61	272	17,215
Magnus Sunesson	72	65	66	70	273	13,750
Ronald Stelten	73	68	67	68	276	11,655
Philip Walton	70	69	71	67	277	8,937
Jose Rivero	67	71	70	69	277	8,937
John Hawksworth	69	68	72	69	278	6,517
Gordon Brand Jnr	68	70	72	68	278	6,517

26-29 April
PEUGEOT SPANISH OPEN *Club de Campo, Madrid*

Rodger Davis	74	69	68	66	277	£50,000
Nick Faldo	70	71	72	65	278	22,360
Bernhard Langer	70	71	69	68	278	22,360
Peter Fowler	72	68	69	69	278	22,360
Stephen McAllister	74	71	65	70	280	12,700
Yago Beamonte	71	75	67	68	281	8,430
Severiano Ballesteros	74	70	68	69	281	8,430
Jose Maria Olazabal	71	67	71	72	281	8,430
Steven Bowman	71	70	68	72	281	8,430

4-7 May
BENSON AND HEDGES INTERNATIONAL OPEN *St Mellion G&CC, Cornwall*

José-Maria Olazabal	69	68	69	73	279	£58,330
Ian Woosnam	69	69	69	73	280	38,860
Bernhard Langer	72	72	68	70	282	21,910
Mark NcNulty	68	68	73	74	283	17,500
John Bland	68	71	75	72	286	12,526
Mike Harwood	71	68	75	72	286	12,526
Philip Walton	70	71	75	70	286	12,526
Ronan Rafferty	67	72	74	74	287	7,507
Colin Montgomerie	69	72	70	76	287	7,507
Gordon Brand Jnr	72	71	71	73	287	7,507
Andrew Oldcorn	75	65	72	75	287	7,507
Richard Boxall	67	70	77	74	288	5,414
Nick Faldo	78	70	71	69	288	5,414
Kenneth Trimble	74	75	65	74	288	5,414
Johan Rystrom	71	68	74	75	288	5,414
Peter Fowler	73	73	74	68	288	5,414
Eamonn Darcy	71	77	68	73	289	4,375
David Feherty	73	70	72	74	289	4,375
Roger Chapman	74	68	76	71	289	4,375
Howard Clark	70	69	76	74	289	4,375
Ross McFarlane	74	69	72	74	289	4,375

10-13 May
PEUGEOT-TRENDS BELGIAN OPEN *Royal Waterloo Golf Club, Brussels*

Ove Sellberg	68	66	67	71	272	£41,660
Ian Woosnam	66	70	70	70	276	27,760
Eduardo Romero	69	72	69	68	278	15,650
Grant Turner	68	74	68	70	280	11,550
José-Maria Olazabal	69	71	71	69	280	11,550
Ronan Rafferty	70	70	74	68	282	7,500
Colin Montgomerie	69	73	72	68	282	7,500
Mike Miller	68	72	74	68	282	7,500
James Spence	68	76	68	71	283	5,600

1990 VOLVO TOUR RESULTS

Bernhard Langer won two tournaments and finished fourth on the Volvo Order of Merit

25-28 May
VOLVO PGA CHAMPIONSHIP *Wentworth Club, West Course*

Mike Harwood	69	68	67	67	271	£66,660
Nick Faldo	67	71	69	65	272	34,720
John Bland	67	67	71	67	272	34,720
José-Maria Olazabal	66	68	69	70	273	18,470
Rodger Davis	68	68	71	66	273	18,470
Eduardo Romero	66	71	69	68	274	14,000
Paul Curry	66	70	72	68	276	11,000
Tony Johnstone	66	72	67	71	276	11,000
Colin Montgomerie	70	70	68	69	277	8,960
Marc Farry	68	71	71	68	278	7,170
Jeff Hawkes	70	69	72	67	278	7,170
Philip Walton	70	67	71	70	278	7,170
David Williams	70	70	70	68	278	7,170

31 May-3 June
DUNHILL BRITISH MASTERS *Woburn G&CC*

Mark James	70	67	66	67	270	£50,000
David Feherty	65	70	68	69	272	33,300
Carl Mason	69	70	68	67	274	18,780
Brett Ogle	70	65	68	73	276	12,733
Mark McNulty	68	70	72	66	276	12,733
Jeff Hawkes	69	69	72	66	276	12,733
Vijay Singh	72	67	71	68	278	9,000
Vicente Fernandez	69	71	69	70	279	5,760
Craig Parry	71	69	69	70	279	5,760
Barry Lane	70	69	75	65	279	5,760
Bill Longmuir	67	67	73	72	279	5,760
Tony Johnstone	71	68	72	68	279	5,760
Peter Senior	68	69	75	67	279	5,760
Roger Chapman	67	70	75	67	279	5,760

17-20 May
LANCIA-MARTINI ITALIAN OPEN *Milano Golf Club, Monza*

Richard Boxall	65	64	70	68	267	£50,000
José-Maria Olazabal	67	69	68	68	272	33,300
Eduardo Romero	72	69	66	68	275	18,780
John Bland	67	74	68	68	277	15,000
Severiano Ballesteros	75	68	66	69	278	12,700
Giuseppe Cali	71	71	67	70	279	8,430
Keith Waters	70	70	71	68	279	8,430
Anders Sorensen	66	72	71	70	279	8,430
Craig Stadler	68	68	71	72	279	8,430

7-10 June
SCANDINAVIAN ENTERPRISE OPEN *Drottning-holm Golf Club*

Craig Stadler	68	72	67	61	268	£66,660
Craig Parry	66	70	69	67	272	44,400
Ronan Rafferty	70	71	65	67	273	25,040
Mats Lanner	69	71	70	64	274	20,000
Miguel Angel Jimenez	67	69	72	67	275	15,470
Mike Harwood	68	69	69	69	275	15,470
Peter McWhinney	67	68	71	70	276	10,320
Gordon Brand Jnr	69	66	68	73	276	10,320
Roger Chapman	72	68	65	71	276	10,320

14-17 June
WANG FOUR STARS NATIONAL PRO-CELEBRITY
Moor Park Golf Club

*Rodger Davis	67	72	65	67	271	£36,500
Mark McNulty	68	69	69	65	271	16,716
Mike Clayton	68	70	66	67	271	16,716
Bill Malley	68	66	67	70	271	16,716
Peter Mitchell	66	66	69	71	272	9,500
Paul Hoad	69	69	67	69	274	8,000
Rick Hartmann	66	66	73	70	275	6,050
Paul Way	69	67	67	72	275	6,050
David J Russell	71	66	71	68	276	4,350
Ken Brown	69	68	72	67	276	4,350
Jeremy Bennett	71	66	67	72	276	4,350

21-24 June
CARROLL'S IRISH OPEN *Portmarnock*

José-Maria Olazabal	67	72	71	72	282	£57,883
Mark Calcavecchia	66	75	72	72	285	30,155
Frank Nobilo	73	70	69	73	285	30,155
Rick Hartmann	72	74	71	69	286	17,369
John Bland	71	69	73	74	287	13,441
Russell Claydon	71	71	72	73	287	13,441
Eamonn Darcy	70	70	74	74	288	9,553
Brian Marchbank	71	73	71	73	288	9,553
David Ray	71	73	72	73	289	7,364
Martin Sludds	72	72	76	69	289	7,364
Peter Mitchell	76	71	75	68	290	5,985
Stephen Bennett	72	73	74	71	290	5,985
Marc Farry	67	73	70	80	290	5,985

Mark McNulty, the European Tour's Mr Consistency, won twice in 1990 and was rarely out of the top ten

28 June-1 July
PEUGEOT FRENCH OPEN *Chantilly, Paris*

*Philip Walton	73	66	67	69	275	£58,330
Bernhard Langer	71	65	72	67	275	38,860
Eduardo Romero	68	69	69	70	276	21,910
Nick Faldo	68	69	68	72	277	16,165
Rick Hartmann	68	65	73	71	277	16,165
Ronan Rafferty	70	70	66	72	278	9,268
Mark McNulty	71	65	69	73	278	9,268
Richard Boxall	70	69	66	73	278	9,268
Bernard Gallacher	70	65	72	71	278	9,268
Malcolm Mackenzie	70	70	70	68	278	9,268

4-7 July
TORRAS MONTE CARLO OPEN *Mont Agel, Monte Carlo*

Ian Woosnam	66	67	65	60	258	£59,158
Costantino Rocca	67	66	67	63	263	39,411
Mark McNulty	67	66	66	65	264	19,984
Mark Mouland	63	67	65	69	264	19,984
Mats Lanner	68	66	72	63	269	13,732
Jeff Hawkes	70	66	67	66	269	13,732
Chris Williams	70	70	66	64	270	9,158
Juan Anglada	70	64	69	67	270	9,158
Severiano Ballesteros	72	66	63	69	270	9,158

1990 VOLVO TOUR RESULTS

Nice win, shame about the jacket! Peter Senior at Sunningdale after his victory in the European Open

119TH OPEN CHAMPIONSHIP *St Andrews, Old Course*

Nick Faldo	67	65	67	71	270	£85,000
Mark McNulty	74	68	68	65	275	60,000
Payne Stewart	68	68	68	71	275	60,000
Ian Woosnam	68	69	70	69	276	40,000
Jodie Mudd	72	66	72	66	276	40,000
Ian Baker-Finch	68	72	64	73	277	28,500
Greg Norman	66	66	76	69	277	28,500
Steve Pate	70	68	72	69	279	22,000
Corey Pavin	71	69	68	71	279	22,000
Donnie Hammond	70	71	68	70	279	22,000
David Graham	72	71	70	66	279	22,000
Vijay Singh	70	69	72	69	280	16,375
Tim Simpson	70	69	69	72	280	16,375
Robert Gamez	70	72	67	71	280	16,375
Paul Broadhurst	74	69	63	74	280	16,375
Mark Roe	71	70	72	68	281	11,150
Steve Jones	72	67	72	70	281	11,150
Sandy Lyle	72	70	67	72	281	11,150
José-Maria Olazabal	71	67	71	72	281	11,150
Peter Jacobsen	68	70	70	73	281	11,150
Frank Nobilo	72	67	68	74	281	11,150

KLM DUTCH OPEN *Kennemer*

Stephen McAllister	69	67	68	70	274	£58,330
Roger Chapman	73	68	66	71	278	38,860
José-Maria Olazabal	73	70	65	71	279	21,910
Colin Montgomerie	71	68	73	68	280	16,165
Danny Mijovic	71	70	71	68	280	16,165
Peter Baker	69	73	71	68	281	9,268
Vicente Fernandez	72	69	69	71	281	9,268
Peter McWhinney	76	69	67	69	281	9,268
Martin Poxon	71	69	68	73	281	9,268
James Spence	71	72	69	69	281	9,268

BELL'S SCOTTISH OPEN *Gleneagles Hotel, King's Course*

Ian Woosnam	72	62	67	68	269	£66,660
Mark McNulty	73	67	64	69	273	44,400
Gordon Brand Jnr	65	67	72	71	275	22,520
Malcolm Mackenzie	71	72	65	67	275	22,520
Nick Faldo	72	73	67	65	277	14,313
David Feherty	69	72	68	68	277	14,313
Derrick Cooper	68	69	68	72	277	14,313
Peter Fowler	74	70	65	69	278	10,000
Craig Parry	67	74	71	67	279	8,106
Ross Drummond	71	69	68	71	279	8,106
Mark Roe	74	68	66	71	279	8,106
Paul Curry	77	65	68	70	280	6,192
Fred Couples	75	69	69	67	280	6,192
Jose Rivero	72	69	69	70	280	6,192
Roger Chapman	72	71	70	67	280	6,192
Richard Boxall	73	67	69	71	280	6,192

PLM OPEN *Bokskogen, Sweden*

Ronan Rafferty	64	67	70	69	270	£58,330
Vijay Singh	69	71	69	65	274	38,860
Bernhard Langer	72	68	67	68	275	21,910
Ove Sellberg	68	66	72	70	276	16,165
Fred Couples	70	72	69	65	276	16,165
Chris Cookson	68	71	72	67	278	10,500
Rodger Davis	70	70	73	65	278	10,500
Jeff Pinsent	71	69	71	67	278	10,500
Frank Nobilo	67	70	72	71	280	7,093
Mike Clayton	73	70	65	72	280	7,093
Jean Van de Velde	68	70	68	74	280	7,093

9-12 August
THE MURPHY'S CUP *Fulford, York*

Tony Johnstone	6	23	6	15	50	£41,660
Malcolm Mackenzie	8	13	16	11	48	27,760
Russell Claydon	10	15	7	12	44	15,650
Sandy Lyle	9	10	8	13	40	12,750
Martin Poxon	7	7	9	16	39	10,800
Barry Lane	5	13	10	9	37	8,900
Glyn Krause	7	17	9	3	36	6,525
Christy O'Connor Jnr	8	8	11	9	36	6,525
Paul Way	4	9	10	13	36	6,525

16-19 August
NM ENGLISH OPEN *The Belfry G&CC (Brabazon Course)*

*Mark James	76	66	65	75	284	£66,660
Sam Torrance	75	67	69	73	284	44,400
David Feherty	73	75	69	68	285	25,040
Severiano Ballesteros	72	72	68	75	287	20,000
Derrick Cooper	77	73	71	67	288	13,235
Stephen McAllister	74	74	72	68	288	13,235
Howard Clark	76	73	69	70	288	13,235
Mike Harwood	74	73	69	72	288	13,235
Gordon Brand Jnr	71	75	72	71	289	8,480
Steven Richardson	71	76	67	75	289	8,480

23-26 August
VOLVO GERMAN OPEN *Hubbelrath GC, Düsseldorf*

Mark McNulty	67	68	70	65	270	£77,896
Craig Parry	66	65	72	70	273	51,953
Eamonn Darcy	66	70	68	70	274	26,310
Anders Forsbrand	64	66	73	71	274	26,310
Jose Rivero	70	71	70	64	275	16,727
Philip Walton	69	67	69	70	275	16,727
Des Smyth	68	66	73	68	275	16,727
Mark James	67	73	66	71	277	9,662
Tony Johnstone	70	70	66	71	277	9,662
Sam Torrance	70	70	70	67	277	9,662
Peter O'Malley	68	73	71	65	277	9,662
Carl Mason	69	68	71	69	277	9,662

30 August-2 September
EBEL EUROPEAN MASTERS—SWISS OPEN
Crans-sur-Sierre, Montana

Ronan Rafferty	70	65	66	66	267	£76,636
John Bland	70	66	66	67	269	51,060
James Spence	66	67	68	69	270	28,796
Craig Parry	72	65	66	68	271	21,252
Howard Clark	64	66	72	69	271	21,252
Mark McNulty	65	72	68	67	272	14,950
José-Maria Canizares	69	67	65	71	272	14,950

Ronan Rafferty stars in the European Masters at Crans-sur-Sierre – music by Rodgers and Hammerstein

Mark Mouland	68	72	66	68	274	8,832
Mats Lanner	73	67	66	68	274	8,832
David Gilford	70	71	64	69	274	8,832
Keith Waters	68	68	69	69	274	8,832
Anders Forsbrand	68	67	71	68	274	8,832
David Williams	69	66	71	68	274	8,832
Sandy Lyle	67	66	71	70	274	8,832

6-9 September
PANASONIC EUROPEAN OPEN *Sunningdale GC, Old Course*

Peter Senior	67	68	66	66	267	£66,660
Ian Woosnam	65	68	68	67	268	44,400
Jose Maria Canizares	69	69	63	68	269	25,040
Tim Simpson	67	72	64	67	270	15,735
José-Maria Olazabal	65	69	70	66	270	15,735
Nick Faldo	68	70	64	68	270	15,735
Gordon J Brand	70	65	65	70	270	15,735
Eduardo Romero	70	65	69	67	271	10,000
David Feherty	73	65	66	68	272	8,480
Jimmy Heggarty	72	70	66	64	272	8,480
Brett Ogle	69	73	68	63	273	7,120
Jose Rivero	70	66	69	68	273	7,120

1990 VOLVO TOUR RESULTS

* Winner in play-off.

13-16 September
LANCÔME TROPHY *St Nom-la-Bretèche, Versailles*

José-Maria Olazabal	68	66	70	65	269	£69,970
Colin Montgomerie	69	63	71	67	270	46,620
Tony Johnstone	68	69	70	64	271	26,290
Rodger Davis	69	66	71	69	275	17,833
Craig Parry	69	70	66	70	275	17,833
Mark James	72	64	68	71	275	17,833
Eamonn Darcy	70	70	67	69	276	10,846
Severiano Ballesteros	70	69	70	67	276	10,846
Eduardo Romero	70	67	71	67	276	10,846
Mike Clayton	71	67	73	66	277	8,025
Jose Rivero	68	70	70	69	277	8,025

20-23 September
BMW INTERNATIONAL OPEN *Golfplatz München Nordekhenried, Munich*

* Paul Azinger	63	73	73	68	277	£66,660
David Feherty	62	72	71	72	277	44,400
Peter O'Malley	70	71	71	66	278	25,040
Russell Claydon	66	76	67	70	279	20,000
Jay Haas	73	70	68	69	280	16,940
David A Russell	66	79	69	67	281	13,000
José-Maria Olazabal	70	73	69	69	281	13,000
Vijay Singh	66	81	69	66	282	8,580
Mike Clayton	69	75	69	69	282	8,580
Philip Walton	71	73	71	67	282	8,580
Jesper Parnevik	71	71	70	70	282	8,580

27-30 September
EPSON GRAND PRIX OF EUROPE *St Pierre G&CC, Chepstow*

Ian Woosnam	65	67	67	72	271	£66,660
José-Maria Olazabal	71	67	67	69	274	34,720
Mark McNulty	67	67	68	72	274	34,720
Miguel Angel Martin	75	72	63	65	275	16,780
Ronan Rafferty	72	71	65	67	275	16,780
Brett Ogle	66	70	71	68	275	16,780
Johan Rystrom	73	69	68	66	276	8,720
Bernhard Langer	71	68	70	67	276	8,720
Mark James	67	71	70	68	276	8,720
Peter Fowler	70	69	69	68	276	8,720
Colin Montgomerie	65	72	70	69	276	8,720
Severiano Ballesteros	67	71	68	70	276	8,720

4-7 October
MERCEDES GERMAN MASTERS *Stuttgart*

Sam Torrance	70	65	64	73	272	£75,000
Bernhard Langer	66	67	74	68	275	39,065
Ian Woosnam	75	69	69	62	275	39,065
José-Maria Olazabal	69	70	69	69	277	20,780
Mike Harwood	71	67	70	69	277	20,780
David Feherty	69	68	74	67	278	15,750
Scott Simpson	72	67	71	70	280	13,500
Mark McNulty	71	68	72	70	281	10,110
Sandy Lyle	69	72	71	69	281	10,110
Paul Broadhurst	67	73	69	72	281	10,110

11-14 October
AUSTRIAN OPEN *Gut Altentann G&CC, Salzburg*

*Bernhard Langer	65	66	72	68	271	£41,660
Lanny Wadkins	67	68	68	68	271	27,760
Des Smyth	70	69	72	62	273	15,650
Manuel Moreno	74	67	67	67	275	11,550
Miguel Angel Martin	68	69	70	68	275	11,550
Gordon Manson	72	67	72	65	276	8,750
Chris Moody	70	69	70	69	278	7,500
David J Russell	70	74	66	69	279	5,925
Rick Hartmann	70	70	66	73	279	5,925

18-21 October
PORTUGUESE OPEN – TPC *Quinta do Lago, Algarve*

Michael McLean	69	69	65	71	274	£45,825
Gordon Brand Jnr	68	70	68	69	275	23,872
Mike Harwood	70	68	71	66	275	23,872
Mark James	68	69	70	69	276	12,702
Paul Broadhurst	70	69	68	69	276	12,702
Rick Hartmann	68	68	73	68	277	8,937
Ove Sellberg	67	68	70	72	277	8,937
Martin Poxon	73	68	69	68	278	6,517
David Williams	72	69	69	68	278	6,517

25-28 October
VOLVO MASTERS *Valderrama, Sotogrande, Spain*

Mike Harwood	70	72	73	71	286	£75,000
Sam Torrance	69	73	72	73	287	39,065
Steven Richardson	71	73	70	73	287	39,065
Bernhard Langer	72	71	72	73	288	17,962
Anders Forsbrand	75	69	71	73	288	17,962
José-Maria Olazabal	72	69	74	73	288	17,962
Mark McNulty	73	73	71	71	288	17,962
Colin Montgomerie	71	72	71	75	289	10,955
David Feherty	70	77	67	75	289	10,955
Rodger Davis	74	71	74	72	291	9,300

Paul Azinger, American winner of the BMW International following a play-off with David Feherty

Early-morning dew at Valderrama, home of the Volvo Masters

1990 PGA EUROPEAN TOUR WINNERS SUMMARY

February	*DUNHILL CUP WORLD QUALIFIER	Thailand	
	VINHO VERDE ATLANTIC OPEN	Stephen McAllister	(Sco)
	EMIRATES AIRLINE DESERT CLASSIC	Eamonn Darcy	(Ire)
March	AMERICAN EXPRESS MEDITERRANEAN OPEN	Ian Woosnam	(Wales)
	OPEN RENAULT DE BALEARES	Severiano Ballesteros	(Sp)
	TENERIFE OPEN	Vicente Fernandez	(Arg)
	VOLVO OPEN, ITALY	Eduardo Romero	(Arg)
	AGF OPEN	Brett Ogle	(Aus)
April	EL BOSQUE OPEN, VALENCIA	Vijay Singh	(Fiji)
	CREDIT LYONNAIS CANNES OPEN	Mark McNulty	(Zimb)
	CEPSA MADRID OPEN	Bernhard Langer	(Ger)
	PEUGEOT SPANISH OPEN	Rodger Davis	(Aus)
May	BENSON AND HEDGES INTERNATIONAL OPEN	José-Maria Olazabal	(Sp)
	PEUGEOT-TRENDS BELGIAN OPEN	Ove Sellberg	(Swe)
	LANCIA-MARTINI ITALIAN OPEN	Richard Boxall	(Eng)
	VOLVO PGA CHAMPIONSHIP	Mike Harwood	(Aus)
	DUNHILL BRITISH MASTERS	Mark James	(Eng)
June	SCANDINAVIAN ENTERPRISE OPEN	Craig Stadler	(US)
	WANG FOUR STARS NATIONAL PRO-CELEB.	Rodger Davis	(Aus)
	CARROLLS IRISH OPEN	José Maria Olazabal	(Sp)
	PEUGEOT FRENCH OPEN	Philip Walton	(Ire)
July	TORRAS MONTE CARLO OPEN	Ian Woosnam	(Wales)
	BELL'S SCOTTISH OPEN	Ian Woosnam	(Wales)
	119TH OPEN CHAMPIONSHIP	Nick Faldo	(Eng)
	KLM DUTCH OPEN	Stephen McAllister	(Sco)
	*VOLVO SENIORS BRITISH OPEN	Gary Player	(SA)
August	PLM OPEN	Ronan Rafferty	(NIre)
	MURPHY'S CUP	Tony Johnstone	(Zimb)
	NM ENGLISH OPEN	Mark James	(Eng)
	VOLVO GERMAN OPEN	Mark McNulty	(Zimb)
	EBEL EUROPEAN MASTERS – SWISS OPEN	Ronan Rafferty	(NIre)
September	PANASONIC EUROPEAN OPEN	Peter Senior	(Aus)
	LANCOME TROPHY	José-Maria Olazabal	(Sp)
	*MOTOROLA CLASSIC	Paul Broadhurst	(Eng)
	*SUNTORY WORLD MATCHPLAY	Ian Woosnam	(Wales)
	BMW INTERNATIONAL OPEN	Paul Azinger	(US)
	*EQUITY & LAW CHALLENGE	Brian Marchbank	(Sco)
	EPSON GRAND PRIX	Ian Woosnam	(Wales)
	*UAP UNDER 25'S EUROPEAN OPEN CHAMP.	Peter Baker	(Eng)
October	MERCEDES GERMAN MASTERS	Sam Torrance	(Sco)
	*DUNHILL CUP	Ireland	
	AUSTRIAN OPEN	Bernhard Langer	(Eng)
	PORTUGUESE OPEN – TPC	Michael McLean	(Eng)
	VOLVO MASTERS	Mike Harwood	(Aus)

* PGA European Tour Approved Special Event

1990 PGA EUROPEAN TOUR

VOLVO ORDER OF MERIT: TOP 100

1	I. Woosnam (Wales)	£574,166	51	J. Spence (England)	£79,929
2	M. McNulty (Zimbabwe)	507,540	52	M. Roe (England)	77,859
3	J.-M. Olazabal (Spain)	434,766	53	D. Cooper (England)	77,772
4	B. Langer (Germany)	320,449	54	M.A. Jimenez (Spain)	75,932
5	R. Rafferty (N. Ireland)	309,851	55	J. Rutledge (Canada)	75,273
6	M. Harwood (Australia)	280,084	56	C. O'Connor Jnr (Ireland)	75,254
7	S. Torrance (Scotland)	248,203	57	M. Persson (Sweden)	72,900
8	D. Feherty (N. Ireland)	237,830	58	J. Rystrom (Sweden)	67,326
9	R. Davis (Australia)	233,841	59	A. Lyle (Scotland)	66,551
10	M. James (England)	229,742	60	P. Curry (England)	65,740
11	E. Romero (Argentina)	200,615	61	P. McWhinney (Australia)	63,708
12	N. Faldo (England)	199,937	62	C. Mason (England)	63,583
13	V. Singh (Fiji)	185,677	63	B. Malley (US)	59,934
14	C. Montgomerie (Scotland)	174,852	64	G.J. Brand (England)	59,094
15	C. Parry (Australia)	170,867	65	R. Drummond (Scotland)	56,722
16	J. Bland (S. Africa)	164,891	66	J. Van De Velde (France)	55,893
17	R. Boxall (England)	148,798	67	T. Charnley (England)	55,862
18	S. Ballesteros (Spain)	148,033	68	B. Lane (England)	55,589
19	S. McAllister (Scotland)	147,238	69	B. Longmuir (Scotland)	51,390
20	P. Walton (Ireland)	142,104	70	M. Poxon (England)	51,259
21	E. Darcy (Ireland)	138,745	71	M. Moreno (Spain)	49,887
22	G. Brand Jnr (Scotland)	135,616	72	J. Parnevik (Sweden)	47,795
23	M. A. Martin (Spain)	133,977	73	B. Marchbank (Scotland)	47,018
24	B. Ogle (Australia)	133,531	74	P. Mitchell (England)	46,956
25	M. Mackenzie (England)	125,307	75	S. Bennett (England)	45,955
26	T. Johnstone (Zimbabwe)	124,826	76	J. Hawkins (S. Africa)	44,952
27	R. Chapman (England)	114,070	77	D.J. Russell (England)	44,897
28	R. Claydon (England)	113,968	78	P. Smith (Scotland)	44,231
29	S. Richardson (England)	109,944	79	D. Durnian (England)	43,428
30	J. Rivero (Spain)	109,176	80	C. Moody (England)	41,624
31	P. Fowler (Australia)	106,452	81	H. Baiocchi (S. Africa)	41,449
32	M. Clayton (Australia)	104,430	82	A. Murray (England)	41,259
33	D. Smyth (Ireland)	103,331	83	J.Q. Segura (Spain)	40,637
34	D. Williams (England)	103,137	84	P. Terevainen (US)	40,315
35	P. Senior (Australia)	99,539	85	K. Waters (England)	40,290
36	O. Sellberg (Sweden)	99,508	86	E. Dussart (France)	39,896
37	V. Fernandez (Argentina)	97,684	87	D.A. Russell (England)	38,797
38	F. Nobilo (NZ)	96,740	88	S. Bowman (US)	38,299
39	R. Hartmann (US)	93,712	89	M. Miller (Scotland)	37,905
40	A. Sorensen (Denmark)	93,285	90	J. Haggerty (N. Ireland)	37,369
41	H. Clark (England)	93,149	91	S. Hamill (N. Ireland)	37,168
42	M. Mouland (Wales)	91,328	92	M. Farry (France)	36,872
43	A. Forsbrand (Sweden)	90,460	93	M. Davis (England)	35,389
44	M. McLean (England)	89,712	94	A. Sherborne (England)	35,169
45	M. Lanner (Sweden)	89,085	95	D. Gilford (England)	34,620
46	J.-M. Canizares (Spain)	86,518	96	M. Sunesson (Sweden)	34,448
47	P. Broadhurst (England)	83,812	97	P. Parkin (Wales)	34,206
48	C. Rocca (Italy)	82,612	98	K. Brown (Scotland)	33,466
49	G. Turner (England)	82,323	99	B. Norton (US)	33,237
50	P. O'Malley (Australia)	81,387	100	P. Carrigill (England)	33,109

THE SUNTORY WORLD MATCHPLAY CHAMPIONSHIP

20–23 September, Wentworth

On paper this was possibly the strongest field that had ever been assembled for the World Matchplay Championship. Nick Faldo, the defending champion and dual Major winner of 1990, was present, as was his arch rival, Greg Norman, making his first appearance since 1987. Ballesteros, a four-time winner over the famous Burma Road Course, was in the line-up, and so was his great adversary of the mid-1980s, Bernhard Langer. Making up the Major Men of 1990 were the triple US Open champion, Hale Irwin, and Wayne Grady, recent winner of the USPGA.

Then there were Europe's Money Men of 1990, Ian Woosnam and Mark McNulty, numbers one and two on the Order of Merit. 1989's Volvo top dog Ronan Rafferty was making his second appearance at Wentworth,

as was Chip Beck, America's star performer in the last Ryder Cup. Making up the twelve were Billy Ray Brown of America and Japan's Ryoken Kawagishi, neither of whom were exactly rabbits, as Brown had only just missed a putt to tie the US Open at Medinah and 23-year-old Kawagishi is being hailed as an 'Oriental Olazabal' after winning three times on the Japanese tour in 1990.

There can be no doubt that under the current World Matchplay format, to be seeded (and therefore given a bye in the first round) is a great advantage. In 1990 that privilege was bestowed upon Messrs Faldo, Norman, Irwin and Woosnam. Having won the tournament more times than anyone else in the field, Ballesteros perhaps had some grounds for feeling a little disgruntled. Well, he had plenty

Greg Norman hits a superb recovery shot at the 36th hole against Wayne Grady. Norman went on to beat his fellow Australian at the second extra hole

Woosnam and McNulty, Europe's number 1 and 2 in 1990, contest the final

more grounds when Ronan Rafferty hammered him 8 and 6 on Thursday. It was Seve's biggest ever defeat at Wentworth. There was a time when British golfers were completely in awe of the Spaniard, but in 1987 he went down narrowly to the Welshman Woosnam; Scotland's Sandy Lyle thrashed him 7 and 6 in 1988, and in 1989 he was soundly beaten by Faldo. With Rafferty now delivering the beating, Ballesteros has been dished by the full set of Brits.

Seve was far from his best at Wentworth last year, but Rafferty did throw an extraordinary 62 at him in the morning. There was still time, however, for a touch of brilliance from Ballesteros: at the par-five 17th he and Rafferty halved the hole in eagle threes; he then won the 18th with a second eagle, and immediately after lunch got a birdie at the long par-four 1st, their 19th – no one could remember when a player last covered those three holes in successive threes.

In the other first-round matches McNulty proved too consistent for Billy Ray Brown, and Chip Beck too experienced for young Kawagishi. Langer and Grady had an intriguing match: in the morning the German played the first nine holes in 29 to go 4 up, but from then on it was Australia all the way, Grady taking the match 4 and 2.

Enter now the seeded players. Two of Friday's matches were close affairs and two were fairly much one-way traffic. There was to be no lap of honour for Hale Irwin; like his compatriot Brown he found McNulty too hot to handle and was swiftly dispatched 6 and 4; Rafferty must have fancied his chances against Woosnam, but he failed to find anything like the form he had produced the previous day, and he too was beaten at the 14th hole in the afternoon. Personable Chip Beck threatened to run away from Faldo, but the Englishman rallied from 5 down to draw level, only to bow out 2 and 1. It was hardly the defence he had wished for, but Faldo was clearly experiencing considerable pain in his wrist and soon after his defeat announced that he was taking an extended break from tournament golf to sort the problem out. So we were to have a new champion. A fourth title for Greg Norman, perhaps? He produced the shot of the week at the final hole of his match with Wayne Grady, hitting a long iron on to the green at the 18th despite having to stand awkwardly with one foot out of bounds. Greg went on to beat his fellow Australian with a birdie at the second extra hole.

In the semi-finals many had expected Beck to give Woosnam a tough match, but the many obviously forgot to tell Woosnam, who went out and overpowered Beck 5 and 3. No American has made it to the final since Crenshaw lost to Ballesteros in 1981. In the other game McNulty always looked to have

the edge, but it was only over the closing holes that he managed to pull away from Norman to win 3 and 2.

So a Woosnam v. McNulty final; power v. precision. Both golfers played, as the Americans would say, 'real solid' for 14 holes, and there was very little in it, then Woosnam unleashed a stunning birdie-birdie-birdie- eagle finish to complete his morning round in 64 strokes. McNulty had produced a very steady 67 but went into lunch 3 down. Showing admirable resilience he clawed his way back in the afternoon and got back on level terms, but could only watch as Woosnam once again stepped up a gear, scoring birdies at the 12th and 15th. At the 16th Woosnam struck his approach to within a foot of the hole and it was all over. All over bar the smiling, that is.

SUNTORY WORLD MATCHPLAY CHAMPIONSHIP

20 – 23 September Wentworth (West Course)

First round
C. BECK (USA) beat R. KAWAGISHI (Jap) 4 and 3
R. RAFFERTY (NIre) beat S. BALLESTEROS (Sp) 8 and 6
W. GRADY (Aus) beat B. LANGER (W. Ger) 4 and 2
M. McNULTY (Zim) beat B.R. BROWN (USA) 4 and 2
   First-round losers received £14,000

Second round
C. BECK beat N. FALDO (Eng) 2 and 1
I. WOOSNAM (Wal) beat R. RAFFERTY 5 and 4
G. NORMAN (Aus) beat W. GRADY at 38th
M. McNULTY beat H. IRWIN (USA) 6 and 4
   Second-round losers received £18,500

Semi-finals
I. WOOSNAM beat C. BECK 5 and 3
N. McNULTY beat G. NORMAN 3 and 2

Play-off for 3rd and 4th places
C. BECK halved with G. NORMAN after 20 holes
   Both players received £30,000

FINAL
I. WOOSNAM beat M. MCNULTY 4 and 2
   I. Woosnam won £100,000; M. McNulty received £60,000

Little Woosie, littler Woosies and giant trophy

THE DUNHILL CUP

11–14 October, St Andrews

The Dunhill Cup has had its critics. No one objects to the venue, that's for sure; moreover the quality of the fields that are regularly attracted to St Andrews is very high. It is the unique medal-matchplay format that seems to upset some people. 'Not proper golf' to the traditionalists and 'not likely to produce exciting finishes', according to the sceptics. 1990's event certainly provided much to get excited over. No one could have asked for a more dramatic climax to the final on Sunday, while the traditionalists were also given plenty to shake their heads at, no doubt in total disbelief when one side halved two of their three matches, won the other, yet still found themselves eliminated. More of which a little later.

The first day produced two almighty shocks. The number one and number two seeds, the United States and Australia, were respectively knocked out by rank outsiders France and New Zealand. The French win was particularly notable, because the American side comprised precisely the same players who had triumphed so emphatically the year before, namely Curtis Strange, Mark Calcavecchia and Tom Kite. On the morning, before they teed off, bookmakers were quoting the United States at 7-4 to win the tournament, France at 125-1. The result was $2^{1}/_{2}$-$^{1}/_{2}$ in favour of the French. Only Curtis Strange could manage to avoid the guillotine, escaping with a half from his match with Jean Van de Velde, and that only when the Frenchman took 6 strokes at the infamous Road Hole 17th.

Australia, winners of the first two Dunhill Cups in 1985 and 1986, had been beaten by the French in 1989, but losing out to their antipodean rivals in 1990 probably hurt a little more. The Kiwis had Frank Nobilo to thank for their unexpected success, as he defeated Greg Norman by 9 strokes.

Those were the big shocks of day one. More predictably, England, Scotland, Ireland and Wales all got over the first hurdle, although Wales struggled against the Chinese, and Japan defeated Argentina.

On Friday, England, for the third year in succession, were drawn against Scotland in the second round, and for the third straight year beat them 2-1. Given that they had also defeated the Scots in the 1987 final, Messrs James, Clark and Boxall did little for Anglo-Scottish golf relations. It was a very close contest though, finally sealed by James with a one-shot victory over his Ryder Cup colleague Sam Torrance. In the battle of the sheep-farming nations, New Zealand overcame Wales 2-1, despite Woosnam's win against Nobilo in the top match. Ireland

Ever since Nakajima's disaster in the 1978 Open, Japanese golfers have dreaded the Road Hole bunker. Hajime Meshiai demonstates the new approach

defeated Spain, also by 2-1, and the Japanese put an end to the French romance, winning all three of their games comfortably.

Both semi-final matches were extremely close affairs. In the six individual contests no player won his match by more than one stroke; indeed three of the six games finished level after 18 holes. The Irish only just squeezed past New Zealand, despite the deceptive $2^1/_2$-$^1/_2$ scoreline: Rafferty and Nobilo halved an excellent match in 68; the Irish captain, Feherty, also recorded a 68 to better Turner's 69; and Walton took 70 to pip Simon Owen, whom many remember for so nearly winning the Open at St Andrews in 1978.

The England *v.* Japan encounter was even tighter. After Clark and Higashi returned matching 70s and Kaneko defeated Boxall by 70-71, Meshiai came down the 18th level with James, believing that if he could manage to stay on equal terms Japan would advance into their third Dunhill Cup final in five years. Meshiai did precisely what was required (or so he thought), and as soon as his par putt disappeared into the hole there were three jubilant Japanese dancing on the most famous green in golf. Unfortunately this was premature: according to the tournament rules – or at least, according to the interpretation given to those poorly drafted rules – if two (or more) of the three games finished level, then the tied matches had to be continued and determined by sudden-death extra holes.

Inevitably England won both the extended matches and so went through to the final against Ireland. For the majority of observers it all seemed more than a little unjust.

Happily, Sunday's 36-hole final revived faith in the competition. In the morning matches there was nothing between the two sides, Walton halving with James, Rafferty defeating Boxall, and Feherty losing to Clark. With everything to play for in the afternoon, Rafferty once again got the better of Boxall, but this time James finished a stroke ahead of Walton. So it was all down to Feherty and Clark. On the home stretch the Irishman looked a likely winner until Clark holed a 20-footer on the 17th to get back on level terms, and as neither could win the 18th it was sudden-death once again. It took three holes to decide the issue and a stroke (to the 17th, where else) described by Feherty as 'the best three-iron I've ever hit.'

Captains Howard Clark of England and David Feherty of Ireland play off for the Dunhill Cup

THE DUNHILL CUP

11-14 October St Andrews (Old Course)

First round

Japan	2	–	1	Argentina
France	2½	–	½	USA
Spain	2	–	1	Sweden
England	3	–	0	Thailand
Scotland	2½	–	½	Mexico
Ireland	3	–	0	Korea
Wales	2	–	1	Chinese Team Taipei
New Zealand	2	–	1	Australia

First-round losers received US$7,500 each

Second round

Japan	3	–	0	France
Ireland	2	–	1	Spain
New Zealand	2	–	1	Wales
England	2	–	1	Scotland

Second-round losers received US$15,000 each

Semi finals

Ireland   2½ –   ½   New Zealand
Philip Walton (70) beat Simon Owen (71)
Ronan Rafferty (68) halved with Frank Nobilo (68)
David Feherty (68) beat Greg Turner (69)

England   2   –   1   Japan
Howard Clark (70) beat Satoshi Higashi (70)
    on the 1st play-off hole
Richard Boxall (70) lost to Yoshinori Kaneko (69)
Mark James (70) beat Hajime Meshiai (70)
    on the 4th play-off hole

Play-off for 3rd and 4th places
New Zealand   2   –   1   Japan
Greg Turner (72) beat Satoshi Higashi (75)
Simon Owen (77) lost to Yoshinori Kaneko (74)
Frank Nobilo (73) beat Hajime Meshiai (77)

FINAL
IRELAND   3½ –   2½ ENGLAND
Philip Walton (72) halved with Mark James (72)
Ronan Rafferty (71) beat Richard Boxall (73)
David Feherty (74) lost to Howard Clark (73)

Philip Walton (77) lost to Mark James (76)
Ronan Rafferty (71) beat Richard Boxall (77)
David Feherty (75) beat Howard Clark (75)
    on the 3rd play-off hole

The Greens have it! Ireland win the Dunhill Cup for the second time in three years

Japan received US$26,666 each
New Zealand received US$36,666 each

England received US$50,000 each
Ireland received US$100,000 each

1990 WPG EUROPEAN TOUR REVIEW

For a long time, in this country at least, it was fashionable to criticize women's professional golf; but today it is women's professional golf that is fashionable. The Women's European tour is still very young; it is only eleven years old, yet in that short timespan total purse money has increased twenty-fold, from the £80,000 on offer in 1979 to approximately £1.6 million in 1990. Geographically it is very much a 'European tour', and the way affairs are conducted would make Jacques Delors extremely proud. The first seven events on 1990's calendar saw the WPGE Tour visit six different countries, and, as on the men's Volvo Tour, there was an extremely international roll of champions, with the first twelve events producing winners from ten different countries.

Given the tour's youth, it is not too surprising that the inaugural Solheim Cup was won by the United States (it is reviewed ahead. But let's face it, the American players are world-beaters. Three weeks before the match against Europe, an LPGA Tour team defeated their Japanese counterparts $22\frac{1}{2}$-$9\frac{1}{2}$ – in Japan. Many people reckon it is an even-money bet that they would defeat America's last Ryder Cup side! Each year the standard of play on the WPGE Tour seems to improve markedly; the leading players are much younger than the top Americans, and in two years' time who knows what might happen?

Returning to the tour, 1990 will go down as Trish Johnson's year. She entered 14 tournaments, only once finished outside the top 10, and won four times. Her wins came in the Hennessy Cup, the Expedier European Open, the Bloor Homes Eastleigh Classic and the Longines Classic. That last win was in the final event of the season and she achieved it most emphatically, winning over the difficult Esterela course at St Raphael by 6 strokes from Gillian Stewart. Not surprisingly it secured first place for her on the Woolmark

Order of Merit. So after two years spent in the proverbial doldrums, Trish Johnson, rookie of the year in 1987, was back with a vengeance.

Only one other player managed to win more than one tournament – that was Belgium's Florence Descampe, and she won three times. Just as Trish Johnson won the last event of the year by 6 shots, so Descampe won the opening tournament, the Valextra Classic, by 6. Twenty-one-year-old Descampe (in fact 20 at the time) unfortunately went slightly off the boil in mid-season and narrowly missed out on making the Solheim Cup side; but late in the year her form returned and she won, in successive weeks, the Italian Classic, which was staged in the beautiful setting of Lake Garda, and the Woolmark Matchplay Championship in Spain. In the Matchplay she came back from being 2 down with 5 to play (don't they all), with a thrilling run of birdies to defeat Solheim Cup team-member Dale Reid, winner of the Stockholm Open.

Florence Descampe surely has a brilliant future ahead of her. So, it would seem, has Helen Alfredsson. The Swedish player has only been on the tour two seasons: in 1989 she was Rookie of the Year, and in 1990 Alfredsson won her first tournament ... the Weetabix British Open, easily the most sought-after title in Europe. It was a stunning victory and it happened in quite dramatic circumstances as she defeated Jane Hill on the fourth hole of a sudden-death play-off; Hill thus became the second Zimbabwean to finish runner-up in a British Open in 1990. After her Woburn success in August, Alfredsson didn't look back, and scored a string of top finishes to end the season in third spot on the Woolmark Order of Merit.

Sandwiching Johnson and Alfredsson on that list was Yorkshire's Alison Nicholas, who had to settle for second place in the table for the third year in a row. She won only once in 1990 (after gaining three wins the year before) but was rarely out of contention all year. The same could be said of Laurette Maritz-Atkins, who won the Laing Charity Classic at Stoke Poges and scored a hole-in-one in the process.

A year of joy for Johnson perhaps, but for 1988 and 1989's leading moneywinner, the phlegmatic French player Marie-Laure de Lorenzi, it was a fairly frustrating year. She added only one win to her ten victories of the previous two years but spent much of the season suffering from tendonitis (sounds familiar?) and an unreliable putter. Her win, a successful defence, came in the Ford Classic, when she, and a very sizeable Woburn crowd, wallowed in April sunshine.

Laura Davies had a similarly disappointing season; however, inspired by the prospect of taking on the Americans at Lake Nona, she found some form late in the year and won the rain-affected AGF Open in Biarritz. Because of the weather the tournament was shortened to two rounds, and Laura's opening 63, in which, according to her playing partner Trish Johnson, she 'played like God', decided the issue. That week, as for most of the year, 'God' played with pink-shafted clubs.

Other wins on tour in 1990 included three by Australian players, Corinne Dibnah, Anne Jones (a first-time winner) and Karen Lunn (who won her second European Masters in three years), and a popular victory for England's Diane Barnard. To emphasize the tour's international flavour, Japanese LPGA star, Ayako Okamoto, won a three-way play-off in the German Open to edge out Cindy Rarick of the United States and Laurette Maritz-Atkins of South Africa.

There is clearly much to look forward to in 1991 on the WPGE Tour. Will it be the year that good pals Florence Descampe and Helen Alfredsson join Laura Davies and Marie-Laure de Lorenzi as the tour's leading lights? Or will Trish Johnson dominate again? Perhaps Alison Nicholas will finally go one better in 1991 and head the Order

Trish Johnson, the WPGE Tour's leading moneywinner in 1990

of Merit? Then again one shouldn't overlook the powerful Australian challenge or the young Spanish stars Xonia Wunsch and Tania Abitbol, or Switzerland's Evelyn Orley, Britain's Barnard and 19-year-old Helen Dobson, Sweden's Sofia Gronberg . . . talk about hedging one's bets!

The lady in pink: Marie-Laure de Lorenzi

Laura Davies: the lady who swings in pink

1990 WPG EUROPEAN TOUR RESULTS

* Winner after play-off

19-22 April
VALEXTRA CLASSIC *Olgiata, Rome*

Florence Descampe	71	71	69	68	279	£10,500
Dale Reid	75	68	70	72	285	7,105
Laura Davies	74	73	69	70	286	4,900
Dennise Hutton	73	74	69	72	288	3,374
Pearl Sinn	73	68	73	74	288	3,374
Kitrina Douglas	72	71	75	71	289	2,450
Alison Nicholas	75	72	72	71	290	1,925
Xonia Wunsch-Ruiz	74	74	72	70	290	1,925
Karen Lunn	75	73	74	69	291	1,568
Trish Johnson	72	77	71	72	292	1,400

25-28 April
FORD LADIES' CLASSIC *Duchess Course, Woburn G&CC*

Marie-Laure de Lorenzi	74	72	68	70	284	£9,750
Laurette Maritz	70	73	71	73	287	6,600
Trish Johnson	73	72	72	73	290	4,550
Rae Hast	72	78	73	68	291	3,133
Alison Nicholas	71	75	70	75	291	3,133
Diane Barnard	70	71	74	78	293	2,112
Sofia Gronberg	73	73	74	73	293	2,112
Maria Navarro Corbachio	74	78	71	71	294	1,540
Evelyn Orley	72	75	71	76	294	1,540
Federica Dassu	73	72	77	73	295	1,300
Kitrina Douglas	75	74	70	77	296	1,091
Debbie Dowling	76	74	72	74	296	1,091
Suzanne Strudwick	72	76	75	73	296	1,091
Helen Alfredsson	69	80	74	73	296	1,091

10-13 May
HENNESSY LADIES' CUP *St Germain, Paris*

Trish Johnson	72	68	71	74	285	£13,500
Marie-Laure de Lorenzi	75	71	69	73	288	7,717
Tammie Green	72	75	66	75	288	7,717
Sofia Gronberg	72	69	73	75	289	4,860
Tania Abitbol	77	69	72	72	290	3,222
Diane Barnard	71	74	71	74	290	3,222
Catherine Panton	74	72	72	72	290	3,222
Beverley New	73	73	74	71	291	2,250
Janice Arnold	73	75	73	72	293	2,016
Corinne Soules	76	73	71	75	295	1,728
Xonia Wunsch-Ruiz	78	74	74	69	295	1,728

24-26 May
WPG EUROPEAN TOUR CLASSIC *Tytherington Club, Macclesfield*

Tania Abitbol	76	69	68	213	£9,000
Anna Oxenstierna	72	73	70	215	6,090
Susan Shapcott	70	70	76	216	4,200
Diane Barnard	73	72	72	217	2,892
Sofia Gronberg	71	75	71	217	2,892
Debbie Dowling	72	74	72	218	1,950
Corinne Soules	75	74	69	218	1,950
Federica Dassu	74	72	73	219	1,348
Kitrina Douglas	72	71	76	219	1,348
Xonia Wunsch-Ruiz	74	74	71	219	1,348

6-9 June
BONMONT LADIES' CLASSIC *Bonmont GC, near Geneva*

*Evelyn Orley	71	72	71	75	289	£10,500
Gillian Stewart	74	72	70	73	289	7,105
Tania Abitbol	72	71	76	71	290	4,340
Dale Reid	70	74	75	71	290	4,340
Florence Descampe	72	72	73	74	291	2,968
Federica Dassu	77	69	71	75	292	2,275
Sofia Gronberg	77	74	68	72	292	2,275
Kitrina Douglas	75	74	75	70	294	1,501
Laurette Maritz	76	71	77	70	294	1,501
Alison Sheard	69	74	78	73	294	1,501
Xonia Wunsch-Ruiz	72	74	74	74	294	1,501

21-24 June
BMW EUROPEAN MASTERS *Bercuit, Brussels*

Karen Lunn	72	71	71	71	285	£18,000
Corinne Soules	69	74	73	73	289	12,180
Gillian Stewart	70	76	73	72	291	8,400
Pearl Sinn	72	77	73	71	293	6,480
Corinne Dibnah	76	74	71	73	294	4,644
Jane Hill	74	75	72	73	294	4,644
Jane Connachan	77	71	73	74	295	3,300
Sofia Gronberg	77	74	72	72	295	3,300
Laurette Maritz	75	76	72	73	296	2,544
Tracey Craik	78	74	73	71	296	2,544
Marie-Laure de Lorenzi	73	74	71	79	297	1,972
Kitrina Douglas	72	77	77	71	297	1,972
Alison Sheard	72	75	76	74	297	1,972
Xonia Wunsch-Ruiz	74	74	75	74	297	1,972
Helen Alfredsson	71	79	71	76	297	1,972

28 June – 1 July
BMW LADIES' CLASSIC *Hubbelrath, Düsseldorf*

Diane Barnard	71	68	70	69	278	£10,500
Corinne Dibnah	66	71	69	73	279	7,105
Alison Nicholas	71	67	70	72	280	4,900
Karen Lunn	67	68	73	72	281	3,780
Marie-Laure de Lorenzi	68	72	70	71	282	2,958
Peggy Conley	69	69	73	72	283	2,450
Debbie Dowling	74	72	73	68	287	2,100
Jane Connachan	68	69	74	78	289	1,442
Laurette Maritz	74	70	69	75	289	1,442
Gillian Stewart	72	73	72	72	289	1,442
Dana Lofland	73	70	71	75	289	1,442
Nadene Hall	76	68	73	71	289	1,442

5-8 July
LAING LADIES' CHARITY CLASSIC *Stoke Poges, Bucks*

*Laurette Maritz	71	67	69	68	275	£9,750
Alison Nicholas	71	70	69	65	275	6,600
Maureen Garner	68	67	71	70	276	4,550
Corinne Soules	70	71	69	67	277	3,510
Patricia Gonzales	71	69	70	73	283	2,756
Diane Barnard	75	68	71	70	284	1,950
Karen Lunn	74	74	69	67	284	1,950
Florence Descampe	73	65	72	74	284	1,950
Jo Rumsey	74	71	69	73	287	1,378
Helen Alfredsson	72	70	71	74	287	1,378

Spain's Xonia Wunsch-Ruiz

12-15 July
BLOOR HOMES EASTLEIGH CLASSIC *Fleming Park, Southampton*

Trish Johnson	61	66	58	64	249	£9,765
Corinne Dibnah	61	69	64	60	254	6,615
Debbie Dowling	65	62	66	62	255	4,565
Kitrina Douglas	62	62	65	67	256	3,148
Dale Reid	62	62	67	65	256	3,148
Florence Descampe	66	66	64	62	258	2,127
Tina Yarwood	61	67	65	65	258	2,127
Dennise Hutton	63	61	69	66	259	1,555
Karen Lunn	64	69	61	65	259	1,555
Diane Barnard	68	60	68	64	260	1,219
Penny Grice-Whittaker	68	62	64	66	260	1,219
Alison Sheard	66	68	62	64	260	1,219

2-5 August
WEETABIX WOMEN'S BRITISH OPEN *Duke's Course, Woburn G&CC*

*Helen Alfredsson	70	71	74	73	288	£20,000
Jane Hill	77	74	69	68	288	13,200
Laura Davies	75	73	73	70	291	7,353
Kitrina Douglas	69	71	75	76	291	7,353
Dana Lofland	73	70	75	73	291	7,353
Marie-Laure de Lorenzi	72	70	72	79	293	4,130
Trish Johnson	71	74	73	75	293	4,130
Myra Blackwelder	73	70	78	72	293	4,130
Diane Barnard	75	70	73	76	294	2,750
Alison Nicholas	75	75	68	76	294	2,750
Pearl Sinn	70	74	77	74	295	2,390
Allison Shapcott	73	74	76	73	296	2,230
Claire Duffy	76	74	74	73	297	2,013
Li Wen-Lin	73	69	76	79	297	2,013
Michelle Estill	77	70	76	74	297	2,013

 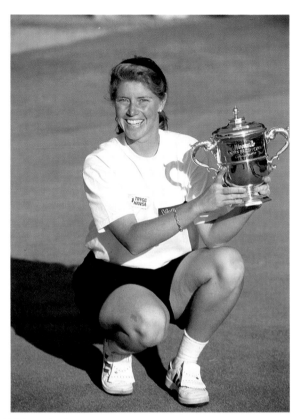

Helen Alfredsson, winner of the Weetabix British Open at Woburn in August

9-12 August
LUFTHANSA LADIES' GERMAN OPEN *Worthsee, Munich*

Ayako Okamoto	68	70	69	67	274	£13,500
Laurette Maritz	70	65	67	72	274	7,717
Cindy Rarick	70	68	67	69	274	7,717
Trish Johnson	67	67	72	70	276	4,860
Alison Nicholas	71	70	71	66	278	3,483
Helen Alfredsson	71	65	71	71	278	3,483
Laura Davies	70	69	70	70	279	2,700
Diane Barnard	70	69	69	72	280	2,250
Ray Bell	71	72	70	68	281	1,908
Liselotte Neumann	70	69	70	72	281	1,908

23-26 August
HANINGE LADIES' OPEN *Haninge, Stockholm*

Dale Reid	74	71	72	74	291	£10,500
Maureen Garner	75	75	70	72	292	5,261
Alison Nicholas	72	73	71	76	292	5,261
Suzanne Strudwick	73	72	73	74	292	5,261
Gillian Stewart	71	74	74	74	293	2,968
Federica Dassu	72	76	72	74	294	2,450
Liselotte Neumann	74	70	76	76	296	1,704
Anna Oxenstierna	78	71	68	79	296	1,704
Tracey Craik	76	76	72	72	296	1,704
Allison Shapcott	72	75	73	76	296	1,704

30 August-2 September
VARIETY CLUB CELEBRITY CLASSIC *Calcot Park, Reading*

Alison Nicholas	68	68	68	71	275	£7,800
Sofia Gronberg	72	70	65	69	276	5,280
Trish Johnson	69	73	67	68	277	4,080
Kitrina Douglas	67	66	70	75	278	3,240
Catherine Panton	72	70	67	71	280	2,520
Gillian Stewart	70	72	68	71	281	2,040
Jane Connachan	74	66	71	71	282	1,620
Laurette Maritz	70	72	71	70	283	1,320
Diane Barnard	69	78	67	70	284	1,110

6-9 September
TEC PLAYERS' CHAMPIONSHIP *Patshull Park, Wolverhampton*

Anne Jones	73	66	69	73	281	£12,000
Laurette Maritz	72	70	70	71	283	8,120
Sofia Gronberg	74	69	72	70	285	4,960
Helen Alfredsson	75	70	68	72	285	4,960
Trish Johnson	71	71	72	72	286	3,392
Tania Abitbol	70	80	69	70	289	2,118
Diane Barnard	78	71	70	70	289	2,118
Jane Connachan	76	74	70	69	289	2,118
Corinne Soules	68	75	72	74	289	2,118

13-16 September
EXPEDIER LADIES' EUROPEAN OPEN *Kingswood, Surrey*

Trish Johnson	71	67	69	69	276	£11,250
Michelle Estill	67	70	68	73	278	6,430
Pearl Sinn	70	68	72	68	278	6,430
Alison Nicholas	69	72	66	74	281	4,050
Laura Davies	69	70	73	70	282	2,902
Stefania Croce	73	66	72	71	282	2,902
Beverly Huke	75	69	73	67	284	1,935
Alison Sheard	73	72	70	69	284	1,935
Nadene Hall	74	70	72	68	284	1,935
Janice Arnold	76	68	72	69	285	1,390
Debbie Dowling	68	72	71	74	285	1,390
Penny Grice-Whittaker	69	71	73	72	285	1,390

20-23 September
TROPHEE INTERNATIONAL COCONUT SKOL *Fourqueux, Paris*

Corinne Dibnah	71	75	72	66	284	£10,500
Trish Johnson	71	73	70	71	285	6,002
Helen Alfredsson	70	73	71	71	285	6,002
Alison Nicholas	72	73	69	74	288	3,780
Marie-Laure de Lorenzi	72	75	72	71	290	2,709
Kitrina Douglas	74	70	74	72	290	2,709
Anne Jones	72	81	66	73	292	2,100
Corinne Soules	71	71	75	76	293	1,572
Florence Descampe	72	75	70	76	293	1,572
Pearl Sinn	72	73	75	73	293	1,572

4-7 October
ITALIAN LADIES' OPEN *Gardagolf, Brescia*

Florence Descampe	72	74	66	70	282	£13,500
Helen Alfredsson	67	75	72	71	285	9,135
Karine Espinasse	72	73	72	70	287	6,300
Dale Reid	69	73	74	72	288	4,860
Marie-Laure de Lorenzi	72	73	71	73	289	3,816
Federica Dassu	72	75	72	71	290	3,150
Claire Duffy	73	75	71	72	291	2,191
Laurette Maritz-Atkins	75	75	72	69	291	2,191
Alison Nicholas	69	74	71	77	291	2,191
Stefania Croce	73	74	74	70	291	2,191

Alison Nicholas celebrates victory in the Variety Classic

1990 WPG EUROPEAN TOUR RESULTS

18-21 October
WOOLMARK LADIES' MATCHPLAY *Club de Campo, Madrid*

Quarter-Finals
A. Jones beat K. Douglas
F. Descampe beat T. Abitbol
X. Wunsch-Ruiz beat S. Moorcraft
D. Reid beat A. Nicholas
   All quarter-final losers won £2,600

Semi-Finals	**Final**
F. Descampe beat A. Jones	F. Descampe beat D. Reid
D. Reid beat X. Wunsch-Ruiz	(£12,000) (£8,000)
Semi-final losers won £5,200	

25-28 October
AGF BIARRITZ LADIES' OPEN *Biarritz, France*

Laura Davies	63	73	136	£12,000
Alison Nicholas	71	66	137	8,120
Kelly Leadbetter	68	70	138	4,960
Laurette Maritz-Atkins	69	69	138	4,960
Marie-Laure de Lorenzi	69	70	139	2,648
Trish Johnson	69	70	139	2,648
Beverley New	69	70	139	2,648
Helen Alfredsson	66	73	139	2,648
Janice Arnold	69	71	140	1,696
Florence Descampe	71	69	140	1,696

1-4 November
BENSON AND HEDGES MIXED TEAM TROPHY
El Bosque, Valencia, Spain

José-Maria Canizares	66	67	66	68	267	£15,250
Tania Abitbol						15,250
Mark Mouland	65	66	69	69	269	11,250
Alison Nicholas						11,250
Brian Barnes	67	67	71	66	271	8,625
Laura Davies						8,625
Gordon J. Brand	68	67	66	71	272	6,010
Jane Hill						6,010
Ove Sellberg	69	64	65	74	272	6,010
Florence Descampe						6,010
Anders Forsbrand	66	71	67	69	273	4,500
Corinne Soules						4,500
Manuel Pinero	65	72	67	70	274	3,860
Marta Figueres Dotti						3,860

8-11 November
LONGINES CLASSIC *Golf Esterel, St Raphael, Nice*

Trish Johnson	72	71	75	68	286	£15,000
Gillian Stewart	71	79	69	73	292	10,150
Karen Lunn	80	71	72	70	293	7,000
Helen Hopkins	74	76	73	71	294	4,820
Helen Alfredsson	72	77	71	74	294	4,820
Kitrina Douglas	77	72	75	71	295	3,500
Federica Dassu	67	76	78	77	298	2,435
Laurette Maritz-Atkins	75	79	69	75	298	2,435
Alison Nicholas	74	75	73	76	298	2,435
Dale Reid	76	73	77	72	298	2,435

Florence Descampe has just played the shot that won her the Woolmark Matchplay Championship in Spain

1990 WPG EUROPEAN TOUR WINNERS SUMMARY

VALEXTRA CLASSIC	Florence Descampe
FORD LADIES' CLASSIC	Marie-Laure de Lorenzi
HENNESSY LADIES' CUP	Trish Johnson
WPG EUROPEAN TOUR CLASSIC	Tania Abitbol
BONMONT LADIES' CLASSIC	Evelyn Orley
BMW EUROPEAN MASTERS	Karen Lunn
BMW LADIES' CLASSIC	Diane Barnard
LAING LADIES' CHARITY CLASSIC	Laurette Maritz-Atkins
BLOOR HOMES EASTLEIGH CLASSIC	Trish Johnson
WEETABIX WOMEN'S BRITISH OPEN	Helen Alfredsson
LUFTHANSA LADIES' GERMAN OPEN	Ayako Okamoto
HANINGE LADIES' OPEN	Dale Reid
VARIETY CLUB CELEBRITY CLASSIC	Alison Nicholas
TEC PLAYERS' CHAMPIONSHIP	Anne Jones
EXPEDIER LADIES' EUROPEAN OPEN	Trish Johnson
TROPHEE COCONUT SKOL	Corinne Dibnah
ITALIAN LADIES' OPEN	Florence Descampe
WOOLMARK LADIES' MATCHPLAY	Florence Descampe
AGF BIARRITZ LADIES' OPEN	Laura Davies
BENSON AND HEDGES TROPHY	Tania Abitbol and José-Maria Canizares
LONGINES CLASSIC	Trish Johnson

WOOLMARK ORDER OF MERIT: TOP 50

1	Trish Johnson	£83,043	26	Anna Oxenstierna	18,008
2	Alison Nicholas	63,199	27	Evelyn Orley	16,482
3	Helen Alfredsson	63,079	28	Karine Espinasse	16,107
4	Laurette Maritz-Atkins	56,273	29	Dennise Hutton	16,035
5	Florence Descampe	51,518	30	Alicia Dibos	15,926
6	Dale Reid	49,343	31	Janice Arnold	15,919
7	Gillian Stewart	43,531	32	Alison Sheard	15,632
8	Marie-Laure de Lorenzi	40,351	33	Michelle Estill	15,498
9	Corinne Dibnah	39,665	34	Catherine Panton	15,380
10	Diane Barnard	39,658	35	Tracey Craik	13,702
11	Kitrina Douglas	38,207	36	Rae Hast	13,377
12	Karen Lunn	36,907	37	Claire Duffy	13,196
13	Laura Davies	36,697	38	Stefania Croce	13,062
14	Sofia Gronberg	34,170	39	Catrin Nilsmark	12,436
15	Corinne Soules	32,936	40	Beverley New	11,587
16	Tania Abitbol	32,600	41	Regine Lautens	11,548
17	Anne Jones	29,387	42	Janet Soulsby	11,247
18	Pearl Sinn	28,407	43	Maria Navarro Corbachio	10,746
19	Jane Hill	25,485	44	Nadene Hall	10,524
20	Debbie Dowling	22,613	45	Dana Lofland	10,261
21	Federica Dassu	22,573	46	Patricia Gonzalez	9,292
22	Xonia Wunsch-Ruiz	21,979	47	Susan Shapcott	9,095
23	Maureen Garner	21,492	48	Peggy Conley	9,032
24	Jane Connachan	20,862	49	Jo Rumsey	8,707
25	Suzanne Strudwick	19,439	50	Joanne Furby	8,498

THE UNITED STATES

PGA West, La Quinta, California

THE 1990 US TOUR

Following the life and times of the US (PGA) Tour in 1990 was, surprisingly, very exciting. Why surprisingly? There were two main reasons for suspecting that the opening year of the decade might be a less than inspiring vintage. Firstly, to all but the most parochial and patriotic American observer it was clear that many of the world's best players were domiciled across the water; yet of the top European stars, only Sandy Lyle had expressed his intention to participate in more than a handful of Tour events – and the Sandy Lyle of 1989–90 was not the same player as the Sandy Lyle of 1987–88, when he won the Players Championship and the Masters. The second reason was that many of America's own stars were now 50 years plus and playing the Seniors Tour (Nicklaus and Trevino having reached that ripe old age around the turn of the year).

It seems likely that 1990 will go down as 'the year of the foreigner': two of the three American Majors were won by overseas players, Britain's Nick Faldo capturing his second successive Masters and the Australian Wayne Grady, the USPGA title. Indeed of all the Majors' silverware, only the US Open was won by an American, Hale Irwin.

Week in, week out, it was a second Australian, Greg Norman, who proved to be the biggest box-office pull by far; he ended the year as leading moneywinner and collected the Vardon Trophy for maintaining the lowest stroke average. The Player of the Year Award went to Faldo. David Frost of South Africa recorded the lowest tournament round, a 60, while the most emphatic win was achieved by a plundering Spaniard from San Sebastian who, as if to rub things in, was only 24 years old.

Ten years ago the Tour's leading moneywinner, for the fourth year running, was Tom Watson. In 1990 Tom finished a disappointing 68th on the list but was only 15 places behind his supposed successor and 'the best player in the world' according to his

friends, Curtis Strange. Poor Curtis, in 1990 all he could win was the Skins Game.

'The year of the foreigner' perhaps, but nowhere else in the world did avid golf fans witness so many thrilling climaxes to tournaments. If Americans needed some consolation to wounded national pride, 1990 at least saw the unearthing of a potential superstar in Robert Gamez, while in the not-too-distant future major things are expected of the 1990 US Amateur champion, left-hander Phil Mickelson.

The first sign of the strong overseas presence came in the opening event of the year, the Tournament of Champions. Paul Azinger won it with four rounds below 70, but three Australians finished in the top six. The next event at Tuscon saw David Frost's second-round 60, but more significant was the emergence of 21-year-old Gamez playing (and winning) his first ever US Tour event. Not since Ben Crenshaw in 1973 had a player achieved such a feat. He won impressively too, by four strokes from the then Open champion Mark Calcavecchia.

The next two tournaments provided popular winners in Peter Jacobsen – still best known in Britain for rugby-tackling a streaker in the 1985 Open – and Tommy Armour III, a grandson of the legendary 'Silver Scot' who won Opens on both sides of the Atlantic in the 1920s and 30s.

In the first week in February the Tour returned to the Californian coast, more specifically to the magnificent Monterey Peninsula. For the third time in six years Mark O'Meara won at Pebble Beach; how he must look forward to 1992, when the US Open returns to America's greatest links. The 25th Hawaiian Open at Waialae was fittingly won by Hawaiian David Ishii, his first Tour victory; then from golf amidst the pineapples to golf amongst the oranges, big-hitting Dan Forsman won at San Diego and the even bigger-hitting Fred Couples won the Los

Angeles Open. A second-round 63 did it for Forsman, but Fred went one better with a third-round 62 at Pacific Palisades. Couples also managed to birdie two of his last three holes on Sunday in a bold attempt to disprove the theory that those handsome features are supported by a glass chin.

The month of March traditionally sees the US Tour head for Florida. Greg Norman now bases himself in America's 'Sunshine State', as does his great pal Jack Nicklaus, and seemingly half of the American Tour. The first event on the Florida run in 1990 was the prestigious Doral Ryder Open, staged just outside Miami. After three rounds Paul Azinger and Fred Couples were the joint leaders; Greg Norman was 7 shots back. After 72 holes Norman had forced himself into a four-way play-off with Azinger, Calcavecchia and Simpson thanks to a brilliant 10-under-par 62. It was an extraordinary round which included 8 birdies and an eagle – this on Doral's revered 'Blue Monster' course. At the first play-off hole Norman chipped in for his second eagle of the day and was now 12 under for 19 holes played. It was an awesome victory.

Calcavecchia also finished runner-up to John Huston in the Honda Classic, and then, for the third week in succession, he was narrowly denied a victory by Jodie Mudd in the Players Championship. Not many people had tipped Mudd to win over the celebrated Sawgrass layout, and that includes Mudd himself. After an impressive first-round 67, Mudd commented: 'I'm not picked to win this tournament; my normal game's not suited to this golf course.' Some Americans like to call the Players Championship golf's fifth Major, yet in 1990 not a single member of Europe's Ryder Cup team was in the field.

They assembled en masse, however, a week later at Bay Hill for the Nestlé Invitational. As it happened, Messrs Faldo, Ballesteros, Woosnam, Olazabal, Lyle and Langer proved to be mere members of the supporting cast as Norman, a white stetson on his head and a huge adoring crowd in tow, cruised towards victory . . . or so it looked with a few holes to go, when up popped that man again, Robert Gamez, who canned a 175-yard 7-iron at the final hole for a winning eagle. It was the most outrageous shot of the year, coming as it did on a hole that is statistically the most difficult on the entire USPGA Tour. It was the first time since 1983 that a US tournament had been won by a player holing out for an eagle from the fairway at the 72nd hole. Watching Gamez, who hails from Las Vegas, strike the jackpot was his playing partner, Larry Mize, someone who knows all about creating miracles to defeat Norman.

The Europeans had been at Bay Hill primarily in preparation for Augusta, and though they hadn't fared well in the Nestlé they found their form the following week on the eve of the Masters in the rain-affected Independent Insurance Agent Open. Woosnam and Ballesteros finished just a stroke behind Sills (the play-off winner) and Morgan. Faldo started slowly but closed with a 65. It was a good portent of things to come. The Masters, like the US Open and USPGA, is chronicled elsewhere in this book. Suffice to say here that as much as the Americans love the British a third successive rendition of Rule Britannia must be a little hard to stomach.

A green blazer is probably one of the few outfits that doesn't hang in Payne Stewart's wardrobe. In 1989 Stewart won the Heritage Classic at Hilton Head. In 1990 he repeated the trick, although this time he needed a play-off to do it. A birdie at the second extra hole was sufficient to defeat two leading members of the US Tour's Bible class, Larry Mize and Steve Jones. It was Payne's first play-off success in six attempts. Aussie Steve Elkington raised a few eyebrows by winning the Greensboro tournament, and then came another astonishing Sunday finish involving Greg Norman. Lying five shots behind David Frost after three rounds of the USF&G Classic at English Turn, near New Orleans, Norman fired eight birdies and an eagle (as well as three bogies) for a best-of-the-week 65. Frost came down the difficult par-4 18th knowing that he needed a par to tie. Only Norman had birdied the hole all day. The South African's second finished in a bunker 60 feet from the flag. Surely he couldn't hole

Greg Norman, leading moneywinner on the US Tour in 1990

out from the sand? Certainly he could; and he did. Gamez's wonderstoke in March had left Greg feeling numb; now in April he had to suffer frostbite! Norman's last four holes at English Turn are worth recounting: on the par-5 15th he hit a 5-iron across the water to an island green to within 6 feet of the flag and sank the putt for an eagle 3; at the 16th he almost holed a full wedge shot. He gave a stroke back by 3-putting the 17th but immediately struck back at the long 18th by smashing a 2-iron that finished 6 inches from the hole. 1990 was an up-and-down year for Norman; it was often desperately frustrating, but one thing is for certain, it was never dull.

Payne Stewart was back in the winners' enclosure in the first week of May, holding off the late challenge of Lanny Wadkins to win the Byron Nelson Classic. A third victory for him in five weeks looked possible until overnight rain washed out the final day's play in the Memorial Tournament.

Benefiting from the weather at Muirfield Village was none other than Greg Norman. On the 13th day of the month Lady Luck had at last smiled on the Australian.

A great big smile was also visible on Ben Crenshaw's face when the popular Texan won the Colonial tournament in his home state at Fort Worth. Playing alongside joint leader Curtis Strange in the final round the famous putting stroke got to work and 'Gentle Ben' reeled off 6 birdies in a front nine of 30.

Two of the next three tournaments were won by the underrated Wayne Levi. Sandwiching his victories in the Atlanta Classic and Western Open was Gil Morgan's win in the Kemper Open. Levi's Western Open success against a very strong field was particularly impressive because only Payne Stewart finished within four strokes of the man who claims his chief interest outside of golf is

Wayne Levi surprised everyone (including himself) by winning four events in 1990

Tom Kite, America's $6m dollar man

playing the money markets. The Western Open was considered a Major championship in the days before the Masters. As long as golf is played the US Open will be one of the game's Grand Slam events. In 1990 Hale Irwin earned himself a prominent place in the history books by becoming the championship's oldest winner.

After Levi and Irwin it was Irwin and Levi. Hale remained on cloud nine throughout the week after Medinah to win the Buick Classic and Levi scored nothing above a 67 in the Greater Hartford Open. Three US Opens for Irwin and three Tour wins in 1990 for Wayne Levi. And Levi still hadn't finished.

When his tail is up, Lanny Wadkins is a difficult man to catch; and in the first week of July at the Anheuser-Busch Classic Lanny's tail was up. Leading all the way, Wadkins won by five strokes from Mize. Morris Hatalsky claimed the Bank of Boston Classic, and at the end of July (following a break for the British Open) Chip Beck found the form which had deserted him for much of the year to win the Buick Open. A Buick Classic–Buick Open double had looked likely for Irwin when the US Open champion scored rounds of 69-63-67, but at this point Hale must have finally come down from the clouds, for he stumbled to an unexpected 74 on the final day.

Talking of being in the clouds, Kite, 1989's leading moneywinner, finally made his presence felt in August with a play-off win in the Federal Express St Jude Classic. Victory also enabled Tom to become the first golfer to pass the $6m winnings mark. A $6m-dollar man perhaps, but not a single Major title to his name. Controversy surrounded the USPGA Championship at Shoal Creek but, as the winner, Wayne Grady, pointed out, 'You can scratch as hard as you like but you will never be able to remove my name from the trophy.'

Davis Love won the International at Castle Rock, Colorado, but it was events a week later that got everybody in golf shaking their heads in disbelief. The World Series is one of America's premier tournaments, perhaps the leading event after the Masters, US Open and USPGA. At the difficult Firestone Course at Akron, Ohio, José-Maria Olazabal won by no fewer than 12 strokes, the biggest winning margin in a US tournament for 15 years. He broke numerous scoring records, never mind his challengers' hearts. His first-round 61 (a new course record) was described by Australian Mike Harwood as 'the best round ever at a tournament I've been playing in.' Only two players got within 8 shots of that opening 61. A second-round 67 followed, and after 36 holes the Spaniard led by 9. Never having won before in America, some wondered whether the Basque might now buckle. Buckle? He didn't drop a single stroke to par! In fact, he added two further 67s. His golf was simply devastating, and the rest of the field was simply devastated. Wadkins finished 12 behind Olazabal; Irwin came third, 15 shots adrift, Greg Norman, in joint sixth place, was 19 strokes behind; Kite was beaten by 20 shots, Payne Stewart by 21.

John Hopkins wrote of Olazabal's achievement in the *Sunday Times* under the heading 'Four Days that Shook the World'. 'Tributes were showered on the popular Spaniard like laurel leaves in ancient Rome,' he reported, and quoted runner-up Wadkins as saying: 'All you have to do is look at what he [Olazabal] did here and you can see what kind of a future he is going to have.'

It might have been fitting if the US Tour had ended on such a glorious note, but it continued for a further nine weeks. Except for Levi's fourth victory of the year, in the Canadian Open at Glen Abbey, September's parade of winners were hardly names to get excited over. Joe Gallagher won the Milwaukee Open; Joey Sindelar the Hardee's Classic; Nolan Henke, a Tour rookie, the BC Open, and Kenny Knox the Southern Open.

October's winning quartet looks a little more familiar. O'Meara landed the Texas Open, his second win of 1990, and in doing so secured the year's lowest aggregate total of 261. A week later the five-round Las Vegas Invitational produced a play-off between Bob Tway and John Cook which Tway won, and in the penultimate event Tim Simpson repeated his 1989 victory in the Walt Disney event at Buena Vista, Florida.

With a prodigious first prize of $450,000 on offer in the final event of the year, the Nabisco Championships, something like ten or a dozen players could have snatched the leading moneywinners' title from under Greg Norman's nose. Fortunately for the sake of Greg's sanity, it didn't happen. Wayne Levi, undoubtedly the surprise package of 1990, made a spirited attempt with a last-round 63 but an opening 75 had left him too much to make up. Levi finished his *annus mirabilis* in second place on the Money List with more than a million dollars to his name; Payne Stewart finished third, Paul Azinger fourth. Jodie Mudd, who had done little since winning the Players Championship in March, claimed the massive final prize after a play-off with Billy Mayfair. The latter had looked a certain winner until Mudd birdied the last two holes and followed that with another at the first extra hole. Mudd may not be the most glamorous of names but it was an exciting end to the season nonetheless, and given the Monopoly-like sums of money they were playing for, it seems appropriate that the game should have been concluded by a player landing on Mayfair.

4-7 January
MONY TOURNAMENT OF CHAMPIONS
Carlsbad, California

P. Azinger	66	68	69	69	272	$135,000
I. Baker-Finch	66	67	72	68	273	82,000
M. O'Meara	69	73	65	69	276	52,000
W. Grady	69	68	72	69	278	36,800
G. Norman	66	72	71	70	279	29,750
S. Hoch	69	68	71	71	279	29,750
C. Strange	71	73	70	67	281	24,666
M. Hulbert	72	68	73	68	281	24,666
M. Calcavecchia	70	68	68	75	281	24,666

11-14 January
NORTHERN TELECOM TUSCON OPEN *Tuscon, Arizona*

R. Gamez	65	66	69	70	270	$162,000
M. Calcavecchia	68	67	70	69	274	79,200
J. Haas	66	64	72	72	274	79,200
B. Sander	68	69	73	65	275	35,437
D. Forsman	70	67	69	69	275	35,437
D. Love III	68	65	73	69	275	35,437
C. Pavin	67	70	69	69	275	35,437
J. Edwards	67	71	71	67	276	27,000
D. Frost	70	60	71	75	276	27,000

17-21 January
BOB HOPE CHRYSLER CLASSIC *La Quinta, California*

P. Jacobsen	67	66	69	66	71	339	$180,000
B. Tennyson	73	68	66	67	66	340	88,000
S. Simpson	68	69	67	68	68	340	88,000
T. Simpson	70	70	67	68	66	341	41,333
T. Schulz	70	66	69	67	69	341	41,333
T. Kite	70	69	64	69	69	341	41,333
D. Love III	67	72	67	69	67	342	32,250
B. Tway	67	68	69	69	69	342	32,250

25-28 January
PHOENIX OPEN *Scottsdale, Arizona*

T. Armour III	65	67	67	68	267	$162,000
J. Thorpe	69	69	66	68	272	97,200
F. Couples	75	66	66	67	274	52,200
B.R. Brown	69	66	70	69	274	52,200
B. Mayfair	73	66	70	66	275	32,850
B. Tway	71	67	71	66	275	32,850
B. Tennyson	70	67	65	73	275	32,850
P. Azinger	69	67	71	70	277	27,000
J. Delsing	69	67	68	73	277	27,000
S. Lyle	67	71	67	73	278	22,500
C. Burroughs	68	67	70	73	278	22,500
D. Barr	67	68	68	75	278	22,500

1-4 February
AT&T PEBBLE BEACH NATIONAL PRO-AM
Monterey, California

M. O'Meara	67	73	69	72	281	$180,000
K. Perry	73	71	69	70	283	108,000
T. Kite	69	69	75	71	284	58,000
P. Stewart	66	71	74	73	284	58,000
D. Frost	74	71	73	67	285	40,000
R. Zokol	75	71	71	69	286	34,750
M. Calcavecchia	69	71	74	72	286	34,750
R. Fehr	70	72	73	72	287	29,000
R. Mediate	69	68	73	77	287	29,000
B. Faxon	75	69	74	69	287	29,000

8-11 February
HAWAIIAN OPEN *Waialae, Honolulu*

D. Ishii	72	67	68	72	279	$180,000
P. Azinger	68	71	71	70	280	108,000
J. Mudd	72	72	68	69	281	52,000
C. Dennis	70	73	68	70	281	52,000
C. Stadler	71	67	72	71	281	52,000
P. Persons	72	68	73	69	282	30,250
T. Simpson	72	69	71	70	282	30,250
B.R. Brown	72	71	69	70	282	30,250
J. Hallet	69	73	70	70	282	30,250
G. Waite	72	67	72	71	282	30,250
B. Mayfair	74	71	67	70	282	30,250

15-18 February
SHEARSON LEHMAN HUTTON OPEN *San Diego, California*

D. Forsman	68	63	72	72	275	$162,000
T. Armour III	66	66	73	72	277	97,200
T. Byrum	70	71	69	68	278	61,200
S. Elkington	72	69	70	68	279	32,625
F. Couples	68	68	74	69	279	32,625
K. Triplett	71	66	72	70	279	32,625
T. Sieckmann	69	64	76	70	279	32,625
M. O'Meara	66	74	67	72	279	32,625
C. Stadler	67	70	70	72	279	32,625

22-25 February
NISSAN LOS ANGELES OPEN *Pacific Pallisades, California*

F. Couples	68	67	62	69	266	$180,000
G. Morgan	67	67	65	70	269	108,000
P. Jacobsen	65	69	70	66	270	58,000
R. Mediate	65	67	67	71	270	58,000
T. Kite	67	70	69	65	271	38,000
H. Sutton	68	67	67	69	271	38,000
T. Sills	70	64	70	68	272	33,500
M. Calcavecchia	71	68	69	65	273	28,000
C. Stadler	68	66	72	67	273	28,000
J. Mahaffey	69	69	67	68	273	28,000
T. Sieckmann	68	68	68	69	273	28,000

Fred Couples won the Los Angeles Open in February and nearly won the USPGA Championship at Shoal Creek

1-4 March
DORAL RYDER OPEN *Miami, Florida*

G. Norman	68	73	70	62	273	$252,000
M. Calcavecchia	68	67	73	65	273	104,533
T. Simpson	70	71	66	66	273	104,533
P. Azinger	68	66	70	69	273	104,533
(Norman won play-off at first extra hole)						
T. Purtzer	67	70	70	68	275	53,200
M. Reid	67	72	66	70	275	53,200
F. Couples	67	67	70	72	276	46,900
P. Jacobsen	68	72	72	65	277	39,200
D. Edwards	69	75	68	65	277	39,200
W. Grady	69	71	71	66	277	39,200
K. Green	68	71	70	68	277	39,200

8-11 March
HONDA CLASSIC *Coral Springs, Florida*

J. Huston	68	73	70	71	282	$180,000
M. Calcavecchia	70	76	69	69	284	108,000
B. Lietzke	75	69	73	68	285	48,000
B.R. Brown	72	76	68	69	285	48,000
R. Floyd	73	72	70	70	285	48,000
M. Brooks	71	71	70	73	285	48,000
D. Rummells	75	73	69	70	287	33,500
B. Bryant	73	71	77	67	288	27,000
G. Burns	75	71	71	71	288	27,000
B. Eastwood	76	67	73	72	288	27,000
K. Green	75	71	70	72	288	27,000
T. Watson	73	69	73	73	288	27,000

15-18 March
THE PLAYERS CHAMPIONSHIP *Ponte Vedra, Florida*

J. Mudd	67	72	70	69	278	$270,000
M. Calcavecchia	67	75	68	69	279	162,000
S. Jones	75	71	69	69	284	87,000
T. Purtzer	71	73	69	71	284	87,000
B.J. Brown	73	72	69	71	285	52,687
T. Kite	72	70	70	73	285	52,687
H. Irwin	70	68	74	73	285	52,687
M. McCumber	73	72	73	68	286	42,000
A. Bean	73	68	72	73	286	42,000
F. Allem	73	70	74	71	288	31,800
R. Mediate	72	67	76	73	288	31,800
S. Pate	69	76	71	72	288	31,800
P. Stewart	71	73	71	73	288	31,800
B. Lietzke	75	70	70	73	288	31,800

22-25 March
NESTLE INVITATIONAL *Bay Hill, Orlando, Florida*

R. Gamez	71	69	68	66	274	$162,000
G. Norman	74	68	65	68	275	97,200
L. Mize	71	70	67	68	276	61,200
S. Hoch	69	68	70	70	277	37,200
F. Allem	74	69	65	69	277	37,200
C. Strange	69	70	68	70	277	37,200
P. Azinger	70	70	70	68	278	30,150
N. Price	69	69	72	70	280	27,000
C. Pavin	69	69	72	70	280	27,000
M. O'Meara	70	73	74	64	281	22,500
J.-M. Olazabal	68	73	71	69	281	22,500
T. Watson	71	68	72	70	281	22,500

Jodie Mudd triumphed in the Players Championship and also landed the tour's biggest pay cheque with a win in the Nabisco Championships in October

29 March-1 April
INDEPENDENT INSURANCE AGENT OPEN *Houston, Texas*

T. Sills	67	72	65	204	$180,000
G. Morgan	67	70	67	204	108,000
(Sills won play-off at first extra hole)					
B. Bryant	68	73	64	205	39,062
I. Woosnam	69	69	67	205	39,062
L. Mize	68	69	68	205	39,062
S. Ballesteros	69	68	68	205	39,062
B. Lietzke	67	70	68	205	39,062
S. Simpson	68	68	69	205	39,062
F. Couples	67	69	69	205	39,062
D. Peoples	67	66	72	205	39,062

5-8 April
THE MASTERS *Augusta, Georgia*

See p. 39.

5-8 April
DEPOSIT GUARANTY CLASSIC *Hattiesburg, Mississippi*

G. Sauers	67	65	68	68	268	$54,000
J. Ferenz	71	64	68	67	270	32,400
M. McCullough	68	67	70	66	271	17,400
D. Ogrin	67	70	69	65	271	17,400
L. Janzen	68	64	71	68	272	12,000

Nick Faldo plays a heroic bunker shot at the 12th during his final round at Augusta

MCI HERITAGE CLASSIC *Hilton Head, South Carolina*

P. Stewart	70	69	66	71	276	$180,000
L. Mize	71	69	70	66	276	88,000
S. Jones	68	73	66	69	276	88,000
(Stewart won play-off at second extra hole)						
S. Pate	67	69	73	68	277	44,000
G. Norman	70	70	67	70	277	44,000
A. Bean	74	68	69	67	278	36,000
G. Sauers	66	72	72	69	279	32,250
L. Roberts	71	70	67	71	279	32,250

19-22 April
K-MART GREATER GREENSBORO OPEN
Greensboro, North Carolina

S. Elkington	74	71	71	66	282	$225,000
J. Sluman	71	74	68	71	284	110,000
M. Reid	72	70	67	75	284	110,000
P. Azinger	72	73	73	67	285	51,666
M. Hulbert	73	70	73	69	285	51,666
F. Couples	71	70	71	73	285	51,666
J. Sindelar	70	73	75	68	286	38,958
J. Huston	74	69	71	72	286	38,958
C. Beck	72	72	70	72	286	38,958

26-29 April
USF&G CLASSIC *New Orleans, Louisiana*

D. Frost	71	70	66	69	276	$180,000
G. Norman	73	68	71	65	277	108,000
R. Cochran	72	69	71	67	279	68,000
B. Tennyson	69	70	69	75	283	48,000
J. Delsing	73	69	73	69	284	40,000
T. Simpson	73	69	71	72	285	36,000
H. Sutton	74	69	74	69	286	29,100
B. Bryant	70	73	73	70	286	29,100
D. Edwards	71	71	72	72	286	29,100
M. Smith	73	72	69	72	286	29,100
T. Moore	73	71	69	73	286	29,100

3-6 May
GTE BYRON NELSON CLASSIC *Las Colinas, Irving, Texas*

P. Stewart	67	68	67	202	$180,000
L. Wadkins	72	67	65	204	108,000
B. Lietzke	71	68	68	207	58,000
M. Calcavecchia	69	69	69	207	58,000
A. Magee	69	68	71	208	38,000
T. Simpson	72	66	70	208	38,000
F. Funk	71	71	67	209	30,125
T. Watson	71	69	69	209	30,125
G. Norman	73	67	69	209	30,125
T. Purtzer	70	67	72	209	30,125

1990 USPGA TOUR RESULTS

Ben Crenshaw got his famous putter working to win the Colonial tournament in May

10-13 May
MEMORIAL TOURNAMENT *Muirfield Village, Dublin, Ohio*

G. Norman	73 74 69 216	$180,000
P. Stewart	74 74 69 217	108,000
M. Brooks	76 70 72 218	48,000
B. Faxon	77 69 72 218	48,000
F. Couples	69 74 75 218	48,000
D. Pooley	73 71 74 218	48,000
P. Jacobsen	76 72 71 219	32,250
B. Sander	75 72 72 219	32,250
G. Morgan	79 72 69 220	26,000
S. Pate	75 75 70 220	26,000
B. Glasson	78 71 71 220	26,000
P. Azinger	74 73 73 220	26,000

17-20 May
SOUTHWESTERN BELL COLONIAL *Fort Worth, Texas*

B. Crenshaw	69 65 72 66 272	$180,000
J. Mahaffey	67 72 70 66 275	74,666
C. Pavin	66 71 70 68 275	74,666
N. Price	72 68 67 68 275	74,666
M. Hulbert	71 70 72 63 276	38,000
C. Strange	68 69 69 70 276	38,000
G. Sauers	72 74 69 62 277	30,125
B. Tennyson	73 68 70 66 277	30,125
A. Magee	71 71 69 66 277	30,125
P. Stewart	70 72 68 67 277	30,125

24-27 May
BELL SOUTH ATLANTA CLASSIC *Marietta, Georgia*

W. Levi	72 66 68 69 275	$180,000
L. Mize	66 69 71 70 276	74,667
K. Clearwater	70 68 66 72 276	74,666
N. Price	68 69 69 70 276	74,666
K. Perry	69 70 70 69 278	38,000
M. Donald	68 72 68 70 278	38,000
B. Clear	69 71 69 70 279	33,500
S. Verplank	70 71 71 68 280	28,000
D. Pooley	72 68 70 70 280	28,000
T. Kite	72 69 68 71 280	28,000
H. Twitty	68 68 72 72 280	28,000

31 May-3 June
KEMPER OPEN *Potomac, Maryland*

G. Morgan	68 67 70 69 274	$180,000
I. Baker-Finch	67 72 70 66 275	108,000
S. Hoch	68 68 69 71 276	58,000
H. Irwin	69 73 65 69 276	58,000
T. Kite	70 70 67 70 277	38,000
D. Watson	67 72 70 68 277	38,000
S. Jones	69 68 65 78 280	28,083
M. Hayes	72 70 70 68 280	28,083
B.R. Brown	68 70 72 70 280	28,083
P. McGowan	65 72 70 73 280	28,083
C. Burroughs	69 70 66 75 280	28,083
J. Edwards	70 71 64 75 280	28,083

7-10 June
CENTEL WESTERN OPEN *Oak Brook, Illinois*

W. Levi	70	66	70	69	275	$180,000
P. Stewart	68	67	72	72	279	108,000
P. Jacobsen	72	70	70	68	280	58,000
L. Roberts	65	75	69	71	280	58,000
G. Norman	71	69	71	70	281	38,000
M. Brooks	71	65	73	72	281	38,000
T. Watson	69	71	69	73	282	33,500
C. Strange	73	71	69	70	283	30,000
J.-M. Olazabal	71	68	72	72	283	30,000
W. Grady	70	71	73	70	284	26,000
S. Pate	71	68	73	72	284	26,000

14-17 June
US OPEN *Medinah, Illinois*

See p. 51.

21-24 June
BUICK CLASSIC *Rye, New York*

H. Irwin	66	69	68	66	269	$180,000
P. Azinger	67	70	69	65	271	108,000
K. Triplett	65	74	67	66	272	68,000
K. Green	70	67	69	67	273	48,000
J. Gallagher Jnr	69	68	70	67	274	38,000
B. McCallister	66	67	70	71	274	38,000
L. Janzen	69	70	69	68	276	30,125
R. Floyd	70	73	65	68	276	30,125
L. Roberts	71	67	69	69	276	30,125
C. Stadler	67	71	68	70	276	30,125

28 June-1 July
CANON GREATER HARTFORD OPEN *Cromwell, Connecticut*

W. Levi	67	66	67	67	267	$180,000
R. Mediate	65	69	70	65	269	66,000
M. Calcavecchia	67	67	68	67	269	66,000
C. Perry	63	69	68	69	269	66,000
B. Fabel	67	65	67	70	269	66,000
B. Lohr	70	68	68	64	270	32,375
B. Tennyson	69	69	65	67	270	32,375
L. Roberts	67	66	68	69	270	32,375
N. Henke	65	67	67	71	270	32,375

5-8 July
ANHEUSER-BUSCH CLASSIC *Williamsburg, Virginia*

L. Wadkins	65	66	67	68	266	$180,000
L. Mize	66	69	68	68	271	108,000
S. Verplank	69	64	69	70	272	58,000
B. Wolcott	69	65	68	70	272	58,000
R. Cochran	66	71	69	67	273	36,500
I. Baker-Finch	69	71	66	67	273	36,500
C. Perry	67	67	68	71	273	36,500
D.A. Weibring	67	70	69	68	274	30,000
C. Strange	67	66	68	73	274	30,000

12-15 July
BANK OF BOSTON CLASSIC *Sutton, Massachusetts*

M. Hatalsky	70	68	69	68	275	$162,000
S. Verplank	67	68	68	73	276	97,200
D.A. Weibring	68	69	72	68	277	46,800
R. Fehr	68	71	68	70	277	46,800
M. Smith	65	72	69	71	277	46,800
B. Mayfair	70	68	72	68	278	27,225
B. Bryant	69	69	70	70	278	27,225
B. Glasson	67	70	70	71	278	27,225
S. Pate	72	65	70	71	278	27,225
W. Wood	69	71	66	72	278	27,225

26-29 July
BUICK OPEN *Grand Blanc, Michigan*

C. Beck	66	70	71	65	272	$180,000
M. Donald	65	69	69	70	273	74,667
F. Zoeller	66	69	66	72	273	74,667
H. Irwin	69	63	67	74	273	74,667
F. Funk	69	71	69	65	274	40,000
K. Green	71	63	71	70	275	36,000
L. Thompson	66	72	67	71	276	30,125
R. Wrenn	67	69	68	72	276	30,125
S. Barr	69	66	68	73	276	30,125
D. Tewell	71	65	66	74	276	30,125

1990 USPGA TOUR RESULTS

2-5 August
FEDERAL EXPRESS ST JUDE CLASSIC *Memphis, Tennesse*

T. Kite	72	68	62	67	269	$180,000
J. Cook	69	67	66	67	269	108,000
(Kite won play-off at first extra hole)						
D. Canipe	66	73	64	69	272	68,000
D. Frost	69	70	68	67	274	41,333
B. Estes	67	69	69	69	274	41,333
T. Simpson	69	68	67	70	275	31,166
B. Andrade	68	70	70	67	275	31,166
L. Roberts	66	68	73	68	275	31,166
B. Mayfair	71	65	69	70	275	31,166

9-12 August
USPGA CHAMPIONSHIP *Shoal Creek, Alabama*

See p. 79.

16-19 August
THE INTERNATIONAL *Castle Rock, Colorado*

D. Love III	+14	$180,000
S. Pate	+11	74,666
P. Senior	+11	74,666
E. Romero	+11	74,666
B. Crenshaw	+9	40,000
S. Utley	+8	33,500
J. Adams	+8	33,500
J. Gallagher Jnr.	+8	33,500

23-26 August
NEC WORLD SERIES OF GOLF *Akron, Ohio*

J.-M. Olazabal	61	67	67	67	262	$198,000
L. Wadkins	70	68	70	66	274	118,600
H. Irwin	70	67	66	74	277	74,600
D. Hammond	73	65	70	71	279	52,600
L. Mize	66	71	73	70	280	44,000
C. Beck	71	69	69	72	281	38,025
G. Norman	71	73	69	68	281	38,025
T. Kite	70	71	72	69	282	31,833
P. Azinger	69	71	72	70	282	31,833
T. Dodds	72	71	68	71	282	31,833
M. O'Meara	71	72	68	72	283	26,400
P. Stewart	65	73	73	72	283	26,400

30 August-2 September
GREATER MILWAUKEE OPEN *Franklin, Wisconsin*

J. Gallagher Jnr.	69	70	66	66	271	$162,000
E. Dougherty	69	69	67	66	271	79,200
B. Mayfair	66	69	68	68	271	79,200
(Gallagher won play-off at first extra hole)						
S. Lowery	69	67	71	65	272	37,200
S. Hoch	70	66	69	67	272	37,200
R. Stewart	63	70	67	72	272	37,200
C. Perry	67	71	68	67	273	29,025
H. Sutton	70	68	66	69	273	29,025

6-9 September
HARDEE'S CLASSIC *Coal Valley, Illinois*

J. Sindelar	70	65	67	66	268	$180,000
W. Wood	68	63	68	69	268	108,000
(Sindelar won play-off at first extra hole)						
I. Baker-Finch	67	69	69	64	269	45,100
D. Barr	67	70	65	67	269	45,100
B. Britton	69	67	68	65	269	45,100
J. Delsing	66	65	70	68	269	45,100
J. Gallagher Jnr	68	66	67	68	269	45,100

12-15 September
CANADIAN OPEN *Glen Abbey, Oakville, Ontario*

W. Levi	68	68	72	70	278	$180,000
J. Woodward	68	71	74	66	279	88,000
I. Baker-Finch	68	70	73	68	279	88,000
A. North	71	71	70	69	281	48,000
P. Azinger	70	71	71	70	282	32,750
B. Tennyson	70	67	73	72	282	32,750
M. Wiebe	69	73	68	72	282	32,750
B. Faxon	65	74	71	72	282	32,750
B. Wadkins	68	72	69	73	282	32,750
B. Gardner	72	68	67	75	282	32,750
D. Love III	69	75	71	68	283	24,000
N. Price	69	70	69	75	283	24,000

20-23 September
BC OPEN *Endicott, New York*

N. Henke	66	64	70	68	268	$126,000
M. Wiebe	70	69	68	64	271	75,600
D. Tewell	71	64	70	67	272	33,600
B. Tennyson	70	70	66	66	272	33,600
J. Benepe	68	69	67	68	272	33,600
B. Jaeckel	70	68	65	69	272	33,600
B. McAllister	71	66	69	68	274	23,450

José-Maria Olazabal takes everything in his stride as he cruises to a magnificent 12-stroke victory in the World Series at Firestone

27-30 September
SOUTHERN OPEN *Columbus, Georgia*

K. Knox	69	62	68	66	265	$108,000
J. Hallet	68	66	65	66	265	64,800

(Knox won play-off at second extra hole)

J. Booros	67	67	68	66	268	40,800
L. Nelson	70	67	68	64	269	23,625
T. Moore	69	68	65	67	269	23,625
D. Peoples	67	62	70	70	269	23,625
J. Wilson	67	64	69	69	269	23,625

4-7 October
TEXAS OPEN *San Antonio, Texas*

M. O'Meara	64	68	66	63	261	$144,000
G. Hallberg	63	69	64	66	262	86,400
N. Price	65	66	63	69	263	54,400
L. Roberts	70	65	64	65	264	38,400
C. Pavin	67	68	62	68	265	32,000
M. Brooks	69	64	65	68	266	28,800
E. Aubrey	63	69	70	65	267	25,800
S. Jones	65	63	70	69	267	25,800

10-14 October
LAS VEGAS INVITATIONAL *Las Vegas, Nevada*

B. Tway	67 67 65 65 70	334	$234,000
J. Cook	64 70 66 67 67	334	140,000

(Tway won play-off at first extra hole)

C. Pavin	72 68 66 68 63	337	75,400
P. Blackmar	67 69 68 66 67	337	75,400
N. Henke	69 69 70 66 64	338	49,400
M. O'Meara	67 64 67 69 71	338	49,400
P. Azinger	69 67 71 68 64	339	43,550
J. Sindelar	72 68 70 66 64	340	37,700
S. Elkington	69 71 71 62 67	340	37,700
R. Zokol	69 68 66 67 70	340	37,700

17-20 October
WALT DISNEY WORLD/OLDSMOBILE CLASSIC
Lake Buena Vista, Florida

T. Simpson	64	64	65	71	264	$180,000
J. Mahaffey	67	66	68	64	265	108,000
D. Love III	68	65	66	67	266	68,000
G. Sauers	68	65	67	67	267	48,000
P. Azinger	67	65	68	69	268	40,000
D. Peoples	68	69	65	67	269	36,000

No wins but five second-place finishes for Mark Calcavecchia in 1990

B. Gilder	68	65	68	69	270	33,500
C. Beck	70	67	65	69	271	28,000
D. Forsman	70	68	65	68	271	28,000
B. Lietzke	68	68	68	67	271	28,000
L. Nelson	72	66	65	67	271	28,000

25-28 October
NABISCO CHAMPIONSHIP *Houston, Texas*

J. Mudd	68	69	68	68	273	$450,000
B. Mayfair	69	66	70	68	273	270,000

(Mudd won play-off at first extra hole)

W. Levi	75	71	67	63	276	146,250
I. Baker-Finch	71	70	67	68	276	146,250
N. Price	68	68	71	70	277	100,000
C. Beck	69	68	71	70	278	90,000
T. Simpson	66	73	70	70	279	82,500
G. Norman	66	71	71	71	279	82,500
W. Grady	72	67	73	69	281	75,000
S. Elkington	72	72	66	72	282	71,000
P. Azinger	73	71	68	71	283	67,500

1990 USPGA TOUR WINNERS SUMMARY

January	MONY TOURNAMENT OF CHAMPIONS	P. Azinger	(US)
	NORTHERN TELECOM TUSCON OPEN	R. Gamez	(US)
	BOB HOPE CHRYSLER CLASSIC	P. Jacobsen	(US)
	PHOENIX OPEN	T. Armour III	(US)
February	AT&T PEBBLE BEACH NATIONAL PRO-AM	M. O'Meara	(US)
	HAWAIIAN OPEN	D. Ishii	(US)
	SHEARSON LEHMAN HUTTON OPEN	D. Forsman	(US)
	NISSAN LOS ANGELES OPEN	F. Couples	(US)
March	DORAL RYDER OPEN	G. Norman	(Aus)
	HONDA CLASSIC	J. Huston	(US)
	THE PLAYERS CHAMPIONSHIP	J. Mudd	(US)
	NESTLE INVITATIONAL	R. Gamez	(US)
	INDEPENDENT INSURANCE AGENT OPEN	T. Sills	(US)
April	THE MASTERS	N. Faldo	(GB)
	DEPOSIT GUARANTY CLASSIC	G. Sauers	(US)
	MCI HERITAGE CLASSIC	P. Stewart	(US)
	K-MART GREATER GREENSBORO OPEN	S. Elkington	(Aus)
	USF&G CLASSIC	D. Frost	(SA)
May	GTE BYRON NELSON CLASSIC	P. Stewart	(US)
	MEMORIAL TOURNAMENT	G. Norman	(Aus)
	SOUTHWESTERN BELL COLONIAL	B. Crenshaw	(US)
	BELL SOUTH ATLANTA CLASSIC	W. Levi	(US)
	KEMPER OPEN	G. Morgan	(US)
June	CENTEL WESTERN OPEN	W. Levi	(US)
	US OPEN	H. Irwin	(US)
	BUICK CLASSIC	H. Irwin	(US)
	CANON GREATER HARTFORD OPEN	W. Levi	(US)
July	ANHEUSER-BUSCH CLASSIC	L. Wadkins	(US)
	BANK OF BOSTON CLASSIC	M. Hatalsky	(US)
	BUICK OPEN	C. Beck	(US)
August	FEDERAL EXPRESS ST JUDE CLASSIC	T. Kite	(US)
	USPGA CHAMPIONSHIP	W. Grady	(Aus)
	THE INTERNATIONAL	D. Love III	(US)
	NEC WORLD SERIES OF GOLF	J.-M. Olazabal	(Sp)
	GREATER MILWAUKEE OPEN	J. Gallagher Jnr	(US)
September	HARDEE'S CLASSIC	J. Sindelar	(US)
	CANADIAN OPEN	W. Levi	(US)
	BC OPEN	N. Henke	(US)
	SOUTHERN OPEN	K. Knox	(US)
October	TEXAS OPEN	M. O'Meara	(US)
	LAS VEGAS INVITATIONAL	B. Tway	(US)
	WALT DISNEY WORLD/OLDSMOBILE CLASSIC	T. Simpson	(US)
	NABISCO CHAMPIONSHIPS	J. Mudd	(US)

Greg Norman

MONEY LIST TOP 100:

1	Greg Norman	$1,165,477	51	Bill Britton	278,977
2	Wayne Levi	1,024,647	52	Craig Stadler	278,482
3	Payne Stewart	976,281	53	Curtis Strange	277,172
4	Paul Azinger	944,731	54	Ken Green	267,172
5	Jodie Mudd	911,746	55	Ray Floyd	264,078
6	Hale Irwin	838,249	56	Jeff Sluman	264,012
7	Mark Calcavecchia	834,281	57	David Peoples	259,367
8	Tim Simpson	809,772	58	Chris Perry	259,108
9	Fred Couples	757,999	59	Morris Hatalsky	253,639
10	Mark O'Meara	707,175	60	Mike Reid	249,148
11	Gil Morgan	702,629	61	Tony Sills	243,350
12	Billy Mayfair	693,658	62	Rocco Mediate	240,625
13	Lanny Wadkins	673,433	63	Scott Simpson	235,309
14	Larry Mize	668,198	64	Billy Andrade	231,362
15	Tom Kite	658,202	65	Russ Cochran	230,278
16	Ian Baker-Finch	611,492	66	Peter Persons	218,505
17	Chip Beck	571,816	67	Mike Hulbert	216,002
18	Steve Elkington	548,564	68	Tom Watson	213,989
19	Peter Jacobsen	547,279	69	Bob Estes	212,090
20	Davis Love III	537,172	70	Jim Thorpe	211,297
21	Wayne Grady	527,185	71	Andrew Magee	210,507
22	Nick Price	520,777	72	Mark Wiebe	210,435
23	Bob Tway	495,862	73	Kenny Knox	209,679
24	Loren Roberts	478,522	74	Jay Delsing	207,740
25	Jim Gallagher Jnr	476,706	75	Hal Sutton	207,084
26	Corey Pavin	468,830	76	Jim Hallet	204,059
27	Robert Gamez	461,407	77	Mark Lye	201,011
28	John Cook	448,112	78	Phil Blackmar	200,796
29	Brian Tennyson	443,508	79	Fuzzy Zoeller	199,629
30	John Huston	435,690	80	Dave Barr	197,979
31	Gene Sauers	374,485	81	Brad Faxon	197,118
32	David Frost	372,485	82	Ted Schulz	193,127
33	Ben Crenshaw	351,193	83	Don Pooley	192,570
34	Steve Jones	350,982	84	Richard Zokol	191,634
35	Tommy Armour	348,658	85	Bobby Wadkins	190,613
36	Mike Donald	348,328	86	Brad Bryant	189,795
37	Nick Faldo	345,262	87	David Ishii	188,000
38	José-Maria Olazabal	337,837	88	Kirk Triplett	183,464
39	Steve Pate	334,505	89	Jay Haas	180,023
40	Scott Hoch	333,978	90	Willie Wood	179,972
41	Bruce Lietzke	329,294	91	Fred Funk	179,346
42	John Mahaffey	325,115	92	Robert Wrenn	174,308
43	Dan Forsman	319,160	93	Bill Sander	172,886
44	Billy Ray Brown	312,466	94	Mike Smith	170,034
45	Mark Brooks	307,948	95	David Edwards	166,028
46	Joey Sindelar	307,207	96	Brad Fabel	165,876
47	Scott Verplank	303,589	97	Mark McCumber	163,413
48	Nolan Henke	294,592	98	Brian Claar	161,356
49	Tom Purtzer	285,176	99	Buddy Gardner	159,737
50	Kenny Perry	279,881	100	Bill Glasson	156,791

1990 LPGA TOUR REVIEW

Between them, Beth Daniel and Betsy King have dominated the LPGA Tour for the past two seasons. From the second half of 1989 until the end of 1990 Daniel won no fewer than twelve tour events. The awesome form she displayed in the Solheim Cup came as no surprise to her team-mates; they were simply relieved not to have to compete against her as they had recently been doing so unsuccessfully week after week. Among Daniel's eight tour victories in 1990 (she also won the J.C. Penney Classic mixed team event with Davis Love) was the Mazda LPGA Championship, her first Major title, which she clinched in brilliant fashion with a final round of 66. Not surprisingly, in addition to being leading money-winner, she enjoyed the tour's lowest stroke average in 1990.

Betsy King had dominated the 1989 season as impressively as Daniel did in 1990. Last year she slipped to third place on the money list behind Patty Sheehan and Daniel but won two of the LPGA's Major events, the Nabisco Dinah Shore and, for the second year running, the Women's US Open. King is regarded as the LPGA's toughest competitor, a player with a calm exterior but an inner steel. This was emphasized late in the year when she won the LPGA Matchplay title. However, the tournament she will surely regard as her greatest triumph was that repeat US Open win at Atlanta, former home club of the great Bobby Jones. She won't forget it, and nor, one suspects, will Patty Sheehan, who led by 8 strokes after superb opening rounds of 66 and 68 but who then completely crumbled on the final day, when because of rain 36 holes had to be played. Sheehan completed those two rounds in 75-76. At one stage on that final day King was 11 strokes behind Sheehan. It was a collapse reminiscent of Arnold Palmer's final round in the 1966 US Open when he allowed Billy Casper to whittle away at a seven-stroke lead with nine holes to play. It was especially cruel

Beth Daniel, the LPGA Tour's leading moneywinner in 1990

for Sheehan, as she had also thrown away a winning opportunity in the 1989 US Open. Her far from modest consolation came in the shape of five LPGA victories and winnings of approximately $750,000.

Following Daniel, Sheehan and King on the money list were Cathy Gerring and three times winner Pat Bradley who in 1990 pushed her career earnings beyond the $3.5 million mark. A little further down the table, but still in the top ten was the most popular player of them all, Nancy Lopez – a person who in the past dozen or so years has been to women's golf in America what Seve Ballesteros has been to golf in Europe – a legend in her own lifetime.

1990 TOURNAMENT WINNERS

Jamaica Classic: Patty Sheehan
Oldsmobile Classic: Pat Bradley
Phar-Mor Inverrary Classic: Jane Crafter
Orix Hawaiian Open: Beth Daniel
Kemper Open: Beth Daniel
Desert Inn International: Maggie Will
Circle K Tucson Open: Colleen Walker
Standard Register Turquoise Classic: Pat Bradley
Nabisco Dinah Shore: Betsy King
Women's Konica Cup: Beth Daniel
Sara Lee Classic: Ayako Okamoto
Crestar Classic: Dottie Mochrie
Corning Classic: Pat Bradley
Lady Keystone Open: Cathy Gerring
McDonald's Championship: Patty Sheehan
Atlantic City Classic: Cathy Johnston
Rochester International: Patty Sheehan

Du Maurier Classic: Cathy Johnston
Jamie Farr Toledo Classic: Tina Purtzer
US Women's Open: Betsy King
Phar-Mor Youngstown: Beth Daniel
Mazda Championship: Beth Daniel
Boston Five Classic: Barbra Mucha
Stratton Mountain LPGA Classic: Cathy Gerring
JAL Big Apple Classic: Betsy King
Northgate Classic: Beth Daniel
Rail Charity Classic: Beth Daniel
Ping Cellular One Championship: Patty Sheehan
Safeco Classic: Patty Sheehan
MBS Classic: Nancy Lopez
Centel Classic: Beth Daniel
Mazda Classic: Debbie Massey
LPGA World Matchplay: Betsy King

1990 LPGA ORDER OF MERIT

1	Beth Daniel	$863,578	21	Catherine J. Johnston	156,240
2	Patty Sheehan	732,618	22	Tammie Green	155,765
3	Betsy King	543,844	23	Barbara Mucha	149,972
4	Cathy Gerring	487,326	24	Dale Eggeling	147,990
5	Pat Bradley	430,018	25	Patti Rizzo	145,377
6	Rosie Jones	353,832	26	Nancy Brown	140,988
7	Ayako Okamoto	302,885	27	Meg Mallon	129,381
8	Nancy Lopez	301,262	28	Penny Hammel	128,753
9	Danielle Ammaccapane	300,231	29	Amy Benz	128,216
10	Cindy Rarick	259,163	30	Sherri Turner	122,937
11	Dawn Coe	240,478	31	Kathy Postlewait	121,063
12	Dottie Mochrie	231,410	32	Sue Ertl	116,422
13	Colleen Walker	225,518	33	Alice Ritzman	112,840
14	Chris Johnson	187,486	34	Jane Crafter	112,225
15	Deb Richard	186,464	35	Kristi Albers	111,515
16	Jane Geddes	181,874	36	Maggie Will	110,488
17	Caroline Keggi	180,197	37	Sherri Steinhauser	109,407
18	Elaine Crosby	169,543	38	Missie Berteotti	107,030
19	Debbie Massey	166,661	39	Susan Sanders	101,446
20	Cindy Figg-Currier	157,651	40	Vicki Fergon	101,049

Atlanta Athletic Club, Duluth, Ga 12-15 July

Betsy King retained her US Women's Open title in Atlanta

B. King	72	71	71	70	284	$85,000
P. Sheehan	66	68	75	76	285	42,500
D. Mochrie	74	74	72	66	286	23,956
D. Ammaccapane	72	73	70	71	286	23,956
M. Murphy	70	74	69	74	287	15,904
E. Crosby	71	74	73	70	288	12,464
T. Green	70	74	73	71	288	12,464
B. Daniel	71	71	74	72	288	12,464
H. Stacy	71	72	77	69	289	8,533
M. Mallon	71	71	77	70	289	8,533
C. Gerring	70	78	70	71	289	8,533
S. Turner	74	72	71	72	289	8,533
C. Walker	69	75	73	72	289	8,533
A. Alcott	72	72	72	73	289	8,533
C. Keggi	67	75	73	74	289	8,533
M. McGeorge	72	74	72	72	290	6,727
R. Jones	72	70	74	74	290	6,727
J. Carner	73	71	70	77	291	6,287
A. Ritzman	77	70	73	72	292	5,424
D. Andrews	75	72	73	72	292	5,424
J. Anschutz	72	73	74	73	292	5,424
P. Bradley	74	70	75	73	292	5,424
N. Lopez	68	76	75	73	292	5,424
J. Geddes	66	74	79	73	292	5,424
C. Rarick	73	74	70	75	292	5,424
C. Figg-Currier	76	72	73	72	293	4,623
B. Mucha	74	72	75	72	293	4,623
L. Davies	73	73	74	73	293	4,623

THE 1st SOLHEIM CUP

16–18 November, Lake Nona, Orlando, Florida

'A large brandy before teeing off and an even larger brandy on reaching the 19th' – that, quite possibly, was the medicine prescribed for the British and Irish team when they had to square up to pairings like Nicklaus and Palmer or Nicklaus and Watson during the Ryder Cup matches in the 1960s and 70s (none of which they won). The members of Europe's 1990 Solheim Cup team can at least sympathize with the way they must have felt: teeing up against such duos as Lopez and Bradley or King and Daniel has to be similarly daunting, especially when the opposition is playing 'in its own back yard'.

Forida's Lake Nona resort must be one of the most impressive back yards in the world.

It provided a glorious setting for the first Solheim Cup encounter, in which Europe's top women players took on the cream of America's LPGA Tour for three days of foursomes, fourballs and singles matches. It was, of course, the inaugural version of the 'women's Ryder Cup'; it had been eagerly awaited all year and in the event proved to be a remarkably successful and popular venture.

The powerful American side triumphed – as just about everyone had predicted – their margin of victory being $11^1/_2$–$4^1/_2$. They won both the foursomes and fourballs series by a score of 3–1 and the singles by $5^1/_2$–$2^1/_2$, but the Europeans, admirably led by non-playing captain Micky Walker, returned home

The mighty pairing of Nancy Lopez and Pat Bradley was the prize scalp of Laura Davies and Alison Nicholas on day one

far from demoralized. They are now able to measure their games against the greatest possible yardstick and they know that from tee to green there was not a great deal between the two sides last November. The Americans outplayed the visitors on and around the greens but in no other department of the game. When the second contest takes place in 1992 they will at least know what they are going to be up against, and you can bet on the Europeans putting up a much stronger showing.

Despite the comprehensive defeat there were one or two outstanding performances from Walker's young team. Laura Davies, for instance, won two of her three matches, the first of which, on day one, was in partnership with Alison Nicholas; and they vanquished none other than Nancy Lopez and Pat Bradley, the LPGA's two leading all-time money winners. Lotte Neumann and Pam Wright produced some inspired golf on the Saturday to defeat Cathy Gerring and Dottie Mochrie 4 and 2, while on the final day, which comprised eight singles matches, in addition to Laura's win Scotland provided the heroines in Dale Reid, who defeated Patty Sheehan 2 and 1, and Pam Wright, who retained her previous day's form to gain a brilliant half against Betsy King. Wright in fact was unlucky not to defeat the double US Open Champion, who scrambled a half at the 18th hole despite clattering her approach into the trees.

At varying times throughout the three days the Europeans were confronted by some phenomenal scoring from the Americans, and in case you are wondering how Trish Johnson, Europe's leading moneywinner in 1990, could lose her 18-hole singles match by 8 and 7, the answer is quite simple – Pat Bradley had seven birdies in the eleven holes she played. Better bring out the brandy to play Bradley next time!

Pam Wright excelled for the European side on days two and three

THE 1st SOLHEIM CUP

16 – 18 November, Lake Nona, Orlando, Florida

Foursomes (US names first)
C. GERRING and D. MOCHRIE beat P. WRIGHT (Sco) and L. NEUMANN (Swe) 6 and 5
P. SHEEHAN and R. JONES beat D. REID (Sco) and H. ALFREDSSON (Swe) 6 and 5
P. BRADLEY and N. LOPEZ lost to L. DAVIES (Eng) and A. NICHOLAS (Eng) 2 and 1
B. DANIEL and B. KING beat T. JOHNSON (Eng) and M.-L. DE LORENZI (Fr) 5 and 4
USA 3   Europe 1

Fourball (US names first)
P. SHEEHAN and R. JONES beat T. JOHNSON and M.-L. DE LORENZI 2 and 1
P. BRADLEY and N. LOPEZ beat D. REID and H. ALFREDSSON 2 and 1
B. DANIEL and B. KING beat L. DAVIES and A. NICHOLAS 4 and 3
C. GERRING and D. MOCHRIE lost to P. WRIGHT and L. NEUMANN 4 and 2
USA 3   Europe 1

Singles (US names first)
C. GERRING beat H. ALFREDSSON 4 and 3
R. JONES lost to L. DAVIES 3 and 2
B. DANIEL beat L. NEUMANN 7 and 6
N. LOPEZ beat A. NICHOLAS 6 and 4
B. KING halved with P. WRIGHT
P. SHEEHAN lost to D. REID 2 and 1
D. MOCHRIE beat M.-L. DE LORENZI 4 and 3
P. BRADLEY beat T. JOHNSON 8 and 7
USA 5½ Europe 2½

USA 11½ EUROPE 4½

The star-studded United States team, winners of the inaugural Solheim Cup, show off the superb Waterford Crystal trophy

(over page) Kingston Heath, near Melbourne, venue for this year's Australian Matchplay Championship

AUSTRALIA

Greg Norman's 1990 campaign couldn't have got off to a better – or worse – beginning. As personifies the man, it was both brilliant, in as much as he opened with rounds of 66 and 63, and desperate, in that during his record-equalling second round he transgressed a minor rule and so disqualified himself from the tournament. It was an extraordinary start to a truly rollercoaster year for Australia's greatest player. The Norman debacle took place in January at the Palm Meadows Cup staged on Queensland's Gold Coast. Rodger Davis won the event after a play-off with double US Open champion Curtis Strange. Davis went on to have a fine year both in Australia and Europe, but strangely Curtis never got closer to winning a regular tournament in 1990.

A week later and nearly a thousand miles away, Ronan Rafferty won the Coca Cola Classic at Royal Melbourne, his fourth Australian tour victory. It would seem that Rafferty now only needs to win in America to be considered a 'world star' – like his young European rival Olazabal.

In the next event David Smith, an Australian tour rookie, defeated Peter Fowler in the final of the Australian Matchplay Championship, and while this was going on, an enormous amount of money was being fought over in Australia's version of America's Skins game. In Queensland, or more particularly in the extravagant Port Douglas Mirage Resort, they obviously think like Texans, for they christened their event the Super Skins. The four contestants were Greg Norman, Nick Faldo, Curtis Strange – at the time ranked 1, 2 and 4 in the world – and Japanese star, Jumbo Ozaki, ranked number 11. It is sometimes said that Ozaki can only perform in Japan: not true, it's just that he rarely chooses to travel. Well, he did for this one, and he veritably skinned his opponents alive, leaving the course with A$370,000 in his pocket. Thank you and goodbye!

Norman, Faldo and Strange had more serious business a week later when they arrived in Melbourne for the prestigious Australian Masters tournament at Huntingdale. Everyone in the field knew that Norman regarded Huntingdale as one of his favourite courses – after all he had already won there five times. As for Faldo, he was bidding to add the Australian Masters crown to the US and British Masters titles he already held. For three rounds Nick played beautifully, scoring 68-67-68 to lead the tournament by two strokes, but he hadn't shaken off Norman: he was the man occupying second place. So it was to be a final-day showdown between the game's Big Two.

Lying two strokes behind, the last thing Norman wanted was a poor start – but that is exactly what happened, and after six holes he trailed his playing partner by four shots. Rather than disheartening Norman, this seemed to inspire him, because he now produced four birdies and an eagle to snatch victory from the stunned Englishman. Not surprisingly, the vast crowd loved every minute of it. This was only the twelfth staging of the Australian Masters, and Norman had now won it six times.

Although only mid-February, and hence still very much summer down under, the Australian tour starts its wind-down after the Masters at Huntingdale. The leading Australian players head off to America, Europe and the Far East, not returning until some time in November. Last May, however, one new event did attract a lot of interest: this was the Ladies' Challenge, the richest women's event ever to be staged in Australia. The venue was one of the country's newest and most spectacularly appointed courses, the wonderfully named Paradise Palms golf course in the far north of Queensland, beyond Cairns. The tournament saw the emergence of 20-year-old Nicole Lowien, an Australian whom several experts are tipping to become the new Jan Stephenson and the female star of the 90s. Blonde, big-hitting and a player who loves to attack a course, there is one other obvious comparison.

One of the first players to make the headlines in November was 69-year-old Kel Nagle in the Air New Zealand Open. It wasn't that the Open Champion of 1960 threatened to win the tournament, it was the fact that in one of his rounds he scored a 67, thus becoming the first golfer for nearly twenty years to better his age in a professional tournament. Wayne Riley actually won that event in New Zealand and the following week it was Mike Harwood's turn to triumph in the South Australian Open. Harwood's win came just 21 days after his splendid victory in the Volvo Masters at Valderrama, the last event on the European tour.

The Australian PGA Championship at Riverside Oaks, just outside Sydney, wasn't so much a contest as a one-man exhibition. Local favourite Brett Ogle took the trophy with an emphatic five-stroke victory – he led from start to finish – with Rodger Davis and Wayne Grady tieing for second place. Ogle is one of Australia's legion of rising young stars; another is Craig Parry, and they were both in the thick of things a week after the PGA in the Australian Open.

A big name was expected to win the Open at the Australian Golf Club, situated again on the outskirts of Sydney. Nick Faldo and Greg Norman were in the starting line-up, and large crowds turned up hoping to see a rerun of their Huntingdale (but not St Andrews!) duel. Unfortunately Nick Faldo was never really in contention but Norman looked to be marching towards his fourth Australian Open title at the halfway stage, after rounds of 70 and 68 had put him two shots clear of the field. His second-day 68 may not sound particularly astonishing, but it included a quite astonishing shot. For the first time in his career Greg scored an albatross two: it came on the 578-yard 5th where he holed out from 279 yards with a 3-wood. For good measure he also had an eagle at the 14th, chipping in from just off the green. But the Midas touch deserted Norman in rounds three and four and he was overtaken by Parry and the little-known John Morse from America. Parry and Morse finished level three ahead of Norman and Riley, and therefore had to play off for the

American John Morse cannot believe he's won the Australian Open; runner-up Craig Parry leads the applause

Greg Norman was up in the clouds during the second round of the Australian Open, scoring an albatross and an eagle, but eventually had to settle for joint third place

championship. Few expected Morse to win it, but he did; and so the player who had failed five times to win his US tour card joined a roll of champions that includes the like of Palmer, Player, Nicklaus and Watson.

There was another turn-up for the books in the penultimate event of the year, the Johnnie Walker Classic at Royal Melbourne. Despite being paid enormous appearance fees, Faldo and Norman didn't feature; in fact Nick was forced to withdraw after three rounds with a recurrence of the wrist injury that dogged him for much of the second half of the year. Ray Floyd, Faldo's play-off victim at Augusta, played at Royal Melbourne and featured prominently throughout. He liked the course so much that he described it as a 'Rembrandt'. On day three it was Ian Baker-Finch who 'painted the beautiful pictures', shooting a course record-equalling 63, to put him two strokes clear. Having been in challenging posi-

tions after three rounds in both the Australian Masters and the Australian Open – only to finish with a 76 and a 74 respectively – Baker-Finch crumbled again, posting a last-round 76. It cost him the title and a lot of money, and it opened the door for Kiwi Greg Turner to become the second surprise winner in as many weeks.

So a miserable Christmas for the likeable Baker-Finch? Not at all – in the season's final tournament, the Coolum Classic, he swept to an impressive 5 stroke victory.

AUSTRALIAN TOUR WINNERS 1990

15-18 February
AUSTRALIAN MASTERS *Huntingdale, Melbourne*

G. Norman	68	67	70	68	273	$A90,000
N. Faldo	68	67	68	72	275	37,800
J. Morse	71	69	68	67	275	37,800
M. Clayton	64	74	69	68	275	37,800
R. Davis	69	71	68	69	277	19,950
D. DeLong	68	71	68	70	277	19,950
P. O'Malley	69	71	70	68	278	15,000
J. Woodland	70	67	71	70	278	15,000
C. Parry	68	71	69	71	279	11,833
R. Mackay	70	68	69	72	279	11,833
B. King	71	67	68	73	279	11,833
C. Strange	69	73	71	67	280	8,600
D. Feherty	68	73	71	68	280	8,600
T. Gale	72	69	70	70	281	7,400
I. Baker-Finch	66	71	69	76	282	7,000

22-25 November
AUSTRALIAN PGA *Riverside Oaks, Sydney*

B. Ogle	65	70	69	69	273	$A90,000
R. Davis	75	68	65	70	278	44,250
W. Grady	65	71	75	67	278	44,250
L. Carter	69	74	64	72	279	24,900
D. Graham	70	71	70	69	280	19,950
L. Stephen	69	73	69	69	280	19,950
W. Riley	71	73	68	69	281	16,000
W. Smith	72	69	69	71	281	16,000
K. Trimble	72	70	68	72	282	11,833
N. Ratcliffe	67	71	72	72	282	11,833
P. Fowler	68	72	70	72	282	11,833
T. Price	73	72	71	67	283	7,900
S. Owen	72	68	72	71	283	7,900
C. Mann	72	72	68	71	283	7,900
M. Harwood	69	69	71	74	283	7,900

29 November-2 December
AUSTRALIAN OPEN *The Australian, Sydney*

J. Morse	72	70	73	68	283	$A108,000
C. Parry	72	70	69	72	283	64,800
(Morse won play-off at first extra hole)						
G. Norman	70	68	76	72	286	35,640
W. Riley	70	72	75	69	286	35,640
I. Baker-Finch	71	71	71	74	287	22,800

J. Maggert	71	69	75	72	287	22,800
R. Davis	70	71	75	71	287	22,800
B. Ogle	71	69	74	76	290	16,080
C. Montgomerie	75	71	73	71	290	16,080
P. Fowler	76	72	73	69	290	16,080
P. McWhinney	74	71	71	75	291	10,960
N. Faldo	74	70	74	73	291	10,960
S. Elkington	75	69	71	76	291	10,960

6-9 December
JOHNNIE WALKER CLASSIC *Royal Melbourne*

G. Turner	69	68	70	69	276	$A180,000
R. Davis	70	69	71	70	280	108,000
I. Baker-Finch	72	70	63	76	281	59,400
P. McWhinney	70	70	70	71	281	59,400
R. Floyd	70	69	71	74	284	41,600
M. Harwood	70	72	72	71	285	36,200
D. Mijovic	69	71	70	75	285	36,200
G. Hjerstedt	70	68	74	74	286	26,800
J. Morse	70	70	73	73	286	26,800
K. Trimble	71	69	72	74	286	26,800
S. Owen	67	75	72	73	287	20,400
B. Lane	70	71	72	75	288	15,800
T. Power	71	77	71	69	288	15,800
S. Bennett	72	72	73	71	288	15,800
M. Bradley	73	71	73	71	288	15,800
G. Norman	71	73	73	72	289	12,900
T. Price	70	75	71	73	289	12,900

Palm Meadows Cup	R. Davis
Coca Cola Classic	R. Rafferty
Vines Classic	J. Maggert
Australian Matchplay	D. Smith
Super Skins	M. Ozaki
Australian Masters	G. Norman
Nedlands Masters	J. Morse
New South Wales Open	K. Trimble
Air New Zealand Open	W. Riley
South Australian Open	M. Harwood
Australian PGA	B. Ogle
Australian Open	J. Morse
Johnnie Walker Classic	G. Turner
Coolum Classic	I. Baker-Finch

JAPAN

Tommy Nakajima returned to form in 1990 and won the Japanese Open. Above he shows a deft touch during the Dunlop Phoenix Open

1990 JAPANESE TOUR REVIEW

1990 on the Japanese tour could be summed up as the year that Nakajima came back, Kawagishi emerged and Jumbo Ozaki continued to belie his years.

Jumbo, properly called Masashi, is now well into his forties; in fact he is almost as old as that other Japanese evergreen, Isao Aoki. He not only looks young but regularly hits the ball 'into next week'. After destroying no less a gathering than Nick Faldo, Greg Norman and Curtis Strange in Australia's Super Skins event at Port Douglas in January (during one amazing sequence there he reeled off nine birdies in ten holes!), Jumbo returned to his beloved Japan, won five tour events and easily retained his leading moneywinner title. The trip to North Queensland was one of the rare occasions when Ozaki left his home country. In Britain and America his considerable skills are rarely properly acknowledged. Nor for that matter do the Sony Rankings do his talent sufficient justice: Ozaki is surely one of the world's top ten players.

Jumbo has been Japan's undisputed number one since 1988. In the fifteen years or so before then the Japanese crown was passed around between himself, Aoki and Tommy Nakajima. After a brilliant run in the mid-1980s, which took him to number four in the world rankings, Nakajima suddenly lost his winning touch. In 1990, however, he bounced back to win three times, and most significantly he snatched the prestigious Japan Open title from under the nose of his great rival Ozaki.

Another triple winner in 1990 was Ryoken Kawagishi, who may well be the successor to Ozaki, Nakajima and Aoki as Japan's leading player. To win three times on a very competitive circuit is a considerable achievement in any event, but 1990 was Kawagishi's rookie year and he is still only 23. Not surprisingly he is being compared with Spain's Olazabal, who in 1986 similarly burst on the scene in his rookie year in Europe. Kawagishi's best win of the year came in the Lark Cup in October: he finished two strokes ahead of Ozaki, whom he partnered on the last day – and they teed off level – and six ahead of the trio in third place, Aoki, Ishii and Britain's Barry Lane.

Aoki, Nakamura and Jumbo's brother, Naomichi Ozaki (also known as Joe Ozaki), once again won regularly on the tour; Naomichi claimed two important victories in the Japanese Matchplay and the end of season Nippon Series, defeating Nakajima in a play-off. Australia's Brian Jones appears to be taking over from Graham Marsh as the tour's leading Aussie Raider; he won twice in 1990, including the tour's opening event, the Fudosan Open, in early March.

Australian golfers had plenty to celebrate in Japan in 1990: for one thing they captured the Asahi Glass Four Tours Championship for the first time. The strong team of Jones, Grady, Davis, Baker-Finch, Senior and Parry were awarded the title after rain had unfortunately foreshortened the proceedings. Ian Baker-Finch received an extra prize for being adjudged the event's 'star performer'.

Overseas players arrived en masse in November when Japan's three-tournament International Tour got under way. In the first tournament Olazabal gained his fifth win of the year, successfully defending his Visa Taiheiyo Masters title. The Spaniard demonstrated why he has risen to number three in the world rankings, comfortably beating a top-class field by five strokes to win a second red jacket. One week later, in Japan's richest event, Larry Mize also managed to repeat his Dunlop Phoenix victory of 1989. Finishing third in the Phoenix was former champion Seve Ballesteros, who came to Japan determined to win again before the year was out. He still had one more chance, in the Casio

World Open at the end of the month. With a round to go he was only two strokes off the lead, but yet again couldn't step up a gear on the final day. Ironically the man who denied Ballesteros was American Mike Reid, who in 1989 twice fell apart when leading Major championships. In 1990 even 'Reid the Crumbler' was able to show Seve a clean pair of heels.

23-year-old Ryoken Kawagishi is being hailed as a Japanese Olazabal

The real thing! Despite this watery hiccup, Olazabal had a successful November in Japan

ASAHI GLASS FOUR TOURS WORLD CHAMPIONSHIP

1-4 November Tokyo Yomiuri

FIRST DAY
PGA European Tour beat USPGA Tour 8-4
Ronan Rafferty (71) beat Mark Calcavecchia (73)
David Feherty (71) beat Payne Stewart (72)
Nick Faldo (69) lost to Fred Couples (65)
Mark James (72) beat Wayne Levi (retired hurt)
Ian Woosnam (68) beat Tim Simpson (71)
Bernhard Langer (70) lost to Jodie Mudd (69)

Australasian PGA Tour halved with PGA Japan 6-6
Peter Senior (70) lost to Nobuo Serizawa (69)
Rodger Davis (71) lost to Saburo Fukiki (68)
Craig Parry (71) beat Hideki Kase (75)
Brian Jones (73) lost to Naomichi Ozaki (71)
Wayne Grady (71) beat Masahiro Kuramoto (72)
Ian Baker-Finch (67) beat Noburo Sugai (68)

SECOND DAY
Australasian PGA Tour beat PGA European Tour 8-4
Davis (69) halved with Rafferty (69)
Jones (72) beat Feherty (74)
Parry (71) halved with James (71)
Baker-Finch (68) beat Woosnam (69)
Grady (69) lost to Faldo (67)
Senior (71) beat Langer (75)

USPGA Tour beat PGA Japan 10-2
Simpson (69) beat Serizawa (71)
Couples (66) beat Fujiki (69)
Stewart (68) halved with Kase (68)
Calcavecchia (68) beat Sugai (73)
Mudd (71) halved with Ozaki (71)
Levi (69) beat Kuramoto (74)

THIRD DAY
USPGA Tour halved with Australasian PGA Tour 6-6
Simpson (69) beat Grady (71)
Calcavecchia (70) beat Senior (74)
Stewart (70) lost to Parry (68)
Couples (69) lost to Davis (67)
Mudd (76) lost to Baker-Finch (68)
Levi (66) beat Jones (70)

PGA European Tour halved with PGA Japan 6-6
Rafferty (72) lost to Kuramoto (68)
James (73) lost to Sugai (70)
Woosnam (69) beat Ozaki (71)
Langer (68) beat Serizawa (70)
Feherty (74) lost to Kase (70)
Faldo (69) beat Fujiki (71)

FINAL STANDINGS
Australasian PGA Tour 20 points
USPGA Tour 20 points
PGA European Tour 18 points
PGA Japan 14 points
Australasia won on countback after the final was washed out

LEADING INDIVIDUAL SCORES
F. Couples	65	66	69	200
I. Baker-Finch	67	68	68	203
N. Faldo	69	67	69	205
I. Woosnam	68	69	69	206
R. Davis	71	69	67	207
S. Fujiki	68	69	71	208
T. Simpson	71	69	69	209
C. Parry	71	71	68	210
N. Serizawa	69	71	70	210
P. Stewart	72	68	70	210
M. Calcavecchia	73	68	70	211
W. Grady	71	69	71	211
N. Sugai	68	73	70	211

The Australasian team, winners of the Asahi Glass Four Tours Championship: (from left to right) Rodger Davis, Ian Baker-Finch, Craig Parry, Brian Jones, Peter Senior and Wayne Grady

8-11 November
VISA TAIHEIYO MASTERS *Taiheiyo*

J.-M. Olazabal	66	68	69	67	270	Y23,400,000
M. Ozaki	67	69	72	67	275	10,920,000
B. Langer	71	68	69	67	275	10,920,000
N. Serizawa	67	71	74	64	276	6,240,000
Y. Isomura	68	70	71	70	279	5,200,000
F. Couples	70	69	72	69	280	4,420,000
M.A. Martin	67	73	69	71	280	4,420,000
G. Marsh	72	68	72	69	281	3,575,000
W. Grady	68	66	75	72	281	3,575,000
S. Maruyamam	68	70	70	73	281	3,575,000
S. Elkington	70	71	72	69	282	2,795,000
I. Shirahama	68	71	71	71	282	2,795,000

22-25 November
CASIO WORLD OPEN *Ibusuki*

M. Reid	69	70	65	70	274	Y21,000,000
Y. Kaneko	70	71	70	65	276	12,000,000
S. Ballesteros	71	67	68	71	277	5,060,000
R. Kawagishi	71	69	66	71	277	5,060,000
D. Ishii	71	71	72	63	277	5,060,000
G. Marsh	72	70	68	67	277	5,060,000
M. Kuramoto	74	68	66	69	277	5,060,000
M. Donald	70	68	69	70	277	5,060,000
T. Watanabe	70	71	69	68	278	2,760,000
M. Ozaki	68	70	70	70	278	2,760,000
Y. Noguchi	71	71	66	70	278	2,760,000

15-18 November
DUNLOP PHOENIX *Miyazaki*

L. Mize	69	65	69	71	274	Y36,000,000
N. Ozaki	67	72	67	71	277	20,000,000
T. Nakajima	69	73	70	66	278	9,600,000
D. Ishii	65	74	71	68	278	9,600,000
S. Ballesteros	71	68	70	69	278	9,600,000
L. Nelson	71	63	73	71	278	9,600,000
G. Marsh	69	71	69	70	279	6,100,000
T. Watson	69	71	69	70	279	6,100,000
R. Mackay	72	71	69	68	280	4,900,000
T. Watanabe	67	70	72	71	280	4,900,000
M. Kuramoto	74	73	68	66	281	3,408,000
J.-M. Olazabal	71	72	71	67	281	3,408,000
Y. Isamura	69	75	67	70	281	3,408,000
S. Jones	71	71	67	72	281	3,408,000
M. Reid	70	69	69	73	281	3,408,000

Larry Mize, winner of the Dunlop Phoenix Open in 1989 and 1990

PGA JAPAN TOUR 1990

TOURNAMENT WINNERS

Dajichi Fudosan B. Jones
Imperial Open T. Nakamura
Shizuoka Open R. Kawagishi
Pocarisweat Open N. Yuhara
Bridgestone Aso T. Sugihara
Chunichi Crowns N. Sugai
Fuki Sankei Open M. Ozaki
Japan PGA Matchplay N. Ozaki
Pepsi Ube Open T. Nakamura
Mitsubishi Galant I. Aoki
JCB Sendai Classic R. Mackay
Sapporo Tokyo Open T. Nakamura
Yomiuri Sapporo S. Fujiki
Mizuno Open B. Jones
Yonex Hiroshima M. Ozaki
Nikkei Cup S. Higashi
NST Nigata Open S. Kanai
Japan PGA Championship H. Kase
Maruman Open M. Ozaki
Daiwa KBC Augusta M. Ozaki
Suntory Open T. Nakamura
ANA Sapporo Open T. Nakajima
Jun Classic N. Ozaki
Tokai Classic G. Marsh
Japan Open Championship T. Nakajima
Golf Digest Open N. Sugai
Bridgestone Tournament S. Fujiki
Lark Cup R. Kawagishi
Acom Stableford B. Gilder
Visa Taiheiyo Masters J.-M. Olazabal
Dunlop Phoenix L. Mize
Casio World Open M. Reid
Nippon Series N. Ozaki
Daikyo Open T. Sugihara

Japan's leading player, Masashi 'Jumbo' Ozaki

PGA Japan Tour Money List

1	M. Ozaki	£504,142
2	T. Nakajima	346,793
3	R. Kawagishi	331,153
4	S. Fujiki	274,061
5	N. Ozaki	273,674
6	N. Sugai	270,597
7	H. Kase	238,556
8	B. Jones	223,996
9	G. Marsh	218,582
10	T. Nakamura	215,861

(over page) Hong Kong's skyline is the backdrop as Nick Faldo drives at the 3rd hole during the Johnnie Walker Asian Classic at Royal Hong Kong last December

153

THE REST OF THE WORLD

ASIA

ASIAN TOUR 1990

Tournament winners

Philippine Open	R. Pactolerin
Hong Kong Open	K. Green
Thailand Open	L. Wen-Ter
Indian Open	A. Debusk
Singapore Open	A. Fernando
Indonesian Open	F. Minoza
Malaysian Open	G. Day
Republic of China Open	F. Minoza
South Korean Open	L. Kang-Sun
Dunlop International Open	F. Minoza

12-15 December
JOHNNIE WALKER ASIAN CLASSIC *Royal Hong Kong GC*

N. Faldo	72	68	62	68	270	$50,000
I. Woosnam	69	68	70	67	274	32,000
M. Clayton	72	70	66	67	275	18,500
L. Porter	69	70	70	67	276	12,500
C. Montgomerie	68	70	68	70	276	12,500
T. Hamilton	69	69	69	69	276	12,500
R. Rafferty	67	69	69	72	277	9,000
R. Gibson	69	69	70	71	279	6,666
R. Zokol	70	68	68	73	279	6,666
K. Hla Han	73	74	66	66	279	6,666
M. Ramayah	72	70	68	71	281	5,850
M. Lanner	71	70	71	69	281	5,850

Who's a happy chappie! Faldo celebrates on the 18th after winning the Johnnie Walker Asian Classic

AFRICA

SOUTH AFRICA TOUR
1990 Tournament winners

ICL International	G. Levenson
Lexington PGA Championship	F. Allem
South African Open	T. Dodds
AECI Classic	J. Daly
Goodyear Classic	P. Jonas
Royal Swazi Sun Classic	J. Daly
Palabora Classic	T. Johnstone
Dewars White Label Trophy	J. Bland
Trustbank Tournament of Champions	T. Dodds
Randfontein Scramble	T. Tolles /J. Daly
Minolta Copiers Matchplay	J. Bland
T J Masters	F. Allem
Skeleton Coast Classic	R. Wessels
Wild Coast Skins	J.-M. Olazabal
Million Dollar Challenge	D. Frost
Bloemfontein Classic	J. Bland

Frosty the dough man! Victory at Sun City earned David Frost this unlikely cheque

SAFARI TOUR 1990
Tournament winners

Zimbabwe Open	G. Turner
Zambia Open	G.J. Brand
Kenya Open	C. O'Connor
Nigerian Open	W. Stephens
Ivory Coast Open	D. Llewellyn

6-9 December
MILLION DOLLAR CHALLENGE *Sun City, Bophuthatswana*

D. Frost	71	71	71	71	284	$1,000,000
J.-M. Olazabal	73	70	73	69	285	300,000
B. Langer	69	74	70	75	288	225,000
S. Elkington	77	68	68	75	288	225,000
F. Allem	73	72	74	71	290	150,000
R. Gamez	79	76	69	69	293	135,000
K. Green	75	72	70	76	293	135,000
S. Lyle	80	67	74	76	297	120,000
T. Armour III	81	71	71	77	300	110,000
T. Simpson	75	74	73	81	303	100,000

THE WORLD CUP OF GOLF

23–26 November, Grand Cypress, Orlando, Florida

Bernhard Langer is a man true to his word. For ten years he had elected not to represent Germany in golf's World Cup because, in his opinion, his country had no hope of winning the competition. During the summer he announced his intention to play at Grand Cypress, Florida, accompanied by Torsten Giedeon. Torsten who? Torsten Giedeon was the player who finished 135th on the 1990 Order of Merit and in the process lost his tour playing card. Langer, however, insisted that Germany had a winning combination, and he must have known something that just about everybody else didn't (and that includes the not exactly over-confident Giedeon).

Favourite to win the 36th World Cup was the United States team of Payne Stewart and Jodie Mudd. Despite playing 'in their own back yard' – almost literally, for Florida-based Stewart – they could do no better than fifth place, largely because Mudd had a wretched time totalling twenty shots more than his flamboyant team-mate, who at least had the consolation of picking up the top individual prize.

For much of the first three days the tournament was led by England's Mark James and Richard Boxall – an unlikely pairing, perhaps, given their contrasting styles but one that played very steadily together. It was on the third day that Langer and Giedeon charged up the leader board, moving from seventh position to second. Langer had a fine 67, but this was eclipsed by an extraordinary 65 from Giedeon, which included one 'fresh-air' shot and a collection of improbable putts.

The German and English sides played together on the final day and initially it was James and Boxall who gained the upper hand when both birdied the 1st hole. But by the 6th the Germans were in the lead and from that point they were never headed. In the end Langer (69) and Giedeon (72) coasted home with 3 strokes to spare. James and Boxall were

Mark James and Richard Boxall line up a putt for England

caught in second place by the fast-finishing Irish team of Rafferty and Feherty, the latter producing the best score of the week, an excellent 63. Finishing fourth were Wales (Ian Woosnam and Mark Mouland), making it a successful event for the Great British and Irish teams. But this was Germany's week: Langer had made the sceptics eat their words, and as for Giedeon, one suspects that this was a week he'll never forget. As a certain famous lady said, 'It's a funny old world!'

LEADING TEAM SCORES

GERMANY	**556**					
B. Langer	71	71	67	69	278	
T. Giedeon	70	71	65	72	278	$120,000 each
ENGLAND	**559**					
M. James	68	71	68	72	279	
R. Boxall	68	69	70	73	280	52,000 each
IRELAND	**559**					
R. Rafferty	72	69	70	72	283	
D. Feherty	70	73	70	63	276	52,000 each
WALES	**561**					
I. Woosnam	72	69	65	70	276	
M. Mouland	68	76	68	73	285	32,000 each
UNITED STATES	**562**					
J. Mudd	69	72	73	77	291	
P. Stewart	69	68	68	66	271	25,000 each
ARGENTINA	**566**					
L. Carbonetti	69	71	74	72	286	
M. Guzman	69	72	69	72	280	15,666 each
AUSTRALIA	**566**					
P. Senior	68	71	70	71	280	
B. Jones	75	74	68	69	286	15,666 each
SPAIN	**566**					
J. Rivero	68	67	73	74	282	
M.A. Jimenez	69	73	72	70	284	15,666 each
CANADA	**570**					
D. Barr	69	70	70	73	282	
R. Gibson	73	69	74	72	288	9,000 each
TAIPEI	**571**					
L. Chen	74	75	70	69	288	
C. Yuan	71	72	70	70	283	7,000 each
MEXICO	**571**					
C. Pelaez	73	76	71	68	288	
C. Espinoza	72	71	70	70	283	7,000 each
SCOTLAND	**571**					
S. Torrance	69	75	66	72	282	
G. Brand Jnr	69	71	74	75	289	7,000 each
DENMARK	**572**					
S. Tinning	77	70	75	77	299	
A. Sorensen	67	67	70	69	273	5,000 each
NEW ZEALAND	**575**					
F. Nobilo	68	73	78	69	288	
G. Turner	74	73	69	71	287	3,750 each
KOREA	**575**					
S. Choi	70	77	67	75	289	
N. Park	71	73	72	70	286	3,750 each

Germany's Torsten Giedeon and Bernhard Langer raise the giant World Cup trophy

LEADING INDIVIDUAL SCORES

P. Stewart	69	68	68	66	271	$75,000
A. Sorensen	67	67	70	69	273	50,000
D. Feherty	70	73	70	63	276	35,000
I. Woosnam	72	69	65	70	276	35,000
B. Langer	71	71	67	69	278	17,500
T. Giedeon	70	71	65	72	278	17,500
M. James	68	71	68	72	279	
N. Guzman	69	71	70	71	280	
P. Senior	68	71	70	71	280	
R. Boxall	68	69	70	73	280	

We can be fairly confident that when he woke up on the morning of the first of January 1990, Lee Trevino had a distinctly mischievous grin on his face. This was the year he had been looking forward to for a long time. Not many people are exactly thrilled when they reach the half-century mark, but for Super Mex, 50 the preceding December, it meant he could now compete on the lucrative US Seniors tour. In 1989 he had joked that he was looking to acquire a giant-sized wheelbarrow, one sufficiently large to transport to the bank all the hundreds of thousands of dollars that he was assuredly going to win on the over-50s circuit.

It didn't take long for that mischievous grin to turn into a smile, and the further we advanced into 1990 the wider the smile became. How wide did it get? How wide is a $1 million smile?

It would be overstating things to say that Trevino 'cleaned up' on the Seniors tour in 1990, but he made a pretty good attempt at it, winning seven times in all; and when he wasn't winning he was invariably in the frame. But wait, you say . . . hadn't a certain Jack Nicklaus also turned 50 before the end of January? Indeed he had, but Jack likes the idea of being 50 about as much as he likes three-putting from six feet, and he only chose to play in four Seniors events in 1990. It is probably just as well for some players that he did: his four finishes in those events were 1st, 3rd, 1st, 2nd. It was just like Nicklaus to win on his debut Senior event, The Tradition at Desert Mountain, near Phoenix; and even more like him to win a Seniors Major in his first year and to challenge strongly in the other two that he entered.

The three American Senior Majors, the PGA Seniors Championship, the Mazda Senior TPC and the US Senior Open, were dominated by Trevino, Nicklaus and Gary Player – now almost a Seniors veteran. The South African remains as fiercely competitive as

Jack Nicklaus played in only four US Seniors tour events – and won two of them

ever; he believes he is entitled to include his Senior Major titles in his total number of Major victories. His goal, he says, is quite simply to win more major titles than anyone else.

An impressive victory in the PGA Seniors championship gave him one more to add to his tally. Nicklaus led after the first round, following a 68, but then uncharacteristically soared to a 78; Trevino, on the other hand, started with a 77 and then added a 67. What won it for Player, however, was his magnificent 65 in the third round. It gave him a five-shot lead over Nicklaus and six over Trevino, and in such a position he was never likely to be caught.

Two months later, on the eve of Medinah's US Open, Nicklaus played sublime golf for four days at Dearborn, Michigan, to win the Mazda Senior TPC. He returned a remarkable 27-under-par total of 261, scoring 65-68-64-64. Trevino finished runner-up, six shots adrift, and there was a further five-shot gap to third place. It was a bit like Nicklaus and Watson at Turnberry, only without Watson.

We didn't have to wait long before Trevino too had won a first Seniors Major. It came in late June at the Ridgewood Country Club, New Jersey, in the US Seniors Open. In a most thrilling finish Trevino held off a spirited challenge from Nicklaus over the final nine holes to win by two strokes. Trevino had now played in 13 Seniors events in 1990 and had won six of them. There was some talk of him exchanging his wheelbarrow for a skip.

A week after the Open at St Andrews, Gary Player was at Turnberry, determined to win a second Volvo Seniors British Open title and so increase his Senior Majors tally to five. Arnold Palmer, so unlucky not to have made the cut at St Andrews, was present; so too was the defending champion, Bob Charles, and several familiar faces, including Christy O'Connor, Neil Coles, Billy Casper and Harold Henning. Sadly, Nicklaus and Trevino had returned to America straight after The Open and missed out on a memorable championship. After three days of low scoring, it looked as if Deane Beman, the holidaying US Tour Commission-er, might emerge as an unlikely winner. Then in the final round the weather changed as a terrific gale blew across the famous Ailsa links. Beman (and most of the field for that matter) just couldn't cope with the conditions; at one point Palmer got his nose in front but in the end, despite dropping two shots at the last, it was the man dressed all in black, Gary Player, who wrestled the title from the unfortunate Beman.

Arnold Palmer finished a gallant fourth at Turnberry; but his high point of the year had occurred back in January when he outgunned Nicklaus, Trevino and Player to win the Senior Skins event in Hawaii. The event reached a terrific climax when Palmer faced up to a three-foot putt to win $215,000. And of course, being Arnie, he rammed it straight into the back of the hole.

Arnold Palmer must have the most expressive face in golf

THE 1990 SENIOR MAJORS

12-15 April
PGA SENIORS CHAMPIONSHIP, *PGA National, Palm Beach, Florida*

G. Player	74	69	65	73	281	$75,000
C.C. Rodriguez	74	70	73	66	283	45,000
J. Nicklaus	68	78	67	72	285	25,000
L. Trevino	77	67	70	71	285	25,000
G. Archer	72	72	73	72	289	16,000
M. Barber	75	73	68	76	292	15,000
D. Douglass	71	73	74	75	293	14,000
A. Kelley	71	77	74	73	295	13,000
H. Henning	74	69	81	72	296	10,500
L. Graham	76	76	72	72	296	10,500
L. Ziegler	73	75	75	73	296	10,500
D. Bies	74	75	73	74	296	10,500

7-10 June
MAZDA SENIOR TPC, *Dearborn, Michigan*

J. Nicklaus	65	68	64	64	261	$150,000
L. Trevino	66	68	66	67	267	88,000
J. Dent	71	70	66	65	272	66,000
C. Coody	68	70	68	66	272	66,000
D. Hill	70	67	68	68	273	44,000
C.C. Rodriguez	70	67	68	68	273	44,000
F. Beard	67	70	67	71	275	36,000
O. Moody	70	69	68	69	276	28,466
L. Mowry	69	67	71	69	276	28,466
H. Henning	69	70	67	70	276	28,466

28 June-1 July
US SENIOR OPEN, *Ridgewood CC, New Jersey*

L. Trevino	67	68	73	67	275	$90,000
J. Nicklaus	71	69	67	70	277	45,000
C.C. Rodriguez	73	74	68	66	281	20,881
M. Hill	72	67	73	69	281	20,881
G. Player	75	65	68	73	281	20,881
H. Henning	71	67	75	69	282	12,828
C. Coody	68	73	72	69	282	12,828
D. Bies	75	69	67	72	283	10,550
B. Miller	75	68	67	73	283	10,550
J. Dent	68	68	72	76	284	9,292
T. Dill	71	73	73	68	285	8,480
O. Moody	75	69	69	72	285	8,480

26-29 July
VOLVO SENIORS BRITISH OPEN, *Turnberry, Scotland*

G. Player	69	65	71	75	280	£25,000
D. Beman	67	66	67	81	281	12,775
B. Waites	66	70	69	76	281	12,775
A. Palmer	66	68	69	79	282	7,350
S. Hobday	67	70	67	79	283	6,150
B. Casper	70	70	70	74	284	4,720
B. Charles	68	67	73	76	284	4,720
D. Simon	71	68	66	80	285	3,422
H. Henning	72	75	62	76	285	3,422
L. Mowry	70	66	71	79	286	2,795
J. Fourie	68	72	69	77	286	2,795
N. Coles	69	71	67	80	287	2,560
C. Mehok	70	68	72	80	290	2,430
D. Butler	70	77	68	76	291	2,310
A. Skerritt	71	71	70	80	292	2,200
A. Grubb	76	74	67	76	293	2,040
C. O'Connor	72	71	74	76	293	2,040

Gary Player won two Senior Majors in 1990, including his second Volvo Seniors British Open at Turnberry

1990 US SENIOR TOUR

TOURNAMENT WINNERS

Mony Senior Tournament of Champions G. Archer
Senior Skins Game A. Palmer
Royal Caribbean Classic L. Trevino
GTE Suncoast Classic M. Hill
Aetna Challenge L. Trevino
Vintage Chrysler Invitational L. Trevino
The Vantage at the Dominion J. Dent
Fuji Electric Grand Slam B. Charles
The Tradition at Desert Mountain J. Nicklaus
PGA Seniors Championship G. Player
Liberty Mutual Legends of Golf D. Douglass
Reunion Murata Pro-Am F. Beard
Las Vegas Senior Classic C.C. Rodriguez
Southwestern Bell Classic J. Powell
Doug Sanders Celebrity Classic L. Trevino
Bell Atlantic Classic D. Douglass
Nynex Commemorative L. Trevino
Mazda Senior TPC J. Nicklaus
Mony Syracuse Classic J. Dent
Digital Seniors Classic B. Charles
USGA Senior Open L. Trevino
Northville Long Island Classic G. Archer
Kroger Classic J. Dent
Ameritech Open C.C. Rodriguez
Newport Cup A. Kelley
Painwebber Invitational B. Crampton
Sunwest Charley Pride Classic C.C. Rodriguez
The Showdown Classic R. McBee
GTE Northwest Classic G. Archer
GTE North Classic M. Hill
Vantage Bank One Classic R. McBee
Greater Grand Rapids Open D. Massengale
Crestar Classic J. Dent
Fairfield Barnett Space Coast Classic M. Hill
Vantage Championship C. Coody
Gatlin Brothers Southwest Golf Classic B. Crampton
Transamerica Championship L. Trevino
Gold Rush at Rancho Murietta G. Archer
Pacific Classic M. Hill
GTE Kaanapali Classic B. Charles
New York Life Championship M. Hill

US Senior Tour Money List

1	L. Trevino	$1,190,518
2	M. Hill	859,678
3	C. Coody	762,901
4	G. Archer	749,691
5	C.C. Rodriguez	729,788
6	J. Dent	693,214
7	B. Charles	584,318
8	D. Douglass	568,198
9	G. Player	507,268
10	R. McBee	480,329
11	B. Crampton	464,569
12	H. Henning	409,879
13	A. Geiberger	373,624
14	D. Hill	354,046
15	J. Nicklaus	340,000
16	F. Beard	327,396
17	L. Mowry	314,657
18	R. Thompson	308,915
19	T. Dill	278,372
20	W. Zembriski	276,292

Seventh Heaven: Lee Trevino won seven tournaments and over a million dollars on the US Seniors tour in 1990

At the beginning of 1990 Great Britain and Ireland held both the Walker Cup and the Curtis Cup (not to mention the Ryder Cup, albeit with a little help from our European cousins). Of course it couldn't last for ever, and in July at Somerset Hills, New Jersey, the Curtis Cup went west. The score of 14-4 looks a bit of a drubbing, to put it mildly, but though the Americans certainly deserved their victory most observers felt that in terms of golfing ability there was not a great deal between the sides – or, in other words, the visitors didn't really do themselves justice. Having won the cup so brilliantly in 1986 and then retaining it in 1988, the British and Irish side, led by Jill Thornhill, came to America in search of an unprecedented hat trick of victories; but it just wasn't to be.

A crucial factor in the Americans' change of fortune is their discovery in the past two years of two outstanding young players, 17-year-old Vicki Goetze and 18-year-old Brandie Burton. It will be interesting to see how they fare on the LPGA circuit, assuming they take the professional plunge – and given that Pat Bradley passed the $3 million earnings mark on that tour in 1990, one couldn't exactly blame them for doing so.

The Eisenhower Trophy was also lost in 1990. The Great Britain and Ireland team of Milligan, Evans, Willison and Coulthart finished a disappointing 9th in Christchurch, New Zealand, behind a powerful Swedish side headed by Mathias Gronberg, the British Youths' Champion. The British women fared better in their World Amateur Team Championships, finishing third behind America, Vicki Goetze taking the leading individual honours.

Some historians claim that golf was invented in Holland. This is pure heresy to the Scots, who have often been at pains to point out that if this was really where the Royal and Ancient game originated, why on earth are there no decent Dutch golfers today? In

Left-hander Phil Mickelson

1990 Rolf Muntz became the first Dutchman to win the Amateur Championship; and he did it, of all places, at Muirfield. Twenty-one-year-old Muntz, a psychology student, defeated Mike Macara of Wales 7 and 6 in the 36-hole final. So the name Rolf Muntz now appears on the famous trophy alongside such familiar names – and here's a nice contrast – as José-Maria Olazabal and Bobby Jones. When Jones won the title in 1930 at St Andrews it was part of his historic grand

Vicki Goetze

slam; while nobody today seriously considers the Amateur Championship to be a 'Major', one of the rewards for winning the title is a place in both the Open Championship and US Masters fields. In Muntz's case, that meant visits to St Andrews and Augusta, both so indelibly linked with the greatest of all amateur golfers.

The final leg of Jones's grand slam in 1930 was the US Amateur Championship (he also won both the US and British Open titles). Sixty years on, great things are being predicted for 1990's US Amateur champion, Phil Mickelson. Twice winner of the prestigious NCAA Championship, and still only 19, Mickelson swept to victory in the US Amateur final, beating South African Manny Zerman 5 and 4; more significant, however, is the statistic that shows he was 15 under par for the 150 holes he played during Championship week. One other fact worth noting is that Mickelson plays left-handed, the first of such a disposition to win the US Amateur title. Perhaps in 1990 we at last witnessed the future successor to Bob Charles, the only left-handed winner of the Open Championship.

Back home again, the British Women's Amateur Championship final saw an intriguing contest between Julie Hall and Helen Wadsworth, which Hall narrowly won; and of a slightly different generation Angela Uzielli became the first 50-year-old to win the English Women's Amateur Championship. Charlie Green made it a hat trick of victories in the British Seniors Championship, while the junior stage was dominated by Michael Welch, who in 1990 swept all before him, winning the English, British, European and World Boys' championships, not to mention a host of other trophies. It would appear that Welch is another name to look out for in the future, along with Goetze and Mickelson. He hails from Shropshire, the county in which Sandy Lyle was raised – prodigious footsteps for him to follow in.

THE 1990 AMATEUR CHAMPIONSHIP

June 4-9, Muirfield and Luffness New

Fourth round

R. Muntz beat A. Sandywell 5 and 4
J. Carvill beat E. Nistri one hole
C. Cassells beat G. Lawrie two holes
G. Winter beat N. Walton one hole
G. Evans beat C. Pottier 2 and 1
O. Edmond beat K. Weeks 2 and 1
R. Johnson beat G. Pooley one hole
M. Macara beat G. Wolstenholme at the 23rd

Quarter-finals

C. Cassells beat G. Winter 5 and 4
R. Johnson beat G. Evans 2 and 1
M. Macara beat O. Edmond at the 20th
R. Muntz beat J. Carvill at the 19th

Semi-finals

R. Muntz beat C. Cassells 2 and 1
M. Macara beat R. Johnson one hole

FINAL (36 holes)

R. Muntz beat M. Macara 7 and 6

Rolf Muntz

PAST CHAMPIONS

Post 1945

1946	J. Bruen	1962	R. Davies	1978	P. McEvoy
1947	W. Turnesa	1963	M. Lunt	1979	J. Sigel
1948	F. Stranahan	1964	G. Clark	1980	D. Evans
1949	S. McCready	1965	M. Bonallack	1981	P. Ploujoux
1950	F. Stranahan	1966	R. Cole	1982	M. Thompson
1951	R. Chapman	1967	R. Dickson	1983	P. Parkin
1952	E. Ward	1968	M. Bonallack	1984	J.-M. Olazabal
1953	J. Carr	1969	M. Bonallack	1985	G. McGimpsey
1954	D. Bachli	1970	M. Bonallack	1986	D. Curry
1955	J. Conrad	1971	S. Melnyk	1987	P. Mayo
1956	J. Beharrell	1972	T. Homer	1988	C. Hardin
1957	R. Reid-Jack	1973	R. Siderowf	1989	S. Dodd
1958	J. Carr	1974	T. Homer		
1959	D. Beaman	1975	M. Giles		
1960	J. Carr	1976	R. Siderowf		
1961	M. Bonallack	1977	P. McEvoy		

Most victories
John Ball (8) between
1888 and 1912

THE 26TH CURTIS CUP

28 – 29 July, Somerset Hills, New Jersey

FIRST DAY

Foursomes (GB and I names first)
H. Dobson (Seacroft) and C. Lambert (North Berwick) lost to
V. Goetze and A. Sander 4 and 3
J. Hall (Felixstowe Ferry) and K. Imrie (Monifieth) beat K.
Noble and M. Platt 2 and I
E. Farquharson (Deeside) and H. Wadsworth (Royal Cinque
Ports) lost to C. Semple-Thompson and R. Weiss 3 and I
Great Britain and Ireland I   USA 2

Singles (GB and I names first)
Hall beat Goetze 2 and I
Imrie lost to K. Peterson 3 and 2
Farquharson lost to B. Burton 3 and I
L. Fletcher (Almouth) lost to Weiss 4 and 3
Lambert lost to Noble I hole
V. Thomas (Pennard) beat Thompson I hole
Great Britain and Ireland 2   USA 4

SECOND DAY

Foursomes (GB and I names first)
Hall and Imrie lost to Goetze and Sander 3 and I
Lambert and Dobson beat Noble and Platt I hole
Farquharson and Wadsworth lost to Peterson and Burton 5
and 4
Great Britain and Ireland I   USA 2

Singles (GB and I names first)
Dobson lost to Goetze 4 and 3
Lambert lost to Burton 4 and 3
Imrie lost to Peterson I hole
Hall lost to Noble 2 holes
Farquharson lost to Weiss 2 and I
Thomas lost to Semple-Thompson 3 and I
Great Britain and Ireland 0   USA 6

MATCH RESULT

GREAT BRITAIN AND IRELAND 4   USA 14

The 1990 Curtis Cup teams pose at Somerset Hills, New Jersey

AMATEUR CHAMPIONS OF 1990

British Amateur R. Muntz bt M. Macara 7 & 6
English Amateur I. Garbutt bt G. Evans 8 & 7
Scottish Amateur C. Everett bt M. Thomson 7 & 5
Welsh Amateur A. Barnett bt A. Jones 1 hole
Irish Amateur D. Clarke bt P. Harrington 3 & 2
British Boys M. Welch bt M. Ellis 3 & 1
British Youths M. Gronberg
British Seniors C. Green
English Amateur Strokeplay G. Evans/O. Edmond (tied)
Scottish Amateur Strokeplay G. Hay
Welsh Amateur Strokeplay G. Houston

English Boys M. Welch
Scottish Boys B. Collier
Welsh Boys M. Ellis
European Juniors M. Welch
World Juniors M. Welch

British Ladies Amateur J. Hall bt H. Wadsworth 3 & 2
English Ladies Amateur A. Uzielli bt L. Fletcher 2 & 1
Scottish Ladies Amateur E. Farquarson bt S. Huggan 3 & 2
Welsh Ladies Amateur S. Roberts bt H. Wadsworth 3 & 2
Irish Ladies Amateur E. McDaid bt L. Callen 2 & 1
British Girls S. Cavalleri bt E. Valera 5 & 4
British Ladies Strokeplay V. Thomas

US Amateur Championship P. Mickelson bt M. Zerman 5 & 4
US Women's Amateur P. Hurst bt S. Davis at 37th

25-28 October
WORLD AMATEUR TEAM CHAMPIONSHIP
(Eisenhower Trophy), *Christchurch, New Zealand*

1.	Sweden	879
2.	New Zealand	892
3.	United States	892
4.	Canada	903
5.	France	903
9.	GB and Ireland	910

LEADING INDIVIDUAL SCORES

M. Gronberg (Sweden)	70	67	77	72	286
G. Hjertstedt (Sweden)	73	71	74	74	292
M. Long (New Zealand)	71	71	79	73	294
S. Maruyama (Japan)	72	75	75	72	294
O. Edmond (France)	75	72	74	75	296

18-21 October
WOMEN'S WORLD AMATEUR TEAM CHAMPIONSHIP *Christchurch, New Zealand*

1.	United States	585
2.	New Zealand	597
3.	GB and Ireland	605
4.	Japan	607

LEADING INDIVIDUAL SCORES

V. Goetze (US)	74	76	74	67	291
J. Higgins (New Zealand)	74	72	74	75	295
J. Won (Korea)	77	77	72	69	295
P. Hurst (US)	74	71	81	74	300
A. Sorenstam (Sweden)	78	71	77	74	300

Michael Welch

4

1991
A YEAR TO
SAVOUR

1991 MAJORS PREVIEW

Dave Hamilton, Associate Editor of *Golf Illustrated Weekly*

There is a feeling among club golfers in Britain that the season doesn't truly get under way until the Major championships come around. Put another way, they don't feel like getting back on the fairways until the US Masters is ready to tee off in early April. By that time both the American Tour and the European circuit are well into their respective schedules, but not until Augusta National throws open its doors to the cream of the world's players do the British get down to the serious action.

Of course, this usually coincides with the better weather, the arrival of British Summer Time and the call of the first cuckoo. Nevertheless, when all is said and done, it is the four Major championships that get us

all fired up, and so they should. They are the glittering prizes that every professional wants to get his hands on, while we lesser mortals can only look on in awe, knowing that, but for a miracle of reincarnation, we will never attain such heights, let alone actually tee off in any of the events.

But we can play the field by staking a few pounds on who might win this year, and, who knows, it could provide a nice little earner, a provision for that new set of clubs you've been promising yourself for so long. For those with the ability – or the luck – to pick three or all four winners, it could mean a fortune. If you had been on all the champions last year, you would now

Nick Faldo will be seeking a Masters hat trick in April

Ronan Rafferty plays to the 13th at Augusta

be sitting pretty. We had Nick Faldo at 13-1 for the Masters, Hale Irwin 100-1 for the US Open, Faldo 10-1 for the Open, and Wayne Grady 80-1 for the USPGA. A fiver wagered would have left you penning your resignation to the boss and calling in your investment manager.

Faldo's successes were probably on the cards, but who would have bet on Irwin becoming the oldest winner of America's top title at 45 after a 19-hole play-off at Medinah, or Grady eclipsing all the fancied runners at Shoal Creek to pick up Australia's first Major since Greg Norman's Open triumph in 1986?

Last year's performances were also cold comfort for the United States, who, for the first time since the Masters was inaugurated in 1934, only picked up one title. But what about 1991? Can Faldo do it again and underline that he is the best in the world? Don't bet against it, because he will surely be among the favourites, while the rest will be looking over their shoulders to see what he is doing. The incentive is there, especially at the Masters, where Faldo will be bidding for

a hat-trick. No one, not even the great Jack Nicklaus, has won three years in succession; so providing he is fit and in form, Faldo will be the man to beat.

Having suffered so many bloody noses in recent years, the Americans will be going flat out to ensure that the Green Jacket doesn't go overseas again. As they tee off, they won't need reminding that it has escaped their clutches on seven of the last 13 occasions or that this is Ryder Cup year. The victories of Gary Player, Seve Ballesteros (twice), Bernhard Langer, Sandy Lyle and Faldo (twice) since 1978 proved that they were able to handle Augusta's lightning-slick greens better than the home players and were less intimidated by the water hazards, especially around Amen Corner, holes 11 to 13, which are flanked by Rae's Creek.

That innocent-looking stream burst its banks under the volume of water flooding through Augusta last October and washed away the 11th green where Faldo clinched both his victories in the past two years' play-offs. Much restoration work has been done to the magnificent course, which is sure to be at its finest again in salute of the new champion. Who will it be? It would be nice to see Faldo create history, but I have a feeling America won't miss out again, with perhaps Paul Azinger or Curtis Strange joining the elite club.

There is a distinct British feel about the US Open, which in June moves to Minnesota and the Hazeltine Club for only the second occasion. It is 21 years since the drama last unfolded there and most of it was created by a 25-year-old called Tony Jacklin. The lad from Scunthorpe had gone to Hazeltine as Open champion but few gave him much of a chance; in fact he was on offer at 18-1 behind firm favourites Billy Casper, Gary Player and Lee Trevino. Jacklin had made his US Open debut the previous year and finished tied 26th, but this time he surprised them all by becoming only the third British winner, following Harry Vardon in 1900 and Ted Ray in 1920. It was generally felt that it was Jacklin's ability to combat the 40mph winds that lashed the course on the first day that paved his way to victory. The conditions 'reminded me of home', said Jacklin as he shot

a one-under-par 71 to open a three-shot lead over a trio who are virtually unknown today, Bobby Mitchell, Rich Crawford and Tony Evans. On that infamous first day, Trevino carded a 77, Arnold Palmer a 79, Player an 80, and Nicklaus 81. It was no comfort to that illustrious band when Jacklin remarked: 'I like to play in this type of weather. I was brought up playing in it and I hope it stays like this.'

No doubt the also-rans felt things would be different on day two in calmer conditions, but Jacklin confounded them by adding a 70 to maintain his three-shot advantage over Dave Hill, who was so critical of the course – 'it lacked acres of corn and a few cows. They ruined a good farm when they built this one' – that he was duly fined. It must have had the desired effect, because Jacklin went round in another 70 on day three to go four in front of Hill and closed with yet another 70 for 281 as Hill slumped to a 73 for second spot, seven shots behind. After collecting the famous silver trophy, Jacklin said: 'This is beyond my wildest dreams. Trying not to think about winning was the toughest job, but I never felt I could be caught.' It would be heartening to

Hazeltine National, Chaska, Minnesota, venue for the 1991 US Open

feel that another Briton might utter similar words this year. Failing that, the Spanish flag could be hoisted, if not by Ballesteros then by José-Maria Olazabal, who surely must claim a Major before long after his stunning victories worldwide last year.

Hill's broadside led to extensive modifications to Robert Trent Jones's Hazeltine creation in the late 1970s but this year's field will still find it a difficult nut to crack with its long par-4s and par-5s topped by large, undulating greens.

When the world's attention switches to Britain in July, the annual Open Championship caravan will come to rest at Royal Birkdale, many players' favourite of all the Open venues. It is often said that the world's premier tournament always produces a great champion, and one glance at Birkdale's roll of honour backs that to the hilt. Peter Thomson (twice), Arnold Palmer, Lee Trevino, Johnny Miller and Tom Watson are from the top flight, and whoever lifts the old trophy this time will be joining an exclusive club.

Royal Birkdale can be classed as one of the Open's newer courses. It was as recently as 1954 that the championship first went there. (It would have been earlier but for a certain Adolf Hitler.) The spacious links lend themselves ideally to the tournament because there are ample spectator vantagepoints over the dunes, while it is conveniently close to major towns to suit most accommodation problems.

Thomson's first victory there in '54 denied Britain another champion, as Dai Rees and Syd Scott shared second spot with South Africa's Bobby Locke one shot behind. Rees was again one off the title in '61 when Palmer clinched his first Open after producing one of golf's master strokes. On the 15th, now the 16th, in the final round, his ball landed under a small bush 140 yards from the green. After deliberating, Palmer pulled out his 6-iron and removed grass, bush *et al.*, his ball finishing on the putting surface. A plaque marks the spot to this day, and in many ways it was a most important stroke in the development of British golf, because Palmer's victory prompted the rest of America's best to embark on an

Langer and Olazabal, both widely fancied to do well at Royal Birkdale in July

annual Open pilgrimage.

In 1965 Thomson triumphed again, this time by two shots over Britons Brian Huggett and Christy O'Connor, while in 1971 again the winning margin was one, this time for Trevino over the gracious Mr Lu from Taiwan. Miller dominated the 1976 Open, romping to a six-stroke success from Nicklaus and a virtually unknown 19-year-old named Ballesteros. The young matador had led at halfway by two from Miller after carding two 69s, but faltered as the American closed with a 66 for the title. But Seve had carved his name with pride, as subsequent years would testify.

Before the 1983 Open, many players felt the course was too difficult, with the rough having grown long and thick, and there were predictions that level par would be good enough to win. Yet this proved groundless, as the leading players scored lower than ever at Birkdale. Watson, by now a firm favourite with British crowds, claimed his fifth Open in nine years after striking a perfect second shot within 20 feet of the flag on the 72nd hole. 'I've never hit a better 2-iron in my life,' he said after rolling his putt to 18 inches and tapping in for par and a one-shot margin over Irwin and Andy Bean.

The Americans will again be a force at Birkdale, but with British players having come so close in the past, it is perhaps time for a first home winner here. Faldo is a clear choice to retain his crown, especially as he has been a winner over the course in the 1978 PGA Championship, while he was also prominent in the '83 Open, after which he felt it was time to remodel his swing. I wouldn't rule out Ian Woosnam or Bernhard Langer this time, as well as the aforementioned Señor Olazabal. The USPGA Championship completes the season of Majors in August and has a history of throwing up first-time winners, as Grady proved last year. Before him there have been John Mahaffey, Hal Sutton, Bob Tway, Jeff Sluman and Payne Stewart.

Many feel it is the easiest of the Majors to win but that isn't borne out by the venues it has visited.

This year it breaks new ground by being staged at the attractively named Crooked Stick in Carmel, Indiana, created in 1964 by Pete Dye, who was also a driving force behind the formation of the club. It is no pushover at 7,075 yards, par-72, and was once described by USGA senior executive director Frank Hannigan as 'the hardest golf course I have ever seen'.

Time will tell if those words were an accurate assessment, but Dye has returned twice to Crooked Stick to upgrade his design. In 1978 he added some fairway bunkers and changed some trees, then in 1980 he recontoured the 11th green and supervised the planting of thousands of trees on the perimeter. In picking a winner, you may not be able to see the wood for the trees, especially when the likes of Grady, Sluman and Tway come out of the pack. But, come August, we shall all be the wiser and, hopefully, richer.

Crooked Stick, Carmel, Indiana – this is where Wayne Grady will defend his USPGA title in August

The magnificent par-3 12th at Royal Birkdale

1991 RYDER CUP AND WALKER CUP PREVIEW

Alistair Tait, Deputy Editor of *Golf Monthly*

If a year makes a big difference in the golfing world, imagine the changes that take place over a decade. As we approach the first Ryder and Walker Cup matches of the 1990s, global golf has been turned on its head.

Ten years ago, amateur and professional players on this side of the Atlantic looked forward to playing their American counterparts with the same enthusiasm as a condemned man contemplating the gallows.

Great Britain and Ireland hadn't won a Ryder Cup match in eleven attempts going into the 1981 matches at Walton Heath. The closest they had come was in 1969, in that contest made famous by Nicklaus graciously conceding Jacklin a two-foot putt on the final green for the first tie in the history of the competition.

That drawn match was merely an aberration, though, because the Americans romped home in every competition during the 70s. Even the inclusion of continental players for the 1979 matches did not stem the American tide. The US team won that match 17–11.

Needless to say, it was no surprise when Europe went down $18^{1}/_{2}$–$9^{1}/_{2}$ at Walton Heath. Another decade of defeat seemed certain. But defeat doesn't sit too easily on the shoulders of Tony Jacklin, the man chosen to guide the European side during the 80s.

Jacklin had been Britain's most successful golfer during the 1960s and 70s, winning both the Open and US Open championships. A combination of his leadership and the blossoming of players such as Woosnam,

Euphoria at The Belfry in 1989 as Europe retains the Ryder Cup

Faldo, Langer, Ballesteros and Lyle made the 1983 matches no mere formality. Indeed, it took a glorious wedge shot by Lanny Wadkins to the 18th green in his singles match with José-Maria Canizares to give the Americans victory by the slimmest of margins, $14\frac{1}{2}$–$13\frac{1}{2}$.

1983 was a turning point in Ryder Cup history. Europe hasn't looked back since. The Belfry was the scene of the start of the European onslaught, and the figure of Sam Torrance standing with his arms stretched victoriously aloft on the 18th green is etched indelibly on the minds of European golfers. Success followed two years later at Muirfield Village, Ohio, when Europe won for the first time on American soil. Then came the drawn match of 1989.

Consequently, when Europe's Captain Bernard Gallacher expressed his belief a year ago that the 1991 event 'will be a great Ryder Cup, a close match between the best players in the world', he does so with the utmost conviction. Similar statements have been uttered by past captains, but until the 80s they were no more than platitudes, so strong was the American grip on Samuel Ryder's trophy.

As veteran of eight matches and Jacklin's deputy for three, Gallacher knows all about the pressure of the Ryder Cup. He is also well aware that his side will enter the competition as favourites, given that the strength of world golf now lies on this side of the Atlantic.

Not only does Gallacher enter the matches confident that the best players are on his side; he know that the course conditions favour his team.

No one could quite understand the rationale when the PGA of America announced that Kiawah Island, South Carolina, not PGA West in California, would be the venue for the 1991 matches. The main reason for deciding against PGA West was to accommodate television coverage. However, the move was made at a time when Kiawah was still just an outline in architect Pete Dye's mind.

Many wondered if the course would be ready in time, but a visit in September 1989 by Gallacher and Dave Stockton, the US Captain, confirmed that, while the course was not quite ready, there would be no problem getting it in top shape for the best players in the world by the dead-line.

Gallacher and Stockton played a few holes together along with Pete Dye, and both praised the course highly. 'It looks like God designed it' was Stockton's reaction, while Gallacher said he was sure Kiawah 'will be ranked among the best in the world when it is finished'.

This is high praise for a course whose architect isn't exactly revered by the players when it comes to course design. Pete Dye has been described as the 'Marquis de Sod' by some professionals because his designs call for pinpoint precision. It's either that or certain calamity. Dye is responsible for perhaps the most notorious par-3 in the world: the 17th on the TPC at Sawgrass, venue for the Players Championship. Although no more than a short iron for the professionals, the green on this 140-yard par-3 is completely surrounded by water. The tournament isn't safely won until this hole has been completed, no matter how big the lead.

The 17th is also Kiawah's signature hole. A par-3 of 215 yards, the tee shot has to carry a lake with no bail out on the left. Gallacher needed a driver to reach this green the day he played the course, even though there was only a slight breeze.

Dye has built a typical links course at Kiawah, and the wind will be a big factor. The par-72 course is a monster, measuring 7,240 from the back tees, with the longest hole being the 605-yard par-5 16th.

The links-type design is something of a surprise and will no doubt favour the European side, a fact recognized by Dave Stockton: 'There is no course in the United States like it, so it will be very difficult for my players to practise the appropriate types of shot.'

The links-type course pleased Gallacher when he first saw it. 'It's like Portmarnock or Portrush with sun,' he said, referring to those two great Irish courses. 'It is built around the wind, and the bump and run shots are going to play a significant part in the Cup matches.'

Gallacher diplomatically stated that he

Sandy Lyle at Muirfield Village in 1987. Kiawah Island will present a very different challenge in 1991 – and it should favour the European side

didn't think the course would help his team, but then he is a confident man, a man with momentum and the best players in the world on his side.

While the European professionals enter their biannual matches as defenders and favourites, the same cannot be said about their amateur counterparts. Although the Great Britain and Ireland side conquered a crack American team at Peachtree two years ago, the Americans will once again enter the matches as the stronger team.

The American grip on the Walker Cup is as firm as it once was on the Ryder Cup. Unlike the professionals, the British and Irish amateurs are still a long way behind their American equivalents. The strong college programme in America provides a good breeding ground for the professional ranks. Indeed, very few American professionals graduate to the US Tour without having first gone to college. Four years of 72-hole stroke play is a good apprenticeship; these players emerge mentally, physically and technically prepared

for golf at the top.

The British and Irish amateur game cannot compete with the American system. It is the chief reason that out of the 32 events the Americans have won 28, drawn one and lost only three.

One of those losses occurred the last time the two sides met, at Peachtree in 1989. The Americans entered the matches as hot favourites, playing on a course tailormade for their style of play. They got a rude awakening the first day, when Great Britain and Ireland forged ahead to a $7^1/_2$–$4^1/_2$ lead. They continued their inspired form in the second-day foursomes matches, when they won $3^1/_2$ out of a possible 4 points, leaving themselves needing to win only $1^1/_2$ points in the afternoon singles to clinch victory.

The climax to those Walker Cup matches couldn't have been more exciting. Rather than cruise home to victory, the visitors seemed destined to lose in dramatic fashion to a US team determined not to be the first side to lose on American soil. At one time the

A jubilant Great Britain and Ireland team celebrate a surprise victory in the 1989 Walker Cup match at Peachtree, Georgia

Americans led in all eight matches. Indeed, the Americans did not lose one singles match, but three halves were enough to give the visitors a $12^1/_2$–$11^1/_2$ victory.

The 1989 victory was a great boost to the amateur game on this side of the Atlantic, and Great Britain and Ireland go into the matches at Portmarnock, Ireland, with the reassuring knowledge that the course will be to their benefit. This great Irish course, venue for many Irish Opens, is a supreme test of golf; it is links golf at its best and will test the best amateurs the game has to offer.

So 1991 is something of an anomaly in the annals of this great game: it is the first time the Americans enter both matches as the vanquished. There was a time when such a scenario would have been unthinkable, but then a lot has happened in a decade.

THE 28TH RYDER CUP

22-24 September 1989
The Belfry

EUROPE	MATCHES	USA	MATCHES
Foursomes: Morning		C. Strange & T. Kite	½
N. Faldo & I. Woosnam	½	L. Wadkins & P. Stewart (1 hole)	1
H. Clark & M. James	0	T. Watson & C. Beck	½
S. Ballesteros & J.-M. Olazabal	½	M. Calcavecchia & K. Green (2 & 1)	1
B. Langer & R. Rafferty	0		
Fourballs: Afternoon			
S. Torrance & G. Brand Jnr (1 hole)	1	C. Strange & P. Azinger	0
H. Clark & M. James (3 & 2)	1	F. Couples & L. Wadkins	0
N. Faldo & I. Woosnam (2 holes)	1	M. Calcavecchia & M. McCumber	0
S. Ballesteros & J.-M. Olazabal (6 & 5)	1	T. Watson & M. O'Meara	0
Foursomes: Morning			
N. Faldo & I. Woosnam (3 & 2)	1	L. Wadkins & P. Stewart	0
G. Brand Jnr & S. Torrance	0	C. Beck & P. Azinger (4 & 3)	1
C. O'Connor & R. Rafferty	0	M. Calcavecchia & K. Green (3 & 2)	1
S. Ballesteros & J.-M. Olazabal (1 hole)	1	T. Kite & C. Strange	0
Fourballs: Afternoon			
N. Faldo & I. Woosnam	0	C. Beck & P. Azinger (2 & 1)	1
B. Langer & J.M. Canizares	0	T. Kite & M. McCumber (2 & 1)	1
H. Clark & M. James (1 hole)	1	P. Stewart & C. Strange	0
S. Ballesteros & J.-M. Olazabal (4 & 2)	1	M. Calcavecchia & K. Green	0
Singles:			
S. Ballesteros	0	P. Azinger (1 hole)	1
B. Langer	0	C. Beck (3 & 1)	1
J.-M. Olazabal (1 hole)	1	P. Stewart	0
R. Rafferty (1 hole)	1	M. Calcavecchia	0
H. Clark	0	T. Kite (8 & 7)	1
M. James (3 & 2)	1	M. O'Meara	0
C. O'Connor (1 hole)	1	F. Couples	0
J. M. Canizares (1 hole)	1	K. Green	0
G. Brand Jnr	0	M. McCumber (1 hole)	1
S. Torrance	0	T. Watson (3 & 1)	1
N. Faldo	0	L. Wadkins (1 hole)	1
I. Woosnam	0	C. Strange (2 holes)	1

EUROPE 14   **USA 14**

PAST RYDER CUP RESULTS

United States 21, Great Britain/Europe 5, Ties 2

1927	Worcester CC, Worcester, Mass.	US 9½, Britain 2½
1929	Moortown, England	Britain 7, US 5
1931	Scioto CC, Columbus, Ohio	US 9, Britain 3
1933	Southport & Ainsdale, England	Britain 6½, US 5½
1935	Ridgewood CC, Ridgewood, NJ	US 9, Britain 3
1937	Southport & Ainsdale, England	US 8, Britain 4
	Ryder Cup not contested during World War II	
1947	Portland Golf Club, Portland, Ore.	US 11, Britain 1
1949	Ganton GC, Scarborough, England	US 7, Britain 5
1951	Pinehurst CC, Pinehurst, NC	US 9½, Britain 2½
1953	Wentworth, England	US 6½, Britain 5½
1955	Thunderbird Ranch & CC, Palm Springs, Ca.	US 8, Britain 4
1957	Lindrick GC, Yorkshire, England	Britain 7½, US 4½
1959	Eldorado CC, Palm Desert, Ca.	US 8½, Britain 3½
1961	Royal Lytham & St Anne's GC, St Anne's-on-the-Sea, England	US 14½, Britain 9½
1963	East Lake CC, Atlanta, Ga.	US 23, Britain 9
1965	Royal Birkdale GC, Southport, England	US 19½, Britain 12½
1967	Champions GC, Houston, Tex.	US 23½, Britain 8½
1969	Royal Birkdale GC, Southport, England	US 16, Britain 16 (TIE)
1971	Old Warson CC, St Louis, Mo.	US 18½, Britain 13½
1973	Muirfield, Scotland	US 18, Britain 13
1975	Laurel Valley GC, Ligonier, Pa.	US 21, Britain 11
1977	Royal Lytham & St Anne's GC, St Annes-on-the-Sea, England	US 12½, Britain 7½
1979	The Greenbrier, White Sulphur Springs, W. Va.	US 17, Europe 11
1981	Walton Heath GC, Surrey, England	US 18½, Europe 9½
1983	PGA National GC, Palm Beach Gdns, Fla.	US 14½, Europe 13½
1985	The Belfry, Sutton Coldfield, England	Europe 16½, US 11½
1987	Muirfield Village, Ohio	Europe 15, US 13
1989	The Belfry, Sutton Coldfield, England	Europe 14, US 14 (TIE)

Captain and first lieutenant – Tony Jacklin and Seve Ballesteros formed a brilliant partnership between 1983 and 1989

JANUARY

The US Tour tees off as early as 3 January with the Tournament of Champions at Carlsbad, but the most glamorous event of the month is undoubtedly the AT&T (formerly Bing Crosby) Pebble Beach Pro-Am, staged over three of California's spectacular Monterey Peninsula courses. Pebble Beach, America's greatest links course (the famous par three 7th pictured above) will also host the 1992 US Open. Other notable tournaments in January are the Hawaiian Open, the South African Open and two events on Queensland's fast-developing Gold Coast, at Palm Meadows and Sanctuary Cove

(Previous page) Portmarnock, near Dublin, venue for the 1991 Walker Cup match

FEBRUARY

Greg Norman crashes a drive down the 1st fairway at Huntingdale in the Australian Masters. In early February Greg will be bidding for a record seventh Australian Masters title and his third in succession. Later in the month he will also be defending the Doral Ryder Open over Miami's notorious 'Blue Monster Course'. In 1990 Greg tamed the monster, setting a course-record 62 in the final round. The European Tour gets under way in February, while in the Far East the Hong Kong Open is hosted by the Royal Hong Kong Golf Club, where again the record is 62, set by Nick Faldo in December's Johnnie Walker Asian Classic

MARCH

An unusual shot of the famous TPC at Sawgrass, Florida, home of the much-vaunted Players Championship. Some Americans like to think of the Players Championship as golf's fifth Major; but then they tend to be pros who've won this event but not one of the Big Four. Jack Nicklaus, who knows a thing or two about Majors, has won the Players Championship three times, and in 1987 Sandy Lyle achieved Europe's solitary success. Two weeks before Sawgrass, Robert Gamez defends the Nestlé Invitational at Bay Hill; in 1990 he holed a full 7-iron shot at the 72nd hole to grab a one-stroke victory over Greg Norman. In Europe the tour journeys to Spain, Portugal and Italy, and in other parts of the world there is championship golf in Thailand, Indonesia, New Zealand and, of course, Japan, where the golfing sun rarely sets

APRIL

'Blue skies and just a hint of a Cornish breeze' is what we asked for in these pages prior to the staging of St Mellion's first Benson and Hedges International. Judging by the picture above we didn't fare too badly. This year we are hoping for a little more rain to fall – before the tournament, that is! A finish similar to 1990's would also be welcome, with two of the world's leading players battling it out over the closing holes. Just seven days before St Mellion, Nick Faldo will be attempting to become the first player ever to win three US Masters titles in succession. Switching back to Europe, the Women's Professional Tour (WPGET) gets under way in April, making its traditional start in Rome, after which comes the popular Ford Ladies' Classic

MAY

All calm on the West Coure at Wentworth. The peace is sure to be shattered in May when vast holiday crowds turn up to watch the PGA Championship. Ballesteros, Langer, Woosnam and Faldo have all won the event in recent years, but in 1990 Australian Mike Harwood surprised the big names by edging out Faldo and Olazabal in a tense final round. The European Tour also stages the Spanish and Italian Opens, and at the end of the month Mark James is due to defend his British Masters title. Also defending titles in May are Greg Norman and Ben Crenshaw in America's Memorial and Colonial tournaments

JUNE

Hale Irwin and a huge gallery watch as Mike Donald putts on the 13th green during last year's US Open play-off at Medinah, which Irwin eventually won. In 1991 the US Open will be played at Hazeltine, Minnesota, the scene of Tony Jacklin's memorable triumph in 1970. A British win in the championship is overdue. In the last three years Faldo and Woosnam have both gone very close. Maybe one of them will pull it off in 1991? A week later is the Irish Open, which in 1991 has an exciting new venue, 'Heaven's Reflex' itself, Killarney

JULY

Just as an Irishman will tell you that Killarney is 'heaven on earth', so a Scotsman will insist that Gleneagles is where the terrestrial angels gather. The vision above was taken at Gleneagles during the Bell's Scottish Open. In 1991 the winner at Gleneagles will want to retain his form the followng week at Royal Birkdale in the 120th Open Championship. Faldo will be hoping for a repeat victory on the great Lancashire links, and Gary Player is sure to put up a strong defence of his Volvo Seniors British Open title at neighbouring Royal Lytham. In the United States, July sees Betsy King attempt to go one better than Curtis Strange by winning the Women's US Open three times in succession

AUGUST

An ecstatic Helen Alfredsson wins the 1990 British Women's Open Championship at Woburn after a four-hole sudden-death play-off with Jane Hill. In 1991 the championship will again be played over the Duke's Course, and large crowds are certain to witness some first-class golf from a very international field. Crooked Stick is the interestingly named venue for the 1991 USPGA Championship; after the trials and tribulations of Shoal Creek one hopes that its name has nothing to do with golf clubs entangling themselves in ferociously thick rough. America's World Series tournament takes place in August; Olazabal won the title last year by a staggering 12 strokes. In Europe The Belfry hosts the NM English Open, and Walton Heath, the GA European Open

SEPTEMBER

How many of The Belfry's magnificent 12 will be in the European side that travels to Kiawah Island in September? One thing's for sure, that magnificent thirteenth member of the team, skipper Tony Jacklin, will not be at the helm this time; instead Bernard Gallacher has the unenviable task of trying to retain a cup that was last won by the United States in 1983. We wish them well! South Carolina will surely seem light-years away when the European Masters–Swiss Open is played at snowy Crans-sur-Sierre in early September. Other big events in September include the Japan Open, the Lancôme Trophy in Paris, the Epson Grand Prix at St Pierre, and, 'back over the pond', the Canadian Open at Glen Abbey

OCTOBER

Both the European and US tours draw to a (hopefully climactic) conclusion in the last week of October. Europe's last event is the Volvo Masters at Valderrama in southern Spain. Valderrama (pictured above) is generally considered to be the toughest course on the entire tour, and last year, when the weather was anything but friendly, it was christened with some rather choice names! The US Tour's final act will be played out at Pinehurst in North Carolina. Earlier in the month the Irish will be seeking their third Dunhill Cup success at St Andrews, and at Wentworth Ian Woosnam will also be going for a hat trick of wins in the World Matchplay Championship

NOVEMBER

Imperious Mount Fuji provides a glorious backdrop to November's Taiheiyo Masters, traditionally the first leg of Japan's yen-laden three-week International Tour. For the last three years the handsome trophy, not to mention the winner's scarlet-coloured blazer, has been captured by a Spanish golfer; in 1988 it was Ballesteros, in 1989 and 1990, Olazabal. The International Tour's second event in 1990, the Dunlop Phoenix, was won by Larry Mize, again for the second year in succession, and the Casio World Open by Mike Reid. Australia will be defending the Four Tours Championship in November and on the beautiful island of Maui a strong, largely American field will assemble for the Kapalua Invitational tournament

DECEMBER

Question: how does a golfer become a millionaire overnight? Answer: he wins the Sun City Million Dollar Challenge. In 1990 David Frost sunk a six-foot putt on the final green at the Gary Player Country Club to hit the jackpot. How could he stand the pressure? Simple – he did it in 1989 as well! There have been rumours that the 1990 event will be the last Million Dollar Challenge, but we shall have to wait and see. There are several big tournaments in Australia in December, including the Australian Open; and, new for 1991, the proposed Johnnie Walker World Championship in Jamaica, scheduled to take place just a few days before Christmas – someone's due to pick up a tremendous present!

USPGA TOUR 1991

JANUARY
3-6 **Tournament of Champions**, Carlsbad, California
10-13 **Northern Telecom Tucson Open**, TPC at Star Pass, Tuscon, Ariz.
17-20 **Hawaiian Open**, Waialae CC, Honolulu
31-3 February **AT & T Pebble Beach National Pro-Am**, Pebble Beach, California

FEBRUARY
6-10 **Bob Hope Chrysler Classic**, La Quinta, California
14-17 **Shearson Lehman Hutton Open**, Torrey Pines GC, La Jolla, California
21-24 **Nissan Los Angeles Open**, Riviera CC, Pacific Palisades, California
28-3 March **Doral Ryder Open**, Doral Hotel & CC, Miami, Florida

MARCH
7-10 **Honda Classic**, TPC at Eagle Trace, Coral Springs, Florida
14-17 **The Nestlé Invitational**, Bay Hill Club & Lodge, Orlando, Florida
21-24 **USF&G Classic**, English Turn G & CC, New Orleans, Louisiana
28-31 **The Players' Championship**, TPC at Sawgrass, Ponte Vedra, Florida

APRIL
4-7 **Independent Insurance Agent Open**, TPC at The Woodlands, Texas
11-14 **The Masters**, Augusta National GC, Augusta, Georgia
11-14 **Deposit Guaranty Golf Classic**, Hattiesburg CC, Hattiesburg, Missouri
18-21 **MCI Heritage Classic**, Harbour Town GL, Hilton Head Island, South Carolina
25-28 **K-Mart Greater Greensboro Open**, Forest Oaks CC, Greensboro, North Carolina

MAY
2-5 **GTE Byron Nelson Classic**, TPC at Las Colinas, Irving, Texas
9-12 **BellSouth Atlanta Classic**, Atlanta CC, Marietta, Georgia
16-19 **Memorial Tournament**, Muirfield Village GC, Dublin, Ohio
23-26 **Southwestern Bell Colonial**, Colonial CC, Fort Worth, Texas
30-2 June **Kemper Open**, TPC at Avenel, Potomac, Maryland

JUNE
6-9 **Buick Classic**, Westchester CC, Rye, NY
13-16 **US Open**, Hazeltine National GC, Chaska, Minnesota
20-23 **Anheuser-Busch Classic**, Kingsmill GC, Williamsburg, Virginia
27-30 **Federal Express St Jude Classic**, TPC at Southwind, Germantown, Tennessee

JULY
4-7 **Centel Western Open**, Cog Hill G.C., Lemont, Illinois
11-14 **Bank of Boston Classic**, Pleasant Valley CC, Sutton, Massachusetts
18-21 **Chattanooga Classic**, Valleybrook G & CC, Hixson, Tennessee
25-28 **Canon Greater Hartford Open**, TPC of Connecticut, Cromwell, Connecticut

AUGUST
1-4 **Buick Open**, Warwick Hills G &CC, Grand Blanc, Michigan
8-11 **USPGA Championship**, Crooked Stick, Carmel, Indiana
15-18 **The International**, Castle Pines GC, Castle Rock, Colorado
22-25 **NEC World Series of Golf**, Firestone CC, Akron, Ohio
29-1 September **Greater Milwaukee Open**, Tuckaway CC, Franklin, Wisconsin

SEPTEMBER
5-8 **Canadian Open**, Glen Abbey GC, Oakville, Ontario
12-15 **Hardee's Classic**, Oakwood CC, Coal Valley, Illinois
19-22 **BC Open**, En-Joie GC, Endicott, NY
26-29 **Buick Southern Open**, Green Island CC, Columbus, Georgia

OCTOBER
3-6 **Texas Open** Oak Hills CC, San Antonio, Texas
9-13 **Las Vegas Invitational**, three courses around Las Vegas, Nevada
16-19 **Walt Disney World/Oldsmobile Classic**, three courses at Disney World, Orlando, Florida
24-27 **TOUR Championship**, Pinehurst, North Carolina

WPG EUROPEAN TOUR 1991

APRIL
18-21 **Valextra Classic**, Olgiata, Rome
25-28 **AFG Open**, Paris

MAY
2-5 **Ford Ladies' Classic**, Woburn
9-12 **TBA**
16-19 **TBA**
23-26 **BMW European Masters** Bercuit, Brussels
30-2 June **TBA**

JUNE
5-8 **Swiss Classic**, Bonmont, Geneva
13-16 **Hennessy Ladies' Cup**, Koln
20-23 **Trophee Coconut Skol**, Paris
27-30 **TBA**

JULY
4-7 **TBA**
11-14 **Bloor Homes Eastleigh Classic**, Fleming Park
25-28 **Lufthansa German Open**, Worthsee

AUGUST
1-4 **Weetabix British Open**, Woburn
8-11 **TBA**
15-18 **Swedish Open**, Haninge, Stockholm
22-25 **European Open**, TBA
29-1 Sept. **TBA**

SEPTEMBER
5-8 **TEC Players' Championship**, TBA
12-15 **Irish Open**, Malahide
19-22 **Italian Open**, TBA
26-29 **Northern Open**, The Tytherington, Cheshire

OCTOBER
3-6 **Japan Festival Cup**, The Belfry
10-13 **Trophee Urban – The World Championship of Women's Golf**, Cely, Paris
17-20 **Woolmark Ladies' Matchplay Championship**, Turin
24-27 **Biarritz Open**, TBA
31-3 November **Longines Classic**, TBA

TBA: to be announced

Alison Nicholas

VOLVO (PGA EUROPEAN) TOUR 1991

FEBRUARY
21-24 **Girona Open**, Pals, Girona
28-3 March **Fujitsu Mediterranean Open**, Nice, France

MARCH
7-10 **Open de Baleares**, Santa Ponsa
14-17 **Catalan Open**, Bonmont, Tarragona
21-24 **Portuguese Open**, Estela Golf Club, Oporto
28-31 **Volvo Firenze**, Ugolino, Florence

APRIL
11-14 **Jersey Open**, La Moye Golf Club, Jersey
18-21 **Benson and Hedges International**, St Mellion, Cornwall
25-28 **Madrid Open**, Puerta de Hierro

MAY
2-5 **Credit Lyonnais Cannes Open**, Cannes Mougins
9-12 **Peugeot Spanish Open**, Club de Campo, Madrid
16-19 **Lancia-Martini Italian Open**, Castelconturbia, Nr Milan
24-27 (Mon) **Volvo PGA Championship**, Wentworth Club, Surrey
30-2 June **Dunhill British Masters**, Woburn, Bucks

JUNE
6-9 **Murphy's Cup**, Fulford, York
13-16 **Belgian Open**, Royal Waterloo, Brussels
20-23 **Carrolls Irish Open**, Killarney, Co. Kerry
27-30 **Peugeot French Open**, National Golf Course, Paris

JULY
3-6 (Sat) **Torras Monte Carlo Golf Open**, Mont Agel
10-13 (Sat) **Bell's Scottish Open**, Gleneagles Hotel, Perthshire
18-21 **120th Open Championship**, Royal Birkdale, Lancs
25-28 **Heineken Dutch Open**, Noordwijk, nr Leiden

AUGUST
1-4 **Scandinavian Masters**, Stockholm
8-11 **European Pro-Celebrity**, TBA
15-18 **NM English Open**, The Belfry, nr Birmingham
22-25 **Volvo German Open**, Hubbelrath, Düsseldorf
29-1 September **GA European Open**, Walton Heath, Surrey

SEPTEMBER
5-8 **European Masters-Swiss Open**, Crans-sur-Sierre
12-15 **Lancôme Trophy**, St Nom-la-Bretèche, Versailles
16-17 *****Equity & Law Challenge**, Royal Mid-Surrey Golf Club
19-22 **Epson Grand Prix**, St Pierre, Chepstow
27-29 *****Ryder Cup**, Kiawah Island, South Carolina
26-29 **Austrian Open**, Gut Altentann, Salzburg

OCTOBER·
3-6 **German Masters**, Stuttgart
10-13 *****Dunhill Cup**, St Andrews
10-13 **BMW International Open**, Munich
17-20 *****Toyota World Match-Play**, Wentworth Club, Surrey
24-27 Nov **Volvo Masters**, Valderrama, Sotogrande

NOVEMBER
7-10 *****Asahi Glass Four Tours Championship**, TBA
7-10 *****Benson and Hedges Trophy (Mixed Team)**, TBA

To Be Scheduled:
*World Cup of Golf
*Motorola Classic

Note:
July 11-14 *****Seniors British Open**, Royal Lytham & St Annes

*PGA European Tour Approved Special Events

Seve Ballesteros

5

GOLF COURSES OF GREAT BRITAIN AND IRELAND

ENGLAND
SCOTLAND
WALES
NORTHERN IRELAND
IRELAND

ENGLAND

AVON

Bath G.C.
(0225) 463834
Sham Castle, North Road,
Bath
(18) 6369 yards

Bristol and Clifton G.C.
(0272) 393474
Beggar Bush Lane, Failand,
Bristol
(18) 6294 yards

Chipping Sodbury G.C.
(0454) 319042
Chipping Sodbury
(18) 6912 yards

Clevedon G.C.
(0272) 874057
Castle Road, Clevedon
(18) 5835 yards

Filton G.C.
(0272) 694169
Golf Course Lane, Filton,
Bristol
(18) 6227 yards

Fosseway C.C.
(0761) 412214
Charlton Lane,
Midsomer Norton
(9) 4246 yards

Henbury G.C.
(0272) 500044
Henbury Hill, Westbury-on-
Trym, Bristol
(18) 6039 yards

Knowle G.C.
(0272) 770660
Brislington, Bristol
(18) 6016 yards

Lansdown G.C.
(0225) 422138
Lansdown, Bath
(18) 6267 yards

Long Ashton G.C.
(0272) 392316
Long Ashton, Bristol
(18) 6051 yards

Mangotsfield G.C.
(0272) 565501
Carsons Road, Mangotsfield
(18) 5337 yards

Mendip G.C.
(0749) 840570
Gurney Slade, Bath
(18) 5982 yards

Saltford G.C.
(0225) 873220
Manor Road, Saltford
(18) 6081 yards

Shirehampton Park G.C.
(0272) 822083
Parkhill, Shirehampton,
Bristol
(18) 5943 yards

Tracy Park G. & C.C.
(027582) 2251
Bath Road, Wick
(18) 6613 yards
(9) 5200 yards

Weston-Super-Mare G.C.
(0934) 621360
Uphill Road, Weston-Super-
Mare
(18) 6225 yards

Worlebury G.C.
(0934) 623214
Worlebury Hill Road,
Weston-Super-Mare
(18) 5945 yards

BEDFORDSHIRE

Aspley Guise & Woburn Sands G.C.
(0908) 583596
West Hill, Aspley Guise
(18) 6248 yards

Beadlow Manor G. & C.C.
(0525) 60800
Shefford
(18) 6231 yards
(9) 3297 yards

Bedford & County G.C.
(0234) 52617
Green Lane, Clapham,
Bedford
(18) 6347 yards

Bedfordshire G.C.
(0234) 53241
Bromham Road, Biddenham,
Bedford
(18) 6172 yards

Dunstable Downs G.C.
(0582) 604472
Whipsnade Road, Dunstable
(18) 6184 yards

John O'Gaunt G.C.
(0767) 260252
Sutton Park, Sandy,
Biggleswade
(18) 6513 yards
(John O'Gaunt)
(18) 5869 yards (Carthagena)

Leighton Buzzard G.C.
(0525) 373811
Plantation Road,
Leighton Buzzard
(18) 5959 yards

Millbrook G.C.
(0525) 712001
Millbrook, Ampthill
(18) 6473 yards

Mowsbury G.C.
(0234) 771042
Kimbolton Road, Bedford
(18) 6514 yards

South Beds G.C.
(0582) 591500
Warden Hill, Luton
(18) 6342 yards
(9) 4954 yards

Stockwood Park G.C.
(0582) 413704
London Road, Luton
(18) 5964 yards

Tilsworth G.C.
(0525) 210721
Dunstable Road, Tilsworth
(9) 5443 yards

Wyboston Lakes G.C.
(0480) 212501
Wyboston
(18) 5688 yards

BERKSHIRE

Bearwood G.C.
(0734) 760060
Mole Road, Sindlesham
(9) 5628 yards

Berkshire G.C.
(0990) 21496
Swinley Road, Ascot
(18) 6356 yards (Red)
(18) 6258 yards (Blue)

Calcot Park G.C.
(0734) 27124
Bath Road, Calcot
(18) 6283 yards

Downshire G.C.
(0344) 424066
Easthampstead Park,
Wokingham
(18) 6382 yards

East Berkshire G.C.
(0344) 772041
Ravenswood Avenue,
Crowthorne
(18) 6315 yards

**Goring &
Streatley G.C.**
(0491) 873229
Rectory Road,
Streatley-on-Thames
(18) 6255 yards

Hawthorn Hill G.C.
(0628) 75588
Drift Road, Maidenhead
(18) 6212 yards

Hurst G.C.
(0734) 345143
Hurst, Wokingham
(9) 3015 yards

Maidenhead G.C.
(0628) 24693
Shoppenhangers Road,
Maidenhead
(18) 6344 yards

**Newbury &
Crookham G.C.**
(0635) 40035
Greenham, Newbury
(18) 5880 yards

Reading G.C.
(0734) 472909
Kidmore End Road, Reading
(18) 6283 yards

Royal Ascot G.C.
(0990) 25175
Winkfield Road, Ascot
(18) 5653 yards

Sonning G.C.
(0734) 693332
Duffield Road,
Sonning-on-Thames
(18) 6355 yards

Sunningdale G.C.
(0990) 21681
Ridgemount Road,
Sunningdale
(18) 6341 yards (Old)
(18) 6676 yards (New)

Sunningdale Ladies G.C.
(0990) 20507
Cross Road, Sunningdale
(18) 3622 yards

Swinley Forest G.C.
(0990) 20197
Coronation Road,
South Ascot
(18) 6001 yards

Temple G.C.
(062882) 4795
Henley Road, Hurley
(18) 6206 yards

West Berks G.C.
(04882) 574
Chaddleworth, Newbury
(18) 7053 yards

Winter Hill G.C.
(06285) 27613
Grange Park, Cookham,
Maidenhead
(18) 6432 yards

BUCKINGHAM-
SHIRE

Abbey Hill G.C.
(0908) 563845
Two Ash, Milton Keynes
(18) 6505 yards

Beaconsfield G.C.
(0494) 676545
Seer Green, Beaconsfield
(18) 6469 yards

Buckingham G.C.
(0280) 815566
Tingewick Road,
Buckingham
(18) 6082 yards

Burnham Beeches G.C.
(06286) 61448
Green Lane, Burnham
(18) 6415 yards

Chesham & Ley Hill G.C.
(0494) 784541
Ley Hill, Chesham
(9) 5147 yards

Chiltern Forest G.C.
(0296) 631267
Halton, Aylesbury
(9) 5724 yards

Datchet G.C.
(0753) 43887
Buccleuch Road, Datchet
(9) 5978 yards

Denham G.C.
(0895) 832022
Tilehouse Lane, Denham
(18) 6439 yards

Ellesborough G.C.
(0296) 622114
Butler's Cross, Aylesbury
(18) 6207 yards

Farnham Park G.C.
(02814) 3332
Park Road, Stoke Poges
(18) 5847 yards

Flackwell Heath G.C.
(06285) 20929
High Wycombe
(18) 6150 yards

Gerrards Cross G.C.
(0753) 885300
Chalfont Park,
Gerrards Cross
(18) 6305 yards

Harewood Downs G.C.
(02404) 2184
Cokes Lane, Chalfont St Giles
(18) 5958 yards

Iver G.C.
(0753) 655615
Hollow Hill Lane, Iver
(9) 6214 yards

Little Chalfont G.C.
(02404) 4877
Lodge Lane, Little Chalfont
(9) 5852 yards

Stoke Poges G.C.
(0753) 26385
Park Road, Stoke Poges
(18) 6654 yards

Weston Turville G.C.
(0296) 24084
New Road, Weston Turville,
Aylesbury
(13) 6782 yards

Wexham Park G.C.
(02816) 3217
Wexham Street, Wexham
(18) 5836 yards
(9) 2383 yards

Whiteleaf G.C.
(08444) 3097
Whiteleaf, Aylesbury
(9) 5391 yards

Windmill Hill G.C.
(0908) 78623
Tattenhoe Lane, Bletchley,
Milton Keynes
(18) 6773 yards

Woburn G. & C.C.
(0908) 370756
Bow Brickhill,
Milton Keynes
(18) 6883 yards Duke's
(18) 6616 yards Duchess

CAMBRIDGE-
SHIRE

Abbotsley G.C.
(0480) 215153
Eynesbury Hardwicke,
St Neots
(18) 6214 yards

**Cambridgeshire
Moat House Hotel G.C.**
(0954) 80555
Bar Hill, Cambridge
(18) 6734 yards

Ely City G.C.
(0353) 662751
Cambridge Road, Ely
(18) 6686 yards

Girton G.C.
(0223) 276169
Dodford Lane, Cambridge
(18) 5927 yards

The Berkshire

Gog Magog G.C.
(0223) 247626
Shelford Bottom, Cambridge
(18) 6354 yards (Old)
(9) 5833 yards (New)

March G.C.
(0354) 52364
Grange Rd, March
(9) 6278 yards

Orton Meadows G.C.
(0733) 237478
Ham Lane, Peterborough
(18) 5800 yards

Peterborough Milton G.C.
(0733) 380489
Milton Ferry, Peterborough
(18) 6431 yards

Ramsey G.C.
(0487) 812600
Abbey Terrace, Ramsey
(18) 6136 yards

St Ives G.C.
(0480) 68392
St Ives, Huntingdon
(9) 6052 yards

St Neots G.C.
(0480) 72363
Crosshall Rd, St Neots
(18) 6027 yards

Thorpe Wood G.C.
(0733) 267701
Nene Parkway, Peterborough
(18) 7086 yards

CHESHIRE

Alderley Edge G.C.
(0625) 585583
Brook Lane, Alderley Edge
(9) 5839 yards

Astbury G.C.
(0260) 272772
Peel Lane, Astbury,
Congleton
(18) 6269 yards

Birchwood G.C.
(0925) 818819
Kelvin Close, Birchwood,
Warrington
(18) 6666 yards

Chapel-en-le-Frith G.C.
(0298) 813943
The Cockyard,
Manchester Road, Chapel-
en-le-Frith
(18) 6065 yards

Chester G.C.
(0244) 677760
Curzon Park, Chester
(18) 6487 yards

Congleton G.C.
(0260) 273540
Biddulph Road, Congleton
(18) 6221 yards

Crewe G.C.
(0270) 584099
Fields Road, Haslington,
Crewe
(18) 6277 yards

Davenport G.C.
(0625) 877319
Worton Hall,
Middlewood Road, Higher
Poynton
(18) 6006 yards

Delamere Forest G.C.
(0606) 882807
Station Road, Delamere,
Northwich
(18) 6287 yards

Eaton G.C.
(0244) 680474
Eaton Park, Eccleston,
Chester
(18) 6446 yards

Ellesmere Port G.C.
(051) 339 7689
Chester Road, Hooton
(18) 6432 yards

Helsby G.C.
(09282) 2021
Towers Lane, Helsby,
Warrington
(18) 6262 yards

Knights Grange G.C.
(06065) 52780
Grange Lane, Winsford
(9) 6210 yards

Knutsford G.C.
(0565) 3355
Mereheath Lane, Knutsford
(9) 6288 yards

Leigh G.C.
(092576) 2943
Kenyon Hall,
Culcheth, Warrington
(18) 5853 yards

Lymm G.C.
(092575) 5020
Whitbarrow Road, Lymm
(18) 6304 yards

Macclesfield G.C.
(0625) 23227
The Hollins, Macclesfield
(9) 5974 yards

Malkins Bank G.C.
(0270) 765931
Betchton Road, Sandbach
(18) 6178 yards

Mere G. & C.C.
(0565) 830219
Mere, Knutsford
(18) 6849 yards

New Mills G.C.
(0663) 43816
Shaw Marsh, New Mills
(9) 5924 yards

Poulton Park G.C.
(0925) 812034
Cinnamon Brow, Warrington
(9) 5512 yards

Prestbury G.C.
(0625) 828241
Macclesfield Road, Prestbury
(18) 6359 yards

Runcorn G.C.
(09285) 74214
Clifton Road, Runcorn
(18) 6012 yards

Sandbach G.C.
(0270) 762117
Middlewich Road, Sandbach
(9) 5533 yards

Sandiway G.C.
(0606) 883247
Chester Road, Sandiway
(18) 6435 yards

The Tytherington Club
(0625) 34562
Macclesfield
(18) 6737 yards

Upton-by-Chester G.C.
(0244) 381183
Upton Lane, Chester
(18) 5875 yards

Vicars Cross G.C.
(0244) 335174
Littleton, Chester
(18) 5804 yards

Walton Hall G.C.
(0925) 66775
Higher Walton, Warrington
(18) 6843 yards

Warrington G.C.
(0925) 61775
Appleton, Warrington
(18) 6217 yards

Widnes G.C.
(051) 424 2995
Highfield Road, Widnes
(18) 5719 yards

Widnes Municipal G.C.
(051) 424 2995
Dundalk Road, Widnes
(9) 5982 yards

Wilmslow G.C.
(056587) 2148
Great Warford, Mobberley,
Knutsford
(18) 6500 yards

CHANNEL ISLANDS

Alderney G.C.
(048182) 2835
Routes des Carriers, Alderney
(9) 2528 yards

La Moye G.C.
(0534) 43401
La Moye, St Brelade
(18) 6464 yards

Royal Guernsey G.C.
(0481) 47022
L'Ancresse, Guernsey
(18) 6206 yards

Royal Jersey G.C.
(0534) 54416
Grouville, Jersey
(18) 6106 yards

St Clements G.C.
(0534) 21938
St Clements, Jersey
(9) 3972 yards

CLEVELAND

Billingham G.C.
(0642) 554494
Sandy Lane, Billingham
(18) 6430 yards

Castle Eden & Peterlee G.C.
(0429) 836220
Castle Eden, Hartlepool
(18) 6297 yards

Cleveland G.C.
(0642) 483693
Queen Street, Redcar
(18) 6707 yards

Eaglescliffe G.C.
(0642) 780098
Yarm Road, Eaglescliffe
(18) 6275 yards

Hartlepool G.C.
(0429) 836510
Hart Warren, Hartlepool
(18) 6325 yards

Middlesborough G.C.
(0642) 316430
Marton, Middlesborough
(18) 6106 yards

Middlesborough Municipal G.C.
(0642) 315533
Ladgate Lane,
Middlesborough
(18) 6314 yards

Saltburn-by-the Sea G.C.
(0287) 22812
Hob Hill, Saltburn-
by-the-Sea
(18) 5803 yards

Seaton Carew G.C.
(0429) 266249
Tees Road, Seaton Carew
(18) 6604 yards

Teeside G.C.
(0642) 616516
Acklam Road, Thornaby
(18) 6472 yards

Wilton G.C.
(0642) 465265
Wilton Castle, Redcar
(18) 5774 yards

CORNWALL

Bude & North Cornwall G.C.
(0288) 352006
Burn View, Bude
(18) 6202 yards

Budock Vean Hotel G.C.
(0326) 250288
Mawnan Smith, Falmouth
(9) 5007 yards

Carlyon Bay Hotel G.C.
(072681) 4228
Carlyon Bay, St Austell
(18) 6463 yards

Falmouth G.C.
(0326) 40525
Swanpool Road, Falmouth
(18) 5581 yards

Isles of Scilly G.C.
(0720) 22692
St Mary's, Isles of Scilly
(9) 5974 yards

Launceston G.C.
(0566) 3442
St Stephen, Launceston
(18) 6409 yards

Looe Bin Down G.C.
(05034) 247
Widegates, Looe
(18) 5875 yards

Mullion G.C.
(0326) 240685
Curry, Helston
(18) 5616 yards

Newquay G.C.
(0637) 874354
Tower Road, Newquay
(18) 6140 yards

Perranporth G.C.
(0872) 573701
Budnick Hill, Perranporth
(18) 6208 yards

Praa Sands G.C.
(0736) 763445
Germoe Cross, Penzance
(9) 4036 yards

St Austell G.C.
(0726) 74756
Tregongeeves Lane, St Austell
(18) 5875 yards

St Enodoc G.C.
(020886) 2402
Rock, Wadebridge
(18) 6188 yards
(18) 4151 yards

St Mellion G. & C.C.
(0579) 50101
St Mellion, Saltash
(18) 6626 yards (Nicklaus)
(18) 5927 yards

Tehidy Park G.C.
(0209) 842208
Camborne
(18) 6222 yards

Trevose G. & C.C.
(0841) 520208
Constantine Bay, Padstow
(18) 6608 yards
(9) 1367 yards

Truro G.C.
(0872) 78684
Treliske, Truro
(18) 5347 yards

West Cornwall G.C.
(0736) 753401
Lelant, St Ives
(18) 6070 yards

Whitsand Bay Hotel G.C.
(0503) 30276
Portwrinkle, Torpoint
(18) 5512 yards

CUMBRIA

Alston Moor G.C.
(0498) 381675
The Hermitage, Alston
(9) 5380 yards

Appleby G.C.
(0930) 51432
Blackenber Moor,
Appleby-in-Westmoreland
(18) 5913 yards

Barrow G.C.
(0229) 24174
Hawcoat, Barrow-in-Furness
(18) 6209 yards

Brampton G.C.
(06977) 2255
Talkin Tarn, Brampton
(18) 6426 yards

Carlisle G.C.
(022872) 303
Aglionby, Carlisle
(18) 6278 yards

Cockermouth G.C.
(059681) 223
Embleton, Cockermouth
(18) 5496 yards

Dunnerholme G.C.
(0229) 62675
Duddon Road, Askam-
in-Furness
(10) 6118 yards

Furness G.C.
(0229) 41232
Central Drive, Barrow-
in-Furness
(18) 6374 yards

Grange Fell G.C.
(04484) 2536
Fell Road, Grange-
over-Sands
(9) 5278 yards

Grange-over-Sands G.C.
(05395) 32536
Meathop Road, Grange-over-
Sands
(18) 5660 yards

Kendal G.C.
(0539) 724079
The Heights, Kendal
(18) 5533 yards

Keswick G.C.
(07687) 72147
Threlkeld Hall, Keswick
(18) 6175 yards

Kirkby Lonsdale G.C.
(0468) 71483
Casterton Road,
Kirkby Lonsdale
(9) 4058 yards

Maryport G.C.
(0900) 812605
Bank End, Maryport
(18) 6272 yards

Penrith G.C.
(0768) 62217
Salkeld Road, Penrith
(18) 6026 yards

St Bees School G.C.
(0946) 812105
Station Road, St Bees
(9) 5082 yards

Seascale G.C.
(09467) 28662
The Banks, Seascale
(18) 6372 yards

Sedbergh G.C.
(0587) 20993
Sedburgh
(9) 4134 yards

Silecroft G.C.
(0657) 4250
Silecroft, Millom
(9) 5627 yards

Silloth-on-Solway G.C.
(0965) 31304
Silloth-on-Solway, Carlisle
(18) 6343 yards

**Stony Holme
Municipal G.C.**
(0228) 34856
St Aidans Road, Carlisle
(18) 5773 yards

Ulverston G.C.
(0229) 52806
Bardsea Park, Ulverston
(18) 6092 yards

Windermere G.C.
(09662) 3123
Cleabarrow, Windermere
(18) 5006 yards

Workington G.C.
(0900) 3460
Branthwaite Road,
Workington
(18) 6202 yards

DERBYSHIRE

Alfreton G.C.
(0773) 832070
Wingfield Road,
Oakerthorpe
(9) 5012 yards

Allestree Park G.C.
(0332) 550616
Allestree Hall, Derby
(18) 5749 yards

Ashbourne G.C.
(0335) 42077
Clifton, Ashbourne
(9) 5388 yards

Bakewell G.C.
(062981) 2307
Station Road, Bakewell
(9) 5240 yards

**Breadsall Priory
G. & C.C.**

(0332) 832235
Moor Road, Morley, Derby
(18) 6402 yards

Burton-on-Trent G.C.

(0283) 44551
Ashby Road East, Burton-on-Trent
(18) 6555 yards

**Buxton &
High Peak G.C.**

(0298) 3453
Fairfield, Buxton
(18) 5954 yards

Cavendish G.C.

(0298) 25052
Gadley Lane, Buxton
(18) 5833 yards

Chesterfield G.C.

(0246) 566032
Walton, Chesterfield
(18) 6326 yards

**Chesterfield
Municipal G.C.**

(0246) 273887
Crow Lane, Chesterfield
(18) 6044 yards

Chevin G.C.

(0332) 841864
Golf Lane, Duffield
(18) 6057 yards

Derby G.C.

(0332) 766462
Shakespeare Street,
Sinfin, Derby
(18) 6183 yards

Erewash Valley G.C.

(0602) 322984
Stanton-by-Dale, Ilkeston
(18) 6487 yards

**Glossop &
District G.C.**

(04574) 3117
Sheffield Road, Glossop
(11) 5726 yards

Ilkeston G.C.

(0602) 320304
West End Drive, Ilkeston
(9) 4116 yards

Kedleston Park G.C.

(0332) 840035
Kedleston, Quarndon
(18) 6636 yards

Matlock G.C.

(0629) 582191
Chesterfield Road, Matlock
(18) 5871 yards

Mickleover G.C.

(0332) 518662
Uttoxeter Road, Mickleover
(18) 5621 yards

**Ormonde Fields
G. & C.C.**

(0773) 42987
Nottingham Road,
Codnor, Ripley
(18) 6007 yards

Pastures G.C.

(0332) 513921
Pastures Hospital,
Mickleover
(9) 5005 yards

Renishaw Park G.C.

(0246) 432044
Station Road,
Renishaw
(18) 6253 yards

Shirlands G. & S.C.

(0773) 834935
Lower Delves,
Shirland
(18) 6021 yards

Sickleholme G.C.

(0433) 51306
Bamford
(18) 6064 yards

Stanedge G.C.

(0246) 566156
Walton, Chesterfield
(9) 4867 yards

DEVON

Axe Cliff G.C.

(0297) 20499
Axemouth, Seaton
(18) 4998 yards

Bigbury G.C.

(0548) 810207
Bigbury-on-Sea,
Kingsbridge
(18) 6038 yards

Chulmleigh G.C.

(0769) 80519
Leigh Road, Chulmleigh
(18) 1440 yards

Churston G.C.

(0803) 842751
Churston, Brixham
(18) 6201 yards

Downes Crediton G.C.

(03632) 3025
Hookway, Crediton
(18) 5858 yards

East Devon G.C.

(03954) 3370
North View Road,
Budleigh Salterton
(18) 6214 yards

**Elfordleigh Hotel
G. & C.C.**

(0752) 336428
Plympton, Plymouth
(9) 5609 yards

Exeter G. & C.C.

(0392) 874139
Countess Wear, Exeter
(18) 5702 yards

Holsworthy G.C.

(0409) 253177
Kilatree, Holsworthy
(18) 5935 yards

Honiton G.C.

(0404) 44422
Honiton
(18) 5900 yards

Ilfracombe G.C.

(0271) 62176
Hele Bay, Ilfracombe
(18) 6227 yards

**Manor House Hotel G. &
C.C.**

(0647) 40355
Princetown Road,
Moretonhampstead
(18) 6016 yards

**Newton Abbot (Stover)
G.C.**

(0626) 62078
Bovey Road, Newton Abbot
(18) 5724 yards

Okehampton G.C.

(0837) 2113
Okehampton
(18) 5307 yards

Royal North Devon G.C.

(0237) 473817
Westward Ho!, Bideford
(18) 6449 yards

Saunton G.C.

(0271) 812436
Saunton, Braunton
(18) 6703 yards (East)
(18) 6356 yards (West)

Sidmouth G.C.

(0395) 513451
Cotmaton Road, Sidmouth
(18) 5188 yards

Staddon Heights G.C.

(0752) 402475
Plymstock, Plymouth
(18) 5861 yards

Tavistock G.C.

(0822) 612049
Down Road, Tavistock
(18) 6250 yards

Teignmouth G.C.

(0626) 773614
Exeter Road, Teignmouth
(18) 6142 yards

Thurlestone G.C.

(0548) 560405
Thurlestone, Kingsbridge
(18) 6337 yards

Tiverton G.C.
(0884) 252187
Post Hill, Tiverton
(18) 6227 yards

Torquay G.C.
(0803) 314591
St Marychurch,
Torquay
(18) 6251 yards

Torrington G.C.
(0805) 22229
Weare Trees, Torrington
(9) 4418 yards

Warren G.C.
(0626) 862255
Dawlish Warren
(18) 5968 yards

Wrangaton G.C.
(03647) 3229
Wrangaton, South Brent
(9) 5790 yards

Yelverton G.C.
(0822) 852824
Golf Links Road, Yelverton
(18) 6288 yards

DORSET

Ashley Wood G.C.
(0258) 452253
Wimborne Road,
Blandford Forum
(9) 6227 yards

Boscombe G.C.
(0202) 36198
Queen's Park, Bournemouth
(18) 6505 yards

Bridport & West Dorset G.C.
(0308) 22597
East Cliff, West Bay, Bridport
(18) 5246 yards

Broadstone G.C.
(0202) 692595
Wentworth Drive,
Broadstone
(18) 6204 yards

Came Down G.C.
(030 581) 2531
Came Down, Dorchester
(18) 6121 yards

Christchurch G.C.
(0202) 473817
Iford Bridge, Christchurch
(9) 4824 yards

Ferndown G.C.
(0202) 874602
119 Golf Links Road,
Ferndown
(18) 6442 yards (Old Course)
(9) 5604 yards (New Course)

Highcliffe Castle G.C.
(04252) 272210
107 Lymington Road,
Highcliffe-on-Sea
(18) 4732 yards

Isle of Purbeck G.C.
(0929) 44361
Studland, Swanage
(18) 6248 yards
(9) 2022 yards

Knighton Heath G.C.
(0202) 572633
Francis Avenue, West Howe,
Bournemouth
(18) 6206 yards

Lakey Hill G.C.
(0929) 471776
Hyde, Wareham
(18) 6146 yards

Lyme Regis G.C.
(02974) 2963
Timber Hill, Lyme Regis
(18) 6262 yards

Meyrick Park G.C.
(0202) 290871
Central Drive, Bournemouth
(18) 5878 yards

Parkstone G.C.
(0202) 707138
Links Road, Parkstone
(18) 6250 yards

Sherborne G.C.
(0935) 814431
Higher Clatcombe, Sherborne
(18) 5768 yards

Weymouth G.C.
(0305) 773981
Links Road, Westham,
Weymouth
(18) 5985 yards

DURHAM

Aycliffe G.C.
(0325) 318390
Newton Aycliffe
(9) 6054 yards

Barnard Castle G.C.
(0833) 38355
Marmire Road, Barnard
Castle
(18) 5838 yards

Beamish Park G.C.
(091) 3701382
Beamish, Stanley
(18) 6205 yards

Birtley G.C.
(091) 4102207
Portobello Road, Birtley
(9) 5154 yards

Bishop Auckland G.C.
(0388) 663648
Durham Road, Bishop
Auckland
(18) 6420 yards

Blackwell Grange G.C.
(0325) 464464
Briar Close, Blackwell,
Darlington
(18) 5609 yards

Brancepeth Castle G.C.
(091) 3780075
Brancepeth Village, Durham
(18) 6300 yards

Chester-le-Street G.C.
(091) 3883218
Lumley Park,
Chester-le-Street
(18) 6054 yards

Consett & District G.C.
(0207) 502186
Elmfield Road, Consett
(18) 6001 yards

Crook G.C.
(0388) 762429
Low Job's Hill, Crook
(18) 6089 yards

Darlington G.C.
(0325) 463936
Haughton Grange,
Darlington
(18) 6272 yards

Dinsdale Spa G.C.
(0325) 332297
Middleton St. George,
Darlington
(18) 6078 yards

Durham City G.C.
(091) 3780069
Langley Moor, Durham
(18) 6118 yards

Mount Oswald G.C.
(091) 3867527
South Road, Durham
(18) 6009 yards

Roseberry Grange G.C.
(091) 3700660
Grange Villa,
Chester-le-Street
(18) 5628 yards

Seaham G.C.
(091) 5812354
Dawdon, Seaham
(18) 5972 yards

South Moor G.C.
(0207) 232848
The Middles, Craghead,
Stanley
(18) 6445 yards

Stressholme G.C.
(0325) 461002
Snipe Lane, Darlington
(18) 6511 yards

EAST SUSSEX

Ashdown Forest Hotel G.C.
(034282) 4866
Chapel Lane, Forest Row
(18) 5433 yards

Brighton and Hove G.C.
(0273) 556482
Dyke Road, Brighton
(9) 5722 yards

Cooden Beach G.C.
(04243) 2040
Cooden, Bexhill
(18) 6411 yards

Crowborough Beacon G.C.
(08926) 61511
Beacon Road, Crowborough
(18) 6279 yards

Dale Hill G.C.
(0580) 200112
Ticehurst, Wadhurst
(18) 6035 yards

The Dyke G.C.
(079156) 296
Dyke Road, Brighton
(18) 6557 yards

Eastbourne Downs G.C.
(0323) 20827
East Dean Road, Eastbourne
(18) 6635 yards

East Brighton G.C.
(0273) 603989
Roedean Road, Brighton
(18) 6291 yards

East Sussex National G.C.
(0825) 86217
Little Horsted, Uckfield
(18) 7112 yards East
(18) 7202 yards West

Hastings G.C.
(0424) 52981
Battle Road, St. Leonards-on-Sea
(18) 6073 yards

Highwoods G.C.
(0424) 212625
Ellerslie Lane, Bexhill-on-Sea
(18) 6218 yards

Hollingbury Park G.C.
(0273) 552010
Ditching Road, Brighton
(18) 6415 yards

Horam Park G.C.
(04353) 3477
Chiddingly Road, Horam
(9) 2600 yards

Lewes G.C.
(0273) 473074
Chapel Hill, Lewes
(18) 5951 yards

Peacehaven G.C.
(0273) 514049
Brighton Road, Newhaven
(9) 5235 yards

Piltdown G.C.
(082572) 2033
Piltdown, Uckfield
(18) 6059 yards

Pyecombe G.C.
(07918) 5372
Clayton Hill, Pyecombe
(18) 6234 yards

Royal Ashdown Forest G.C.
(034282) 2018
Chapel Lane, Forest Row
(18) 6439 yards

Royal Eastbourne G.C.
(0323) 29738
Paradise Drive, Eastbourne
(18) 6084 yards
(9) 2147 yards

Rye G.C.
(0797) 225241
Camber, Near Rye
(18) 6301 yards
(18) 6141 yards (Jubilee)

Seaford G.C.
(0323) 892442
East Blatchington, Seaford
(18) 6241 yards

Seaford Head G.C.
(0323) 894843
Southdown Road, Seaford
(18) 5812 yards

Waterhall G.C.
(0273) 508658
Mill Road, Brighton
(18) 5615 yards

West Hove G.C.
(0273) 419738
Old Shoreham Road, Hove
(18) 6130 yards

Willingdon G.C.
(0323) 32383
Southdown Road,
Eastbourne
(18) 6049 yards

ESSEX

Abridge G. & C.C.
(04028) 396
Stapleford Tawney, Abridge
(18) 6703 yards

Ballards Gore G.C.
(0702) 258917
Gore Road, Canewdon,
Rochford
(18) 7062 yards

Basildon G.C.
(0268) 533297
Clay Hill Lane, Basildon
(18) 6122 yards

Belfairs Park G.C.
(0702) 525345
Eastwood Road,
Leigh-on-Sea
(18) 5871 yards

Belhus Park G.C.
(0708) 854260
Belhus Park, South Ockendon
(18) 5501 yards

Bentley G.C.
(0277) 373179
Ongar Road, Brentwood
(18) 6709 yards

Birch Grove G.C.
(0206) 34276
Layer Road, Colchester
(9) 2828 yards

Boyce Hill G.C.
(0268) 793625
Vicarage Hill, South Benfleet
(18) 5882 yards

Braintree G.C.
(0376) 24117
Kings Lane, Stisted, Braintree
(18) 6026 yards

Bunsay Downs G.C.
(024541) 2648
Woodham Walter, Maldon
(18) 5826 yards

Burnham-on-Crouch G.C.
(0621) 782282
Creeksea, Burnham-on-Crouch
(9) 5866 yards

Canon's Brook G.C.
(0279) 21482
Elizabeth Way, Harlow
(18) 6745 yards

Channels G.C.
(0245) 440005
Belsteads Farm Lane, Little Waltham, Chelmsford
(18) 6033 yards

Chelmsford G.C.
(0245) 256483
Widford, Chelmsford
(18) 5912 yards

Clacton G.C.
(0255) 421919
West Road, Clacton-on-Sea
(18) 6217 yards

Colchester G.C.
(0206) 853396
Braiswick, Colchester
(18) 6319 yards

Forrester Park G.C.
(0621) 891406
Great Totham, Maldon
(9) 5350 yards

Frinton G.C.

(02556) 4618
Esplanade, Frinton-on-Sea
(18) 6259 yards

Harwich & Dovercourt G.C.

(0255) 503616
Parkeston, Harwich
(9) 5692 yards

Havering G.C.

(0708) 22942
Lower Bedfords Road, Romford
(18) 5687 yards

Maldon G.C.

(0621) 53212
Beeleigh Landford, Maldon
(9) 6197 yards

Maylands G. & C.C.

(04023) 73080
Harold Park, Romford
(18) 6351 yards

Orsett G.C.

(0375) 891352
Brentwood Road, Orsett
(18) 6575 yards

Pipps Hill G.C.

(0268) 523456
Cranes Farm Road, Basildon
(9) 5658 yards

Quietwaters G.C.

(0621) 860410
Colchester Road, Tolleshunt
D'Arcy
(18) 6201 yards
(18) 6855 yards

Rochford Hundred G.C.

(0702) 544302
Rochford Hall, Rochford
(18) 6255 yards

Romford G.C.

(0708) 740986
Gidea Park, Romford
(18) 6377 yards

Saffron Walden G.C.

(0799) 22786
Windmill Hill, Saffron Walden
(18) 6608 yards

Skips G.C.

(04023) 48234
Tysea Hill, Stapleford
Abbotts
(18) 6146 yards

Stoke-by-Nayland G.C.

(0206) 262836
Leavenheath, Colchester
(18) 6471 yards
(Gainsborough)
(18) 6498 yards (Constable)

Theydon Bois G.C.

(0378) 3054
Theydon Road, Epping
(18) 5472 yards

Thorndon Park G.C.

(0277) 811666
Ingrave, Brentwood
(18) 6455 yards

Thorpe Hall G.C.

(0702) 582205
Thorpe Hall Avenue, Thorpe
Bay
(18) 6259 yards

Three Rivers G. & C.C.

(0621) 828631
Stow Road, Purleigh
(18) 6609 yards (Kings)
(9) 2142 yards

Towerlands G.C.

(0376) 26802
Panfield Road, Braintree
(9) 5396 yards

Upminster G.C.

(04022) 22788
Hall Lane, Upminster
(18) 5926 yards

Warley Park G.C.

(0277) 224891
Little Warley, Brentwood
(18) 6261 yards
(9) 3166 yards

Warren G.C.

(024541) 3258
Woodham Walter, Maldon
(18) 6211 yards

GLOUCESTER-SHIRE

Cirencester G.C.

(0285) 652465
Cheltenham Road,
Bagendon,
Cirencester
(18) 6021 yards

Cleeve Hill G.C.

(0242) 672592
Cleeve Hill, Cheltenham
(18) 6217 yards

Cotswold Hills G.C.

(0242) 515264
Ullenwood, Cheltenham
(18) 6716 yards

Gloucester Hotel G. & C.C.

(0452) 411331
Robinswood Hill, Gloucester
(18) 6135 yards

Lilley Brook G.C.

(0242) 526785
Cirencester Road, Charlton
Kings, Cheltenham
(18) 6226 yards

Lydney G.C.

(0594) 42614
Lakeside Avenue, Lydney
(9) 5382 yards

Minchinhampton G.C.

(045383) 3866 (New)
(045383) 2642 (Old)
Minchinhampton, Stroud
(18) 6295 yards (Old Course)
(18) 6675 yards (New
Course)

Painswick G.C.

(0452) 812180
Painswick, Stroud
(18) 4780 yards

Royal Forest of Dean G.C.

(0594) 32583
Lords Hill, Coleford
(18) 5519 yards

Stinchcombe Hill G.C.

(0453) 2015
Stinchcombe Hill, Dursley
(18) 5710 yards

Tewkesbury Park Hotel G.C.

(0684) 295405
Lincoln Green Lane,
Tewkesbury
(18) 6533 yards

Westonbirt G.C.

(066) 688242
Westonbirt, Tetbury
(9) 4504 yards

GREATER LONDON

The Addington G.C.

(081) 777 6057
Shirley Church Road,
Croydon
(18) 6242 yards

Addington Court G.C.

(081) 657 0281
Featherbed Lane,
Addington, Croydon
(18) 5577 yards (Old)
(18) 5513 yards (New)

Addington Palace G.C.

(081) 654 3061
Gravel Hill, Addington,
Croydon
(18) 6262 yards

Arkley G.C.

(081) 449 0394
Rowley Green Road, Barnet
(9) 6045 yards

Aquarius G.C.

(081) 693 1626
Marmora Road, Honor Oak
SE22
(9) 5035 yards

Ashford Manor G.C.

(0784) 252049
Fordbridge Road, Ashford
(18) 6343 yards

Banstead Downs G.C.

(081) 642 2284
Burdon Lane, Belmont,
Sutton
(18) 6169 yards

Beckenham Place Park G.C.
(081) 658 5374
Beckenham Hill Road, Beckenham
(18) 5722 yards

Bexley Heath G.C.
(081) 303 6951
Mount Road, Bexley Heath
(9) 5239 yards

Brent Valley G.C.
(081) 567 1287
Church Road, Hanwell W7
(18) 5426 yards

Bushey G.C.
(081) 950 2215
High Street, Bushey
(9) 6000 yards

Bush Hill Park G.C.
(081) 360 5738
Winchmore Hill, N21
(18) 5809 yards

Chigwell G.C.
(081) 500 2059
High Road, Chigwell
(18) 6279 yards

Chingford G.C.
(081) 529 5708
Station Road, Chingford E4
(18) 6136 yards

Chislehurst G.C.
(081) 467 2782
Camden Place, Chislehurst
(18) 5128 yards

Coombe Hill G.C.
(081) 942 2284
Golf Club Drive, Kingston Hill
(18) 6286 yards

Coombe Wood G.C.
(081) 942 0388
George Road, Kingston Hill
(18) 5210 yards

Coulsdon Court G.C.
(081) 660 0468
Coulsdon Road, Coulsdon
(18) 6030 yards

Crews Hill G.C.
(081) 363 6674
Cattlegate Road, Crews Hill
(18) 6208 yards

Croham Hurst G.C.
(081) 657 2075
Croham Road, South Croydon
(18) 6274 yards

Cuddington G.C.
(081) 393 0952
Banstead Road, Banstead
(18) 6282 yards

Dulwich & Sydenham Hill G.C.
(081) 693 3961
College Road, SE21
(18) 6051 yards

Dyrham Park G.C.
(081) 440 3361
Galley Lane, Barnet
(18) 6369 yards

Ealing G.C.
(081) 997 0937
Perivale Lane, Greenford
(18) 6216 yards

Elstree G.C.
(081) 953 6115
Watling Street, Elstree
(18) 5245 yards

Eltham Warren G.C.
(081) 850 4477
Bexley Road, Eltham SE9
(9) 5840 yards

Enfield G.C.
(081) 363 3970
Old Park Road South, Windmill Hill, Enfield
(18) 6137 yards

Fairlop Waters G.C.
(081) 500 9911
Barkingside, Ilford
(18) 6288 yards

Finchley G.C.
(081) 346 2436
Frith Lane, NW7
(18) 6411 yards

Fulwell G.C.
(081) 977 2733
Hampton Hill
(18) 6490 yards

Greenford G.C.
(081) 578 3949
Rockware Avenue, Greenford
(9) 4418 yards

Grim's Dyke G.C.
(081) 428 4539
Oxhey Lane, Hatch End, Pinner
(18) 5598 yards

Hadley Wood G.C.
(081) 449 4328
Beech Hill, Hadley Wood
(18) 6473 yards

Hainault Forest G.C.
(081) 500 0385
Chigwell Row, Hainault Forest
(18) 5754 yards (No. 1)
(18) 6445 yards (No. 2)

Hampstead G.C.
(081) 455 7089
Winnington Road, N2
(9) 5812 yards

Harefield Place G.C.
(0895) 31169
The Drive, Harefield Place, Uxbridge
(18) 5711 yards

Hartsbourne G. & C.C.
(081) 950 1113
Bushey Heath
(18) 6305 yards
(9) 5432 yards

Haste Hill G.C.
(09274) 22877
The Drive, Northwood
(18) 5794 yards

Hatfield London C.C.
(0707) 42624
Bedwell Park, Essendon
(18) 6878 yards

Hendon G.C.
(081) 346 6023
Devonshire Road, NW7
(18) 6241 yards

Highgate G.C.
(081) 340 3745
Denewood Road, Highgate N6
(18) 5964 yards

Hillingdon G.C.
(0895) 33956
Dorset Way, Hillingdon
(9) 5469 yards

Home Park G.C.
(081) 977 2423
Hampton Wick, Kingston
(18) 6497 yards

Horsenden Hill G.C.
(081) 902 4555
Woodland Rise, Greenford
(9) 1618 yards

Hounslow Heath G.C.
(081) 570 5271
Staines Road, Hounslow
(18) 5820 yards

Ilford G.C.
(081) 554 0094
Wanstead Park Road, Ilford
(18) 5710 yards

Langley Park G.C.
(081) 658 6849
Barnfield Wood Road, Beckenham
(18) 6488 yards

Lime Trees G.C.
(081) 845 3180
Ruislip Road, Northolt
(9) 5815 yards

London Scottish G.C.
(081) 788 0135
Windmill Enclosure, Wimbledon Common SW19
(18) 5486 yards

Magpie Hall Lane G.C.
(081) 462 7014
Magpie Hall Lane, Bromley
(9) 5538 yards

Royal Ashdown Forest

Malden G.C.
(081) 942 0654
Traps Lane, New Malden
(18) 6315 yards

Mill Hill G.C.
(081) 959 2339
Barnet Way, Mill Hill NW7
(18) 6294 yards

Mitcham G.C.
(081) 648 4197
Carshalton Road, Mitcham
Junction
(18) 5931 yards

Muswell Hill G.C.
(081) 888 1764
Rhodes Avenue, Wood Green
N22
(18) 6470 yards

North Middlesex G.C.
(081) 445 1604
Friern Barnet Lane, N20
(18) 5611 yards

Northwood G.C.
(09274) 21384
Rickmansworth Road,
Northwood
(18) 6464 yards

**Oaks Park Sports Centre
G.C.**
(081) 643 8363
Woodmansterne Road,
Carshalton
(18) 5873 yards

Old Ford Manor G.C.
(081) 440 9185
Hadley Green, Barnet
(18) 6449 yards

Perivale Park G.C.
(081) 575 8655
Ruislip Road East, Greenford
(9) 5334 yards

Picketts Lock G.C.
(081) 803 3611
Picketts Lock Lane,
Edmonton
(9) 2496 yards

Pinner Hill G.C.
(081) 866 0963
South View Road, Pinner Hill
(18) 6293 yards

Purley Downs G.C.
(081) 657 8347
Purley Downs Road, Purley
(18) 6237 yards

Richmond G.C.
(081) 940 4351
Sudbrook Park, Richmond
(18) 5965 yards

Richmond Park G.C.
(081) 876 1795
Richmond Park, SW15
(18) 5940 yards (Dukes)
(18) 5969 yards (Princes)

Roehampton G.C.
(081) 876 5505
Roehampton Lane
(18) 6057 yards

Royal Blackheath G.C.
(081) 850 1795
Court Road, Eltham
(18) 6216 yards

Royal Epping Forest G.C.
(081) 529 2195
Forest Approach, Chingford
(18) 6220 yards

Royal Mid-Surrey G.C.
(081) 940 1894
Old Deer Park, Richmond
(18) 6331 yards (Outer)
(18) 5446 yards (Inner)

Royal Wimbledon G.C.
(081) 946 2125
29 Camp Road, Wimbledon
(18) 6300 yards

Ruislip G.C.
(0895) 638835
Ickenham Road, Ruislip
(18) 5235 yards

Sandy Lodge G.C.
(09274) 25429
Sandy Lodge Lane,
Northwood
(18) 6340 yards

Selsdon Park Hotel G.C.
(081) 657 8811
Addington Road,
Sanderstead
(18) 6402 yards

Shirley Park G.C.
(081) 654 1143
Addiscombe Road, Croydon
(18) 6210 yards

Shooters Hill G.C.
(081) 854 6368
Eaglesfield Road,
Shooters Hill
(18) 5736 yards

Shortlands G.C.
(081) 460 2471
Meadow Road, Shortlands,
Bromley
(9) 5261 yards

Sidcup G.C.
(081) 300 2150
Hurst Road, Sidcup
(9) 5692 yards

South Herts G.C.
(081) 445 2035
Links Drive, Totteridge
(18) 6470 yards

Stanmore G.C.
(081) 954 2599
Gordon Avenue, Stanmore
(18) 5982 yards

Strawberry Hill G.C.
(081) 894 0165
Wellesley Road, Twickenham
(9) 4762 yards

Sudbury G.C.
(081) 902 3713
Bridgewater Road, Wembley
(18) 6282 yards

Sundridge Park G.C.
(081) 460 0278
Garden Road, Bromley
(18) 6410 yards (East)
(18) 6027 yards (West)

Surbiton G.C.
(081) 398 3101
Woodstock Lane,
Chessington
(18) 6211 yards

**Thames Ditton & Esher
G.C.**
(081) 398 1551
Portsmouth Road, Esher
(9) 5415 yards

Trent Park G.C.
(081) 366 7432
Bramley Road, Southgate
(18) 6008 yards

Twickenham G.C.
(081) 892 5579
Staines Road, Twickenham
(9) 6014 yards

Wanstead G.C.
(081) 989 3938
Overton Drive, Wanstead
(18) 6211 yards

West Essex G.C.
(081) 529 7558
Stewardstonebury, Chingford
(18) 6289 yards

West Middlesex G.C.
(081) 574 3450
Greenford Road, Southall
(18) 6242 yards

Whitewebbs G.C.
(081) 363 2951
Clay Hill, Enfield
(18) 5755 yards

**Wimbledon Common
G.C.**
(081) 946 7571
Camp Road, Wimbledon
Common
(18) 5486 yards

Wimbledon Park G.C.
(081) 946 1250
Home Park Road,
Wimbledon
(18) 5465 yards

Woodcote Park G.C.
(081) 668 2788
Meadow Hill, Coulsdon
(18) 6624 yards

Woodford G.C.
(081) 504 3330
Sunset Avenue,
Woodford Green
(9) 5806 yards

Wyke Green G.C.
(081) 560 8777
Syon Lane, Isleworth
(18) 6242 yards

GREATER MANCHESTER

Altrincham Municipal G.C.
(061) 928 0761
Stockport Road, Timperley,
Altrincham
(18) 6204 yards

Ashton-in-Makerfield G.C.
(0942) 727745
Gardwood Park,
Liverpool Road, Ashton-in-Makerfield
(18) 6160 yards

Ashton-on-Mersey G.C.
(061) 973 3220
Church Lane, Sale
(9) 6242 yards

Ashton-under-Lyne G.C.
(061) 330 1537
Kings Road, Ashton-under-Lyne
(18) 6157 yards

Blackley G.C.
(061) 643 4116
Victoria Avenue East,
Blackley
(18) 6235 yards

Bolton G.C.
(0204) 43067
Lostock Park, Bolton
(18) 6215 yards

Bolton Municipal G.C.
(0204) 42336
Links Road, Lostock,
Bolton
(18) 6012 yards

Bolton Old Links G.C.
(0204) 42307
Chorley Old Road, Bolton
(18) 6406 yards

Brackley G.C.
(061) 790 6076
Bullows Road, Little Hulton
(9) 6006 yards

Bramhall G.C.
(061) 439 6092
Ladythorn Road, Bramhall
(18) 6293 yards

Bramhall Park G.C.
(061) 485 3119
Manor Road, Bramhall
(18) 6214 yards

Breightmet G.C.
(0204) 27381
Redbridge, Ainsworth
(9) 6407 yards

Brookdale G.C.
(061) 681 4534
Woodhouses, Failsworth
(18) 5878 yards

Bury G.C.
(061) 766 2213
Blackford Bridge, Bury
(18) 5961 yards

Castle Hawk G.C.
(0706) 40841
Castleton, Rochdale
(18) 6316 yards

Cheadle G.C.
(061) 428 2160
Shiers Drive, Cheadle
(9) 5006 yards

Chorlton-Cum-Hardy G.C.
(061) 881 5830
Barlow Hall Road, Chorlton
(18) 6004 yards

Crompton & Royton G.C.
(061) 624 2154
High Barn, Royton, Oldham
(18) 6121 yards

Davyhulme Park G.C.
(061) 748 2260
Gleneagles Road, Davyhulme
(18) 6237 yards

Deane G.C.
(0204) 651808
Junction Road, Deane,
Bolton
(18) 5511 yards

Denton G.C.
(061) 336 3218
Manchester Road, Denton
(18) 6290 yards

Didsbury G.C.
(061) 998 2811
Ford Lane, Northenden
(18) 6273 yards

Disley G.C.
(0663) 62071
Jackson's Edge, Disley
(18) 5977 yards

Dukinfield G.C.
(061) 338 2669
Yew Tree Lane, Dukinfield
(18) 5544 yards

Dunham Forest G. & C.C.
(061) 928 2605
Oldfield Lane, Altrincham
(18) 6636 yards

Dunscar G.C.
(0204) 53321
Bromley Cross, Bolton
(18) 5995 yards

Ellesmere G.C.
(061) 790 7108
Old Clough Lane, Worsley
(18) 5957 yards

Fairfield G. & S.C.
(061) 370 2292
Booth Road, Andenshaw
(18) 5664 yards

Flixton G.C.
(061) 748 2116
Church Road, Flixton,
Urmston
(9) 6441 yards

Gathurst G.C.
(02575) 2432
Shevington
(9) 6308 yards

Gatley G.C.
(061) 437 2091
Styal Road, Heald Green
(9) 5934 yards

Great Lever & Farnworth G.C.
(0204) 72550
Lever Edge Lane, Bolton
(18) 5859 yards

Greenmount G.C.
(020488) 3712
Greenmount, Bury
(9) 4920 yards

Hale G.C.
(061) 980 4225
Rappax Road, Hale
(9) 5734 yards

Harwood G.C.
(0204) 28028
Harwood, Bolton
(9) 6028 yards

Hazel Grove G.C.
(061) 483 7272
Buxton Road, Hazel Grove
(18) 6300 yards

Heaton Moor G.C.
(061) 432 6458
Heaton Mersey, Stockport
(18) 5876 yards

Heaton Park G.C.
(061) 798 0295
Heaton Park, Prestwich
(18) 5849 yards

Horwich G.C.
(0204) 696298
Horwich, Bolton
(9) 5404 yards

Houldsworth G.C.
(061) 224 4571
Wingate House, Levenshulme
(18) 6078 yards

Lowes Park G.C.
(061) 764 1231
Walmersley, Bury
(9) 6003 yards

Manchester G.C.
(061) 643 3202
Rochdale Road, Middleton
(18) 6450 yards

Marple G.C.
(061) 427 6364
Hawk Green, Marple,
Stockport
(18) 5506 yards

**Mellor & Townscliffe
G.C.**
(061) 427 2208
Mellor, Stockport
(18) 5925 yards

Mirrlees G.C.
(061) 483 1000
Bramhall Moor Lane,
Hazel Grove
(9) 6102 yards

North Manchester G.C.
(061) 643 9033
Manchester Old Road,
Middleton
(18) 6542 yards

Northenden G.C.
(061) 998 4738
Palatine Road, Northenden
(18) 6435 yards

Oldham G.C.
(061) 624 4986
Lees New Road, Oldham
(18) 5045 yards

Pike Fold G.C.
(061) 740 1136
Cooper Lane,
Victoria Avenue,
Blackley
(9) 5789 yards

Prestwich G.C.
(061) 773 2544
Hilton Lane, Prestwich M25
(18) 4712 yards

Reddish Vale G.C.
(061) 480 2359
Southcliffe Road, Reddish,
Stockport
(18) 6048 yards

Ringway G.C.
(061) 980 2630
Hale Barns, Altrincham
(18) 6494 yards

Rochdale G.C.
(0706) 43818
Bagslate, Rochdale
(18) 5981 yards

Romiley G.C.
(061) 430 7257
Goosehouse Green, Romiley
(18) 6357 yards

Saddleworth G.C.
(04577) 3653
Uppermill, Oldham
(18) 5961 yards

Sale G.C.
(061) 973 1638
Golf Road, Sale
(18) 6351 yards

Springfield Park G.C.
(0706) 49801
Marland, Rochdale
(18) 5209 yards

Stamford G.C.
(04575) 4829
Huddersfield Road,
Stalybridge
(18) 5619 yards

Stand G.C.
(061) 766 2388
Ashbourne Grove,
Whitefield
(18) 6411 yards

Stockport G.C.
(061) 427 4425
Offerton Road, Offerton,
Stockport
(18) 6319 yards

Swinton Park G.C.
(061) 794 0861
East Lanes Road, Swinton
(18) 6675 yards

Tunshill G.C.
(0706) 342095
Milnrow, Rochdale
(9) 5812 yards

Turton G.C.
(0204) 852235
Bromley Cross, Bolton
(9) 5805 yards

Walmersley G.C.
(061) 764 0018
Garretts Close, Walmersley
(9) 6114 yards

Werneth G.C.
(061) 624 1190
Garden Suburb, Oldham
(18) 5296 yards

Werneth Low G.C.
(061) 368 7388
Werneth Low, Hyde
(9) 5734 yards

Westhoughton G.C.
(0942) 811085
Westhoughton, Bolton
(9) 5834 yards

Whitefield G.C.
(061) 766 2904
Higher Lane, Whitefield
(18) 6106 yards

Wigan G.C.
(0257) 421360
Arley Hall, Haigh, Wigan
(9) 6058 yards

Wigan Metropolitan G.C.
(0942) 401107
Haigh Hall Park, Wigan
(18) 6423 yards

William Wroe G.C.
(061) 748 8680
Pennybridge Lane, Flixton
(18) 4395 yards

Withington G.C.
(061) 445 9544
Palatine Road,
West Didsbury
(18) 6411 yards

Worsley G.C.
(061) 789 4202
Monton Green, Eccles
(18) 6217 yards

HAMPSHIRE

Alresford G.C.
(0962) 733746
Cheriton Road, Alresford
(18) 5986 yards

Alton G.C.
(0420) 82042
Old Odiham Road, Alton
(9) 5699 yards

Ampfield Par Three G.C.
(0794) 68480
Winchester Road, Ampfield
(18) 2478 yards

Andover G.C.
(0264) 58040
Winchester Road, Andover
(9) 5933 yards

Army G.C.
(0252) 540638
Laffans Road, Aldershot
(18) 6579 yards

Barton-on-Sea G.C.
(0425) 615308
Marine Drive, Barton-on-Sea
(18) 5565 yards

Basingstoke G.C.
(0256) 465990
Kempshott Park, Basingstoke
(18) 6309 yards

**Basingstoke Hospitals
G.C.**
(0256) 20347
Aldermaston Road,
Basingstoke
(9) 5480 yards

Bishopswood G.C.

(07356) 5213
Bishopswood Lane, Tadley,
Basingstoke
(9) 6474 yards

Blackmoor G.C.

(04203) 2775
Golf Lane, White Hill,
Bordon
(18) 6213 yards

Bramshaw G.C.

(0703) 813433
Brook, Lyndhurst
(18) 6233 yards (Manor)
(18) 5774 yards (Forest)

Brockenhurst Manor G.C.

(0590) 23332
Sway Road, Brockenhurst
(18) 6216 yards

Burley G.C.

(04253) 2431
Burley, Ringwood
(9) 6224 yards

Corhampton G.C.

(0489) 877279
Sheeps Pond Lane, Droxford,
Southampton
(18) 6088 yards

Dibden G.C.

(0703) 845596
Dibden, Southampton
(18) 6206 yards

Dunwood Manor G.C.

(0794) 40549
Shootash Hill, Romsey
(18) 5959 yards

Fleming Park G.C.

(0703) 612797
Magpie Lane, Eastleigh
(18) 4436 yards

Gosport and Stokes Bay G.C.

(0705) 527941
Haslar, Gosport
(9) 5806 yards

Great Salterns G.C.

(0705) 664549
Eastern Road, Portsmouth
(18) 5970 yards

Hartley Wintney G.C.

(025126) 4211
London Road,
Hartley Wintney
(9) 6096 yards

Hayling G.C.

(0705) 464446
Ferry Road,
Hayling Island
(18) 6489 yards

Hockley G.C.

(0962) 713165
Twyford, Winchester
(18) 6260 yards

Lee-on-the-Solent G.C.

(0705) 551170
Brune Lane,
Lee-on-the-Solent
(18) 6022 yards

Liphook G.C.

(0428) 723785
Wheatsheaf Enclosure,
Liphook
(18) 6207 yards

Meon Valley Hotel G. & C.C.

(0329) 833455
Sandy Lane, Shedfield
(18) 6519 yards

New Forest G.C.

(042128) 2450
Lyndhurst
(18) 5748 yards

North Hants G.C.

(0252) 616443
Minley Road, Fleet
(18) 6257 yards

Old Thorns Hotel & G.C.

(0428) 724555
Longmoor Road, Liphook
(18) 6447 yards

Petersfield G.C.

(0730) 62386
Heath Road, Petersfield
(18) 5751 yards

Portsmouth G.C.

(0705) 372210
Crookhorn Lane, Woodley,
Portsmouth
(18) 6259 yards

Romsey G.C.

(0703) 732218
Nursling, Southampton
(18) 5752 yards

Rowlands Castle G.C.

(070541) 2784
Links Lane, Rowlands Castle
(18) 6627 yards

Royal Winchester G.C.

(0962) 52462
Sarum Road, Winchester
(18) 6218 yards

Southampton G.C.

(0703) 768407
Golf Course Road, Bassett,
Southampton
(18) 6218 yards
(9) 2391 yards

Southwick Park G.C.

(0705) 380131
Pinsley Drive, Southwick
(18) 5970 yards

Southwood G.C.

(0252) 548700
Ively Road, Farnborough
(18) 5553 yards

Stoneham G.C.

(0703) 769272
Bassett, Southampton
(18) 6310 yards

Tylney Park G.C.

(0256) 722079
Rotherwick, Basingstoke
(18) 6150 yards

Waterlooville G.C.

(0705) 263388
Idsworth Road, Cowplain,
Portsmouth
(18) 6647 yards

HEREFORD & WORCESTER

Abbey Park G. & C.C.

(0527) 63918
Dagnell End Road, Redditch
(18) 6400 yards

Belmont House G.C.

(0432) 277445
Belmont, Hereford
(18) 6448 yards

Blackwell G.C.

(021) 445 1994
Blackwell, Bromsgrove
(18) 6105 yards

Broadway G.C.

(0386) 853683
Willersey Hill, Broadway
(18) 6211 yards

Churchill & Blakedown G.C.

(0562) 700200
Blakedown, Kidderminster
(9) 5399 yards

Droitwich G. & C.C.

(0905) 774344
Ford Lane, Droitwich
(18) 6036 yards

Evesham G.C.

(0386) 860395
Fladbury Cross,
Pershore
(9) 6418 yards

Habberley G.C.

(0562) 745756
Habberley, Kidderminster
(9) 5440 yards

Herefordshire G.C.

(0432) 71219
Wormsley, Hereford
(18) 6036 yards

Kidderminster G.C.

(0562) 822303
Russell Road, Kidderminster
(18) 6156 yards

Kington G.C.
(0544) 230340
Bradnor Hill, Kington
(18) 5830 yards

Leominster G.C.
(0568) 2863
Ford Bridge, Leominster
(18) 6084 yards

Little Lakes G.C.
(0299) 266385
Lye Head, Bewdley
(9) 6204 yards

Redditch G.C.
(0527) 43309
Callow Hill, Redditch
(18) 6671 yards

Ross-on-Wye G.C.
(098982) 267
Gorsley, Ross-on-Wye
(18) 6500 yards

Tolladine G.C.
(0905) 21074
Tolladine Road, Worcester
(9) 5630 yards

Worcester G. & C.C.
(0905) 422555
Boughton Park, Worcester
(18) 5890 yards

Worcestershire G.C.
(0684) 575992
Wood Farm, Malvern Wells
(18) 6449 yards

HERTFORDSHIRE

Aldenham G. & C.C.
(0923) 853929
Radlett Road, Aldenham
(18) 6455 yards

Ashridge G.C.
(044284) 2244
Little Gaddesden,
Berkhamsted
(18) 6508 yards

Batchwood Hall G.C.
(0727) 33349
Batchwood Drive,
St. Albans
(18) 6463 yards

Berkhamsted G.C.
(0442) 865832
The Common,
Berkhamsted
(18) 6568 yards

Bishop's Stortford G.C.
(0279) 654715
Dunhow Road,
Bishop's Stortford
(18) 6440 yards

Boxmoor G.C.
(0442) 42434
Box Lane,
Hemel Hempstead
(9) 4854 yards

Brickendon Grange G.C.
(099286) 258
Brickendon, Hertford
(18) 6315 yards

Brookman's Park G.C.
(0707) 52487
Golf Club Road, Hatfield
(18) 6438 yards

Bushey Hall G.C.
(0923) 225802
Bushey Hall Drive,
Bushey
(18) 6071 yards

Chadwell Springs G.C.
(0920) 463647
Hertford Road, Ware
(9) 6418 yards

Cheshunt Park G.C.
(0992) 24009
Park Lane, Cheshunt
(18) 6608 yards

Chorleywood G.C.
(09278) 2009
Common Road,
Chorleywood
(9) 5676 yards

East Herts G.C.
(0920) 821978
Hammels Park,
Buntingford
(18) 6449 yards

Harpenden G.C.
(0582) 712580
Hammonds End,
Harpenden
(18) 6363 yards

Harpenden Common G.C.
(0582) 712856
East Common,
Harpenden
(18) 5613 yards

Knebworth G.C.
(0438) 812752
Deards End Lane,
Knebworth
(18) 6428 yards

Letchworth G.C.
(0462) 683203
Letchworth Lane,
Letchworth
(18) 6082 yards

Little Hay G.C.
(0442) 833798
Bovingdon,
Hemel Hempstead
(18) 6610 yards

Mid Herts G.C.
(058283) 2242
Gustard Wood,
Wheathampstead
(18) 6094 yards

Moor Park G.C.
(0923) 773146
Moor Park,
Rickmansworth
(18) 6713 yards (High)
(18) 5815 yards (West)

Panshanger G.C.
(0707) 333350
Herns Lane,
Welwyn Garden City
(18) 6538 yards

Porters Park G.C.
(0923) 854127
Shenley Hill, Radlett
(18) 6313 yards

Potters Bar G.C.
(0707) 52020
Darkes Lane, Potters Bar
(18) 6273 yards

Redbourn G.C.
(058285) 3493
Kingsbourne Green Lane,
Redbourn
(18) 6407 yards

Rickmansworth G.C.
(0923) 773163
Moor Lane, Rickmansworth
(18) 4412 yards

Royston G.C.
(0763) 42696
Baldock Road, Royston
(18) 6032 yards

Stevenage G.C.
(043888) 424
Aston, Stevenage
(18) 6451 yards

Verulam G.C.
(0727) 53327
London Road, St Albans
(18) 6432 yards

Welwyn Garden City G.C.
(0707) 325243
High Oaks Road,
Welwyn Garden City
(18) 6200 yards

West Herts G.C.
(0923) 224264
Cassiobury Park, Watford
(18) 6488 yards

Whipsnade Park G.C.
(044284) 2330
Studham Lane, Dagnall
(18) 6812 yards

HUMBERSIDE

Beverley & East Riding G.C.
(0482) 869519
The Westwood, Beverley
(18) 5937 yards

Boothferry G.C.
(0430) 430364
Spaldington, Goole
(18) 6651 yards

Bridlington G.C.
(0262) 606367
Belvedere Road, Bridlington
(18) 6320 yards

Brough G.C.
(0482) 667374
Cave Road, Brough
(18) 6012 yards

Cleethorpes G.C.
(0472) 812059
Kings Road, Cleethorpes
(18) 6015 yards

Driffield G.C.
(0377) 44069
Sunderlandwick, Driffield
(18) 6227 yards

Elsham G.C.
(0652) 680291
Barton Road, Elsham
(18) 6420 yards

Flamborough Head G.C.
(0262) 850333
Flamborough, Bridlington
(18) 5438 yards

Ganstead Park G.C.
(0482) 811280
Coniston, Hull
(9) 5769 yards

Grimsby G.C.
(0472) 356981
Littlecoates Road, Grimsby
(18) 6058 yards

Hainsworth Park G.C.
(0964) 542362
Driffield
(9) 5350 yards

Hessle G.C.
(0482) 650171
Cottingham, Hull
(18) 6638 yards

Holme Hall G.C.
(0724) 862078
Bottesford, Scunthorpe
(18) 6475 yards

Hornsea G.C.
(0964) 534989
Rolston Road, Hornsea
(18) 6470 yards

Hull G.C.
(0482) 658919
Packman Lane, Kirk Ella, Hull
(18) 6242 yards

Immingham G.C.
(0469) 75493
Church Lane, Immingham
(18) 5809 yards

Normanby Hall G.C.
(0724) 720226
Normanby Park, Scunthorpe
(18) 6398 yards

Scunthorpe G.C.
(0724) 866561
Burringham Road, Scunthorpe
(18) 6281 yards

Sutton Park G.C.
(0482) 74242
Holderness Road, Hull
(18) 6251 yards

Withernsea G.C.
(0964) 612214
Chesnut Avenue, Withernsea
(9) 5112 yards

ISLE OF MAN

Castletown G.C.
(0624) 822125
Fort Island, Castletown
(18) 6804 yards

Douglas G.C.
(0624) 75952
Pulrose Road, Douglas
(18) 6080 yards

Howstrake G.C.
(0624) 20430
Grondle Road, Onchan
(18) 5367 yards

Peel G.C.
(0624) 843456
Rheast Lane, Peel
(18) 5914 yards

Ramsey G.C.
(0624) 812244
Brookfield Avenue, Ramsey
(18) 6019 yards

Rowany G.C.
(0624) 834108
Rowany Drive, Port Erin
(18) 5813 yards

ISLE OF WIGHT

Cowes G.C.
(0983) 292303
Crossfield Avenue, Cowes
(9) 5880 yards

Freshwater Bay G.C.
(0983) 752955
Afton Downs, Freshwater Bay
(18) 5628 yards

Newport G.C.
(0983) 525076
St. George's Down, Newport
(9) 5704 yards

Osborne G.C.
(0983) 295421
Osborne, East Cowes
(9) 6286 yards

Ryde G.C.
(0983) 614809
Binstead Road, Ryde
(9) 5220 yards

Shanklin & Sandown G.C.
(0983) 403217
The Fairway, Sandown
(18) 6000 yards

Ventnor G.C.
(0983) 853326
Steephill Down Road, Ventnor
(9) 5910 yards

KENT

Ashford G.C.
(0233) 620180
Sandyhurst Lane, Ashford
(18) 6246 yards

Barnehurst G.C.
(0322) 523746
Mayplace Road, East Barnehurst
(9) 5320 yards

Bearsted G.C.
(0622) 38198
Ware Street, Bearsted, Maidstone
(18) 6253 yards

Broome Park G. & C.C.
(0227) 831701
Barham, Canterbury
(18) 6610 yards

Canterbury G.C.
(0227) 453532
Scotland Hills, Canterbury
(18) 6209 yards

Cherry Lodge G.C.
(0959) 72250
Jail Lane, Biggin Hill
(18) 6908 yards

Chestfield G.C.
(022779) 2365
Chestfield, Whitstable
(18) 6126 yards

Cobtree Manor Park G.C.
(0622) 53276
Chatham Road, Boxley, Maidstone
(18) 5701 yards

Cranbrook G.C.
(0580) 712833
Benenden Road, Cranbrook
(18) 6128 yards

Cray Valley G.C.
(0689) 37909
Sandy Lane, St Paul's Cray,
Orpington
(18) 6338 yards

Darenth Valley G.C.
(09592) 2922
Station Road, Shoreham
(18) 6356 yards

Dartford G.C.
(0322) 26455
Dartford Heath, Dartford
(18) 5914 yards

Deangate Ridge G.C.
(0634) 251180
Hoo, Rochester
(18) 6300 yards

Edenbridge G. & C.C.
(0732) 865097
Crouch House Road,
Edenbridge
(18) 6635 yards

Faversham G.C.
(079589) 561
Belmont Park, Faversham
(18) 5979 yards

Gillingham G.C.
(0634) 53017
Woodlands Road,
Gillingham
(18) 5911 yards

Hawkhurst G.C.
(0580) 752396
High Street, Hawkhurst
(9) 5769 yards

Herne Bay G.C.
(0227) 373964
Eddington, Herne Bay
(18) 5466 yards

High Elms G.C.
(0689) 58175
High Elms Road, Downe
(18) 6210 yards

Holtye G.C.
(034286) 635
Holtye Common, Cowden,
Edenbridge
(9) 5289 yards

Hythe Imperial G.C.
(0303) 67554
Princes Parade, Hythe
(9) 5583 yards

Knole Park G.C.
(0732) 452150
Seal Hollow Road,
Sevenoaks
(18) 6249 yards

Lamberhurst G.C.
(0892) 890241
Church Road, Lamberhurst
(18) 6277 yards

Leeds Castle G.C.
(0622) 880467
Leeds Castle, Maidstone
(9) 6017 yards

Littlestone G.C.
(0679) 63355
St Andrews Road,
Littlestone,
New Romney
(18) 6417 yards

Lullingstone Park G.C.
(0959) 34542
Park Gate, Chelsfield,
Orpington
(18) 6674 yards
(9) 2432 yards

Mid Kent G.C.
(0474) 568035
Singlewell Road,
Gravesend
(18) 6206 yards

Nevill G.C.
(0892) 25818
Benhall Mill Road,
Tunbridge Wells
(18) 6336 yards

North Foreland G.C.
(0843) 62140
Convent Road, Broadstairs
(18) 6382 yards

Poult Wood G.C.
(0732) 364039
Higham Lane, Tonbridge
(18) 5569 yards

Prince's G.C.
(0304) 613797
Sandwich Bay, Sandwich
(18) 6923 yards
(9) 3134 yards

**Rochester & Cobham
Park G.C.**
(047482) 3411
Park Dale, Rochester
(18) 6467 yards

Royal Cinque Ports G.C.
(0304) 374007
Golf Road, Deal
(18) 6744 yards

Royal St George's G.C.
(0304) 613090
Sandwich
(18) 6857 yards

Ruxley G.C.
(0689) 71490
St Paul's Cray, Orpington
(18) 5017 yards

St Augustine's G.C.
(0843) 590333
Cliffsend, Ramsgate
(18) 5138 yards

Sene Valley G.C.
(0303) 268514
Sene, Folkestone
(18) 6320 yards

Sheerness G.C.
(0795) 662585
Powe Station Road, Sheerness
(18) 6500 yards

**Sittingbourne & Milton
Regis G.C.**
(0795) 842261
Newington, Sittingbourne
(18) 6121 yards

Tenterden G.C.
(05806) 3987
Woodchurch Road,
Tenterden
(9) 5119 yards

Tudor Park C.C.
(0622) 34334
Ashford Road, Bearsted
(18) 6041 yards

Tunbridge Wells G.C.
(0892) 23034
Langton Road,
Tunbridge Wells
(9) 4684 yards

**Walmer & Kingsdown
G.C.**
(0304) 373256
Kingsdown, Deal
(18) 6451 yards

**Westgate & Birchington
G.C.**
(0843) 31115
Domneva Road,
Westgate-on-Sea
(18) 4926 yards

West Kent G.C.
(0689) 51323
Downe, Orpington
(18) 6392 yards

West Malling G.C.
(0732) 844785
Addington, Maidstone
(18) 6142 yards

**Whitstable & Seasalter
G.C.**
(0227) 272020
Collingwood Road,
Whitstable
(18) 5276 yards

Wildernesse G.C.
(0732) 61199
Seal, Sevenoaks
(18) 6478 yards

Woodlands Manor G.C.
(09592) 3806
Woodlands, Sevenoaks
(18) 5858 yards

Wrotham Heath G.C.
(0732) 884800
Comp, Sevenoaks
(9) 5823 yards

LANCASHIRE

Accrington & District G.C.
(0254) 35070
West End, Oswaldtwistle,
Accrington
(18) 5954 yards

Ashton & Lea G.C.
(0772) 720374
Blackpool Road, Lea, Preston
(18) 6286 yards

Bacup G.C.
(0706) 873170
Maden Road, Bacup
(9) 5652 yards

Baxenden & District G.C.
(0254) 34555
Top o' th' Meadow,
Baxenden,
Accrington
(9) 5740 yards

Beacon Park G.C.
(0695) 622700
Dalton, Up Holland, Wigan
(18) 5996 yards

Blackburn G.C.
(0254) 55942
Beardwood Brow, Blackburn
(18) 6099 yards

Blackpool North Shore G.C.
(0253) 52054
Devonshire Road, Blackpool
(18) 6440 yards

Blackpool Park G.C.
(0253) 31004
North Park Drive, Blackpool
(18) 6060 yards

Burnley G.C.
(0282) 24328
Glen View, Burnley
(18) 5891 yards

Chorley G.C.
(0257) 480263
Charnock, Chorley
(18) 6277 yards

Clitheroe G.C.
(0200) 22292
Whalley Road, Clitheroe
(18) 6311 yards

Colne G.C.
(0282) 863391
Skipton Old Road, Colne
(9) 5961 yards

Darwen G.C.
(0254) 701287
Winter Hill, Darwen
(18) 5752 yards

Dean Wood G.C.
(0695) 622219
Lafford Lane, Up Holland,
Skelmersdale
(18) 6097 yards

Duxbury Park G.C.
(02572) 65380
Duxbury Park, Chorley
(18) 6390 yards

Fairhaven G.C.
(0253) 736741
Lytham Hall Park, Ansdell,
Lytham St Annes
(18) 6883 yards

Fishwick Hall G.C.
(0772) 796866
Farringdon Park, Preston
(18) 6203 yards

Fleetwood G.C.
(03917) 3661
Princes Way, Fleetwood
(18) 6437 yards

Green Haworth G.C.
(0254) 37580
Green Haworth, Accrington
(9) 5513 yards

Heysham G.C.
(0254) 51011
Trumacar Park, Heysham
(18) 6224 yards

Hindley Hall G.C.
(0942) 55991
Hall Lane, Hindley
(18) 5875 yards

Ingol G. & S.C.
(0772) 734556
Ingol, Preston
(18) 6345 yards

Knott End G.C.
(0253) 810576
Wyreside, Knott End on Sea,
Blackpool
(18) 5852 yards

Lancaster G. & C.C.
(0524) 751247
Ashton-with-Stodday,
Lancaster
(18) 6442 yards

Lansil G.C.
(0524) 67143
Caton Road, Lancaster
(9) 5608 yards

Leyland G.C.
(0772) 436457
Wigan Road, Leyland
(18) 6105 yards

Longridge G.C.
(0772) 783291
Jeffrey Hill, Longridge
(18) 5678 yards

Lytham Green Drive G.C.
(0253) 737390
Ballam Road, Lytham
(18) 6043 yards

Marsden Park G.C.
(0282) 67525
Townhouse Road, Nelson
(18) 5806 yards

Morecambe G.C.
(0254) 412841
Bare, Morecambe
(18) 5766 yards

Nelson G.C.
(0282) 64583
Brierfield, Nelson
(18) 5961 yards

Ormskirk G.C.
(0695) 72227
Lathom, Ormskirk
(18) 6333 yards

Penwortham G.C.
(0772) 744630
Penwortham, Preston
(18) 5915 yards

Pleasington G.C.
(0254) 22177
Pleasington, Blackburn
(18) 6445 yards

Poulton-le-Fylde G.C.
(0253) 892444
Breck Road, Poulton-le-Fylde
(9) 5752 yards

Preston G.C.
(0772) 700011
Fulwood, Preston
(18) 6249 yards

Rishton G.C.
(0254) 884442
Eachill Links, Rishton
(9) 6094 yards

Rossendale G.C.
(0706) 213056
Haslinden, Rossendale
(18) 6267 yards

Royal Lytham & St Annes G.C.
(0253) 724206
Links Gate, Lytham St Annes
(18) 6673 yards

St Annes Old Links G.C.
(0253) 723597
Highbury Road, St Annes,
Lytham
(18) 6616 yards

Shaw Hill G. & C.C.
(02572) 69221
Whittle-le-Woods,
Chorley
(18) 6467 yards

Silverdale G.C.
(0524) 701300
Redbridge Lane, Silverdale,
Carnworth
(9) 5262 yards

Todmorden G.C.
(070681) 2986
Stone Road, Todmorden
(9) 5818 yards

Towneley G.C.
(0282) 38473
Towneley Park, Burnley
(9) 5840 yards

Whalley G.C.
(025482) 2236
Whalley, Blackburn
(9) 5953 yards

Whittaker G.C.
(0706) 78310
Whittaker Lane,
Littleborough
(9) 5636 yards

Wilpshire G.C.
(0254) 248260
Wilpshire, Blackburn
(18) 5911 yards

LEICESTERSHIRE

Birstall G.C.
(0533) 674322
Station Road, Birstall,
Leicester
(18) 6203 yards

Charnwood Forest G.C.
(0509) 890259
Breakback Lane, Woodhouse
Eaves
(9) 6202 yards

Cosby G.C.
(0533) 864759
Chapel Lane, Cosby
(18) 6277 yards

Enderby G.C.
(0533) 849388
Mill Lane, Enderby
(9) 4356 yards

Glen Gorse G.C.
(0533) 714159
Glen Road, Oadby, Leicester
(18) 6641 yards

Hinckley G.C.
(0455) 615014
Leicester Road, Hinckley
(18) 6578 yards

**Humberstone Heights
G.C.**
(0533) 764674
Gipsy Lane, Leicester
(18) 6444 yards

Kibworth G.C.
(0533) 792301
Weir Road,
Kibworth Beauchamp
(18) 6282 yards

Kirby Muxloe G.C.
(0533) 393457
Kirby Muxloe,
Leicester
(18) 6303 yards

Leicestershire G.C.
(0533) 738825
Evington Lane,
Leicester
(18) 6312 yards

Lingdale G.C.
(0509) 890035
Joe Moores Lane,
Woodhouse Eaves
(18) 6114 yards

Longcliffe G.C.
(0509) 239129
Snell's Nook Lane,
Loughborough
(18) 6551 yards

Luffenham Heath G.C.
(0780) 720205
Ketton, Stamford
(18) 6254 yards

Lutterworth G.C.
(0455) 552532
Rugby Road,
Lutterworth
(18) 5570 yards

Market Harborough G.C.
(0858) 63684
Oxenden Road,
Market Harborough
(9) 6080 yards

Melton Mowbray G.C.
(0664) 62118
Waltham Road,
Melton Mowbray
(9) 6168 yards

Oadby G.C.
(0533) 709052
Leicester Road, Oadby
(18) 6228 yards

Rothley Park G.C.
(0533) 302809
Westfield Lane,
Rothley
(18) 6487 yards

R.A.F. North Luffenham
(0780) 720041
North Luffenham, Oakham
(18) 5629 yards

Rushcliffe G.C.
(050982) 2959
Stocking Lane, East Leake,
Loughborough
(18) 6057 yards

Scraptoft G.C.
(0533) 419000
Beeby Road, Scraptoft
(18) 6166 yards

Ullesthorpe G.C.
(0455) 209023
Ullesthorpe, Luttersworth
(18) 6048 yards

Western Park G.C.
(0533) 872339
Scudmore Road, Leicester
(18) 6532 yards

Whetstone G.C.
(0533) 861424
Cosby, Leicester
(18) 5795 yards

Willesley Park G.C.
(0530) 414596
Tamworth Road,
Ashby-de-la-Zouch
(18) 6310 yards

LINCOLNSHIRE

Belton Park G.C.
(0476) 67399
Londonthorpe Road,
Grantham
(9) 6412 yards
(9) 6101 yards
(9) 5857 yards

Blankney G.C.
(0526) 20202
Blankney, Lincoln
(18) 6232 yards

Boston G.C.
(0205) 350589
Horncastle Road,
Boston
(18) 5795 yards

Burghley Park G.C.
(0780) 53789
Stamford
(18) 6133 yards

Canwick Park G.C.
(0522) 22166
Canwick Park, Lincoln
(18) 6257 yards

Carholme G.C.
(0522) 33263
Carholme Road, Lincoln
(18) 6086 yards

Lincoln G.C.
(042771) 721
Torksey, Lincoln
(18) 6400 yards

Louth G.C.
(0507) 603681
Crowtree Lane, Louth
(18) 6502 yards

**Market Rasen and District
G.C.**
(0673) 842416
Legsby Road, Market Rasen
(18) 6031 yards

North Shore G.C.
(0754) 3298
North Shore Road, Skegness
(18) 6134 yards

Sandilands G.C.
(0521) 41617
Sandilands, Mablethorpe
(18) 5995 yards

Seacroft G.C.
(0754) 3020
Seacroft, Skegness
(18) 6478 yards

Sleaford G.C.
(05298) 273
South Rauceby, Sleaford
(18) 6443 yards

Spalding G.C.
(077585) 386
Surfleet, Spalding
(18) 5807 yards

Stoke Rochford G.C.
(047683) 275
Stoke Rochford, Grantham
(18) 6204 yards

Sutton Bridge G.C.
(0406) 350323
Sutton Bridge, Spalding
(9) 5850 yards

Thonock G.C.
(0427) 3088
Thonock, Gainsborough
(18) 5824 yards

Toft Hotel G.C.
(0778) 33616
Toft, Nr. Bourne
(18) 6539 yards

Woodhall Spa G.C.
(0526) 52511
The Broadway,
Woodhall Spa
(18) 6899 yards

MERSEYSIDE

Allerton Municipal G.C.
(051) 428 1046
Allerton, Liverpool
(18) 5459 yards

Alt G.C.
(0704) 35268
Park Road West, Southport
(18) 5939 yards

Arrowe Park G.C.
(051) 677 1527
Arrow Park, Woodchurch,
Birkenhead
(18) 6377 yards

Bidston G.C.
(051) 630 6650
Leasowe, Wirral
(18) 6207 yards

Bootle G.C.
(051) 928 1371
Dunningsbridge Road, Bootle
(18) 6362 yards

Bowring G.C.
(051) 489 5985
Roby Road, Huyton
(9) 5592 yards

Brackenwood G.C.
(051) 608 3093
Bebington, Wirral
(18) 6285 yards

Bromborough G.C.
(051) 334 2978
Raby Hall Road,
Bromborough
(18) 6650 yards

Caldy G.C.
(051) 625 1818
Links Hey Road,
Caldy, Wirral
(18) 6665 yards

Childwall G.C.
(051) 487 9871
Naylor's Road,
Liverpool
(18) 6425 yards

Eastham Lodge G.C.
(051) 327 3003
Ferry Road, Eastham,
Wirral
(15) 5826 yards

Formby G.C.
(07048) 72164
Golf Road, Formby
(18) 6871 yards

Formby Ladies G.C.
(07048) 73493
Golf Road, Formby
(18) 5374 yards

Grange Park G.C.
(0744) 26318
Prescot Road, St Helens
(18) 6480 yards

Haydock Park G.C.
(09252) 6944
Golborne Park,
Newton-le-Willows
(18) 6014 yards

Hesketh G.C.
(0704) 36897
Cambridge Road,
Southport
(18) 6478 yards

Heswall G.C.
(051) 342 1237
Cottage Lane, Heswall,
Wirral
(18) 6472 yards

Hillside G.C.
(0704) 67169
Hastings Road,
Southport
(18) 6850 yards

Hoylake Municipal G.C.
(051) 632 2956
Carr Lane, Hoylake
(18) 6312 yards

Huyton & Prescot G.C.
(051) 489 3948
Hurst Park, Huyton
(18) 5738 yards

Leasowe G.C.
(051) 677 5852
Leasowe Road, Moreton,
Wirral
(18) 6204 yards

Lee Park G.C.
(051) 487 3882
Childwall Valley Road,
Liverpool
(18) 6024 yards

Liverpool Municipal G.C.
(051) 546 5435
Ingoe Lane, Kirkby
(18) 6571 yards

Prenton G.C.
(051) 608 1053
Golf Links Road, Prenton,
Birkenhead
(18) 6379 yards

Royal Birkdale G.C.
(0704) 67920
Waterloo Road, Southport
(18) 6968 yards

Royal Liverpool G.C.
(051) 632 3101
Meols Drive, Hoylake,
Wirral
(18) 6780 yards

Sherdley Park G.C.
(0744) 813149
Elton Road, St. Helens
(18) 5941 yards

**Southport &
Ainsdale G.C.**
(0704) 78000
Bradshaws Lane,
Ainsdale,
Southport
(18) 6603 yards

Southport Municipal G.C.
(0704) 35286
Park Road West,
Southport
(18) 6253 yards

Southport Old Links G.C.
(0704) 24294
Moors Lane, Southport
(9) 6486 yards

Wallasey G.C.
(051) 691 1024
Bayswater Road, Wallasey
(18) 6607 yards

Warren G.C.
(051) 639 5730
Grove Road, Wallasey
(9) 5914 yards

West Derby G.C.
(051) 228 1034
Yew Tree Lane, West Derby,
Liverpool
(18) 6333 yards

Royal Liverpool (Hoylake)

West Lancashire G.C.
(051) 924 1076
Hall Road West,
Blundellsands,
Liverpool
(18) 6756 yards

Wirral Ladies G.C.
(051) 652 1255
Budston Road, Oxon,
Birkenhead
(18) 4966 yards

Woolton G.C.
(051) 486 2298
Doe Park, Woolton,
Liverpool
(18) 5706 yards

NORFOLK

**Barnham Broom
Hotel G.C.**
(060545) 393
Honingham Road,
Barnham Broom
(18) 6470 yards (Valley)
(18) 6628 yards (Hill)

Bawburgh G.C.
(0603) 746390
Long Lane, Bawburgh
(9) 5278 yards

Dereham G.C.
(0362) 693122
Quebec Road, Dereham
(9) 6255 yards

Diss G.C.
(0379) 642847
Stuston, Diss
(9) 5900 yards

Eaton G.C.
(0603) 51686
Newmarket Road, Norwich
(18) 6125 yards

Fakenham G.C.
(0328) 2867
The Racecourse, Fakenham
(9) 5879 yards

Gorleston G.C.
(0493) 661911
Warren Road, Gorleston
Great Yarmouth
(18) 6279 yards

**Great Yarmouth &
Caister G.C.**
(0493) 728699
Beach House, Caister-on-Sea
(18) 6235 yards

Hunstanton G.C.
(04853) 2811
Golf Course Road,
Old Hunstanton
(18) 6670 yards

Kings Lynn G.C.
(0533) 987654
Castle Rising, Kings Lynn
(18) 6552 yards

**Links Country Park
Hotel & G.C.**
(026375) 691
West Runton
(9) 4814 yards

Mundesley G.C.
(0263) 720095
Mundesley, Norwich
(9) 5376 yards

Hollinwell (Notts)

Royal Cromer G.C.
(0263) 512884
Overstrand Road, Cromer
(18) 6508 yards

Royal Norwich G.C.
(0603) 429928
Hellesdon, Norwich
(18) 6603 yards

Royal West Norfolk G.C.
(0485) 210087
Brancaster
(18) 6302 yards

Ryston Park G.C.
(0366) 382133
Denver, Downham Market
(9) 6292 yards

Sheringham G.C.
(0263) 823488
Weybourne Road,
Sheringham
(18) 6430 yards

Sprowston Park G.C.
(0603) 410657
Wroxham Road, Sprowston,
Norwich
(18) 5985 yards

Swaffham G.C.
(0760) 21611
Clay Road, Swaffham
(9) 6252 yards

Thetford G.C.
(0842) 752169
Brandon Road, Thetford
(18) 6504 yards

NORTH YORKSHIRE

Aldwark Manor G.C.
(03473) 8146
Alne, York
(18) 5172 yards

Bedale G.C.
(0677) 22451
Leyburn Road, Bedale
(18) 5599 yards

Bentham G.C.
(0468) 61018
Robin Lane, Bentham
(9) 5752 yards

Catterick Garrison G.C.
(0748) 833268
Leyburn Road, Catterick
Garrison
(18) 6336 yards

Easingwold G.C.
(0347) 21486
Stillington Road,
Easingwold
(18) 6222 yards

Filey G.C.
(0723) 513293
West Avenue, Filey
(18) 6030 yards

Fulford G.C.
(0904) 412882
Heslington Lane,
Fulford, York
(18) 6779 yards

Ganton G.C.
(0944) 70329
Ganton, Scarborough
(18) 6720 yards

Ghyll G.C.
(0282) 842466
Ghyll Brow, Barnoldswick
(9) 5708 yards

Harrogate G.C.
(0423) 862999
Starback, Harrogate
(18) 6183 yards

Heworth G.C.
(0904) 424618
Mancastergate, York
(11) 6078 yards

Kirkbymoorside G.C.
(0751) 31525
Manor Vale, Kirkbymoorside
(18) 5958 yards

Knaresborough G.C.
(0423) 862690
Boroughbridge Road,
Knaresborough
(18) 6281 yards

Malton & Norton G.C.
(0653) 697912
Norton, Malton
(18) 6411 yards

Masham G.C.
(0765) 89379
Masham, Ripon
(9) 5338 yards

Oakdale G.C.
(0423) 67162
Oakdale, Harrogate,
(18) 6456 yards

Pannal G.C.
(0423) 872628
Follifoot Road, Pannal,
Harrogate
(18) 6659 yards

Pike Hills G.C.
(0904) 708756
Copmanthorpe, York
(18) 6048 yards

Richmond G.C.
(0748) 4775
Bend Hagg, Richmond
(18) 5704 yards

Ripon City G.C.
(0765) 700411
Palace Road, Ripon
(9) 5752 yards

Scarborough North Cliff G.C.
(0723) 360786
Burniston Road, Scarborough
(18) 6425 yards

Scarborough South Cliff G.C.
(0723) 374737
Deepdale Avenue,
Scarborough
(18) 6085 yards

Selby G.C.
(075782) 785
Mill Lane, Selby
(18) 6246 yards

Settle G.C.
(07292) 3921
Giggleswick, Settle
(9) 4900 yards

Skipton G.C.
(0756) 792128
Grassington Road, Skipton
(18) 6087 yards

Thirsk & Northallerton G.C.
(0845) 22170
Thornton-le-Street, Thirsk
(9) 6087 yards

Whitby G.C.
(0947) 600660
Low Straggleton, Whitby
(18) 5710 yards

York G.C.
(0904) 490304
Lords Manor Lane, Strensall,
York
(18) 6275 yards

NORTHAMPTON-SHIRE

Cherwell Edge G.C.
(0295) 711591
Chacombe, Nr. Banbury
(18) 5925 yards

Cold Ashby G.C.
(0604) 740548
Cold Ashby
(18) 5957 yards

Collingtree Park G.C.
(0604) 700000
Windingbrook Lane,
Northampton
(18) 6692 yards

Daventry & District G.C.
(0327) 702829
Norton Road, Daventry
(9) 5555 yards

Delapre G.C.
(0604) 764036
Nene Valley Way,
Northampton
(18) 6293 yards

Farthingstone Hotel G.C.
(032736) 291
Farthingstone,
Towcester
(18) 6330 yards

Kettering G.C.
(0536) 511104
Headlands, Kettering
(18) 6035 yards

Kingsthorpe G.C.
(0604) 710610
Kingsley Road,
Northampton
(18) 6006 yards

Northampton G.C.
(0604) 719453
Kettering Road,
Northampton
(18) 6002 yards

Northamptonshire County G.C.
(0604) 843025
Church Brampton,
Northampton
(18) 6503 yards

Oundle G.C.
(0832) 273267
Oundle
(18) 5507 yards

Priors Hall G.C.
(0536) 67546
Stamford Road, Weldon
(18) 6677 yards

Rushden & District G.C.
(0933) 312197
Kimbolton Road, Chelveston
(9) 6381 yards

Staverton Park G.C.
(0327) 705911
Staverton, Daventry
(18) 6634 yards

Wellingborough G.C.
(0933) 677234
Harrowden Hall,
Wellingborough
(18) 6604 yards

NORTHUMBER-LAND

Allendale G.C.
(091) 2675875
Allendale, Hexham
(9) 4488 yards

Alnmouth G.C.
(0665) 830368
Foxton Hall, Alnmouth
(18) 6414 yards

Alnmouth Village G.C.
(0665) 830370
Marine Road, Alnmouth
(9) 6078 yards

Alnwick G.C.
(0665) 602499
Swansfield Park, Alnwick
(9) 5379 yards

Arcot Hall G.C.
(091) 236 2794
Dudley, Cramlington
(18) 6389 yards

Bamburgh Castle G.C.
(06684) 321
Bamburgh
(18) 5465 yards

Bedlingtonshire G.C.
(0670) 822457
Acorn Bank, Bedlington
(18) 6825 yards

Bellingham G.C.
(0660) 20530
Boggle Hole, Bellingham
(9) 5226 yards

**Berwick-upon-Tweed
G.C.**
(0289) 87348
Goswick, Berwick-
upon-Tweed
(18) 6399 yards

Blyth G.C.
(0670) 356514
New Delaval, Blyth
(18) 6533 yards

**Dunstanburgh Castle
G.C.**
(066576) 562
Embleton
(18) 6357 yards

Hexham G.C.
(0434) 603072
Spital Park, Hexham
(18) 6272 yards

Magdalene Fields G.C.
(0289) 306384
Berwick-upon-Tweed
(18) 6551 yards

Morpeth G.C.
(0670) 512065
The Common, Morpeth
(18) 6215 yards

**Newbiggin-by-the Sea
G.C.**
(0670) 817833
Newbiggin-by-the-Sea
(18) 6444 yards

Prudhoe G.C.
(0661) 32466
Eastwood Park, Prudhoe
(18) 5812 yards

Rothbury G.C.
(0669) 20718
Old Race Course, Rothbury
(9) 5650 yards

Seahouses G.C.
(0665) 720794
Bednell Road, Seahouses
(18) 5399 yards

Slaley Hall G. & C.C.
(0434) 673691
Slaley, Hexham
(18) 6995 yards

Stocksfield G.C.
(0661) 843041
New Ridley, Stocksfield
(18) 5594 yards

Tynedale G.C.
(0434) 605701
Tyne Green, Hexham
(9) 5706 yards

Warkworth G.C.
(0665) 711596
Warkworth, Morpeth
(9) 5817 yards

NOTTINGHAM-
SHIRE
Beeston Fields G.C.
(0602) 257062
Beeston Fields, Nottingham
(18) 6404 yards

Bulwell Forest G.C.
(0602) 278008
Hucknall Road, Bulwell,
Nottingham
(18) 5606 yards

Bulwell Hall Park G.C.
(0602) 278021
Lawton Drive, Bulwell
(18) 6218 yards

Chilwell Manor G.C.
(0602) 258958
Meadow Lane, Chilwell,
Nottingham
(18) 6379 yards

Coxmoor G.C.
(0623) 557359
Coxmoor Road, Sutton-
in-Ashfield
(18) 6501 yards

Edwalton Municipal G.C.
(0602) 234775
Edwalton, Nottingham
(9) 3336 yards

Kilton Forest G.C.
(0909) 486563
Blyth Road, Worksop
(18) 6569 yards

Lindrick G.C.
(0909) 475282
Lindrick Common, Worksop
(18) 6377 yards

**Mansfield Woodhouse
G.C.**
(0623) 23521
Leeming Lane, Mansfield
(9) 2150 yards

Mapperley C.C.
(0602) 265611
Mapperley Plains,
Nottingham
(18) 6224 yards

Newark G.C.
(0636) 626241
Coddington, Newark
(18) 6486 yards

Notts G.C.
(0623) 753225
Hollinwell, Derby Road,
Kirby-in-Ashfield
(18) 7020 yards

Oxton G.C.
(0602) 653545
Oxton, Southwell
(18) 6630 yards

Radcliffe-on-Trent G.C.
(06073) 3000
Cropwell Road, Radcliffe-on-
Trent
(18) 6423 yards

Retford G.C.
(0777) 703733
Ordsall, Retford
(9) 6230 yards

Sherwood Forest G.C.
(0623) 26689
Eakring Road, Mansfield
(18) 6709 yards

**Stanton-on-the-Wolds
G.C.**
(06077) 2044
Stanton-on-the-Wolds,
Keyworth
(18) 6379 yards

Wollaton Park G.C.
(0602) 787574
Wollaton Park, Nottingham
(18) 6494 yards

Worksop G.C.
(0909) 477731
Windmill Lane, Worksop
(18) 6651 yards

OXFORDSHIRE
Badgemore Park G.C.
(0491) 572206
Henley-on-Thames
(18) 6112 yards

Burford G.C.
(099 382) 2583
Burford
(18) 6405 yards

Chesterton County G.C.
(0869) 241204
Chesterton, Bicester
(18) 6496 yards

Chipping Norton G.C.
(0608) 642383
Southcombe,
Chipping Norton
(9) 5280 yards

Frilford Heath G.C.
(0865) 390865
Frilford Heath, Abingdon
(18) 6768 yards (Red)
(18) 6006 yards (Green)

Henley G.C.
(0491) 575742
Harpsden,
Henley-on-Thames
(18) 6329 yards

Huntercombe G.C.
(0491) 641207
Nuffield, Henley-on-Thames
(18) 6257 yards

North Oxford G.C.
(0865) 54924
Banbury Road, Oxford
(18) 5805 yards

Southfield G.C.
(0865) 242158
Hill Top Road, Oxford
(18) 6230 yards

Tadmarton Heath G.C.
(0608) 737278
Wiggington, Banbury
(18) 5917 yards

SHROPSHIRE

Bridgnorth G.C.
(07462) 2400
Stanley Lane, Bridgnorth
(18) 6673 yards

Church Stretton G.C.
(0694) 722281
Trevor Hill, Church Stretton
(18) 5008 yards

Hawkstone Park Hotel & G.C.
(093924) 611
Weston-under-Redcastle, Shrewsbury
(18) 6465 yards (Hawkstone)
(18) 5368 yards (Weston)

Hill Valley G. & C.C.
(0948) 3584
Terrick Road, Whitchurch
(18) 6884 yards
(9) 5106 yards

Lilleshall Hall G.C.
(0952) 604776
Lilleshall, Newport
(18) 5891 yards

Llanymynech G.C.
(0691) 830542
Pant, Oswestry
(18) 6114 yards

Ludlow G.C.
(058477) 285
Bromfield, Ludlow
(18) 6239 yards

Market Drayton G.C.
(0630) 2266
Sutton, Market Drayton
(18) 6170 yards

Meole Brace G.C.
(0743) 64050
Meole Brace
(9) 5830 yards

Oswestry G.C.
(069188) 535
Aston Park, Oswestry
(18) 6046 yards

Patshull Park G.C.
(0902) 700342
Pattingham
(18) 6412 yards

Shifnal G.C.
(0952) 460330
Decker Hill, Shifnal
(18) 6422 yards

Shrewsbury G.C.
(074372) 2976
Condover, Shrewsbury
(18) 6212 yards

Telford Hotel G. & C.C.
(0952) 585642
Greay Hay, Telford
(18) 6228 yards

Wrekin G.C.
(0952) 44032
Wellington, Telford
(18) 5699 yards

SOMERSET

Brean G.C.
(027875) 467
Brean, Burnham-on-Sea
(18) 5566 yards

Burnham and Berrow G.C.
(0278) 785760
St Christopher's Way, Burnham-on-Sea
(18) 6547 yards
(9) 6550 yards

Enmore Park G.C.
(027867) 481
Enmore, Bridgewater
(18) 6443 yards

Minehead and West Somerset G.C.
(0643) 2057
The Warren, Minehead
(18) 6131 yards

Taunton and Pickeridge G.C.
(082342) 240
Corfe, Taunton
(18) 5927 yards

Vivary Park G.C.
(0823) 333875
Taunton
(18) 4620 yards

Wells G.C.
(0749) 72868
East Horrington Road, Wells
(18) 5288 yards

Windwhistle G. & S.C.
(046030) 231
Cricket St Thomas, Chard
(12) 6055 yards

Yeovil G.C.
(0935) 22965
Sherborne Road, Yeovil
(18) 6139 yards

SOUTH YORKSHIRE

Abbeydale G.C.
(0742) 360763
Twentywell Lane, Dore, Sheffield
(18) 6419 yards

Austerfield Park G.C.
(0302) 710850
Cross Lane, Austerfield
(18) 6824 yards

Barnsley G.C.
(0226) 382954
Staincross, Barnsley
(18) 6048 yards

Beauchief Municipal G.C.
(0742) 367274
Abbey Lane, Sheffield
(18) 5428 yards

Birley Wood G.C.
(0742) 389198
Birley Lane, Sheffield
(18) 6275 yards

Concord Park G.C.
(0742) 456806
Shiregreen Lane, Sheffield
(18) 4280 yards

Crookhill Park G.C.
(0709) 863466
Conisbrough, Doncaster
(18) 5846 yards

Doncaster G.C.
(0302) 868404
Bescarr, Doncaster
(18) 6230 yards

Doncaster Town Moor G.C.
(0302) 535458
Belle Vue, Doncaster
(18) 6081 yards

Dore & Totley G.C.
(0742) 369872
Broadway Road, Sheffield
(18) 6301 yards

Grange Park G.C.
(0709) 559497
Upper Wortley Road, Rotherham
(18) 6461 yards

Hallamshire G.C.
(0742) 302153
Sandygate, Sheffield
(18) 6396 yards

Hallowes G.C.
(0246) 413734
Hallowes Lane, Dronfield, Sheffield
(18) 6366 yards

Hickleton G.C.
(0709) 895170
Hickleton, Doncaster
(18) 6401 yards

Burnham and Berrow

Hillsborough G.C.
(0742) 349151
Worrall Road, Sheffield
(18) 6100 yards

Lees Hall G.C.
(0742) 552900
Hemsworth Road, Norton,
Sheffield
(18) 6137 yards

Phoenix G.C.
(0709) 370759
Brinsworth, Rotherham
(18) 6170 yards

Rotherham G.C.
(0709) 850812
Thrybergh Park, Rotherham
(18) 6324 yards

Serlby Park G.C.
(0777) 818268
Serlby, Doncaster
(18) 5325 yards

Silkstone G.C.
(0226) 790328
Field Head, Silkstone,
Barnsley
(18) 6045 yards

Sitwell Park G.C.
(0709) 541046
Shrogswood Road,
Rotherham
(18) 6203 yards

**Stocksbridge & District
G.C.**
(0742) 882408
Royd Lane, Townend,
Deepcar
(15) 5055 yards

Tankersley Park G.C.
(0742) 468247
High Green, Sheffield
(18) 6241 yards

Tinsley Park G.C.
(0742) 560237
Darnall, Sheffield
(18) 6045 yards

Wath G.C.
(0709) 878677
Abdy Rawmarsh, Rotherham
(9) 5606 yards

Wheatley G.C.
(0302) 831655
Armthorpe Road, Doncaster
(18) 6345 yards

Wortley G.C.
(0742) 885294
Hermit Hill Lane, Wortley,
Sheffield
(18) 5960 yards

SUFFOLK

Aldeburgh G.C.
(0728) 452890
Saxmundham Road,
Aldeburgh
(18) 6330 yards
(9) 2114 yards

Beccles G.C.
(0502) 712479
The Common, Beccles
(9) 5392 yards

**Bungay &
Waveny Valley G.C.**
(0986) 2337
Outney Common, Bungay
(18) 5944 yards

Bury St Edmunds G.C.
(0284) 755979
Tuthill,
Bury St Edmunds
(18) 6615 yards

Felixstowe Ferry G.C.
(0394) 286834
Ferry Road, Felixstowe
(18) 6042 yards

Flempton G.C.
(028484) 291
Flempton,
Bury St Edmunds
(9) 6050 yards

Fornham Park G.C.
(0284) 706777
Fornham St. Martin,
Bury St. Edmunds
(18) 6212 yards

Haverhill G.C.
(0440) 61951
Coupals Road, Haverhill
(9) 5708 yards

Ipswich G.C.
(0473) 78941
Purdis Heath, Ipswich
(18) 6405 yards
(9) 3860 yards

Links G.C.
(0638) 663000
Cambridge Road,
Newmarket
(18) 6402 yards

Newton Green G.C.
(0787) 77501
Newton Green, Sudbury
(9) 5442 yards

Rookery Park G.C.
(0502) 560380
Carlton Colville,
Lowestoft
(18) 6649 yards

**Royal Worlington
& Newmarket G.C.**
(0638) 712216
Worlington,
Bury St Edmunds
(9) 6218 yards

Rushmere G.C.
(0473) 75648
Rushmere Heath, Ipswich
(18) 6287 yards

Southwold G.C.
(0502) 723248
The Common, Southwold
(9) 6001 yards

Stowmarket G.C.
(04493) 473
Onehouse, Stowmarket
(18) 6119 yards

Thorpeness G.C.
(0728) 452176
Thorpeness
(18) 6241 yards

Waldringfield Heath G.C.
(0473) 726821
Waldringfield, Woodbridge
(18) 5837 yards

Woodbridge G.C.
(03943) 2038
Bromeswell Heath,
Woodbridge
(18) 6314 yards
(9) 4486 yards

STAFFORDSHIRE

Alsager G. & C.C.
(0270) 875700
Alsager Road, Alsager
(18) 6192 yards

Beau Desert G.C.
(05438) 2626
Hazel Slade, Cannock
(18) 6285 yards

Branston G.C.
(0283) 43207
Branston, Burton-on-Trent
(18) 6480 yards

Brocton Hall G.C.
(0785) 661901
Brocton, Stafford
(18) 6095 yards

Burslem G.C.
(0782) 837006
High Lane, Tunstall,
Stoke-on-Trent
(9) 5354 yards

Craythorne G.C.
(0283) 64329
Stretton, Burton-on-Trent
(18) 5230 yards

Drayton Park G.C.
(0827) 251139
Drayton Park, Tamworth
(18) 6414 yards

Greenway Hall G.C.
(0782) 503158
Stockton Brook,
Stoke-on-Trent
(18) 5676 yards

Ingestre Park G.C.
(0889) 270845
Ingestre, Weston,
Stafford
(18) 6376 yards

Leek G.C.
(0538) 385889
Cheadle Road, Leek
(18) 6240 yards

Leek Westwood G.C.
(0538) 383060
Newcastle Road, Leek
(9) 5501 yards

**Newcastle-under-Lyme
G.C.**
(0782) 617006
Whitmore Road, Newcastle
(18) 6450 yards

**Newcastle Municipal
G.C.**
(0782) 627596
Keele Road, Newcastle
(18) 6301 yards

Stafford Castle G.C.
(0785) 3821
Newport Road, Stafford
(9) 6347 yards

Stone G.C.
(0785) 813103
Filleybrooks, Stone
(9) 6272 yards

Tamworth G.C.
(0827) 53850
Eagle Drive, Tamworth
(18) 6695 yards

Trentham G.C.
(0782) 658109
Barlaston Old Road,
Trentham,
Stoke-on-Trent
(18) 6644 yards

Trentham Park G.C.
(0782) 658800
Trentham Park,
Trentham,
Stoke-on-Trent
(18) 6403 yards

Uttoxeter G.C.
(08893) 4844
Wood Lane, Uttoxeter
(9) 5695 yards

**Whittington Barracks
G.C.**
(0543) 432317
Tamworth Road, Lichfield
(18) 6457 yards

Wolstanton G.C.
(0782) 622413
Dimsdale Old Hall,
Newcastle
(18) 5807 yards

SURREY

Barrow Hills G.C.
(0276) 72037
Longcross, Chertsey
(18) 3090 yards

Betchworth Park G.C.
(0306) 882052
Reigate Road, Dorking
(18) 6266 yards

Bramley G.C.
(0483) 892696
Godden Hill, Bramley
(18) 5910 yards

Burhill G.C.
(0932) 227345
Walton-on-Thames
(18) 6224 yards

Camberley Heath G.C.
(0276) 23258
Golf Drive, Camberley
(18) 6402 yards

Chipstead G.C.
(0737) 555781
How Lane, Coulsdon
(18) 5454 yards

Crondall G.C.
(0252) 850880
Oak Park, Heath Lane,
Crondall
(18) 6233 yards

Dorking G.C.
(0306) 886917
Chart Park, Dorking
(9) 5106 yards

Drift G.C.
(04865) 4641
The Drift, East Horsley
(18) 6404 yards

Effingham G.C.
(0372) 52203
Guildford Road,
Effingham
(18) 6488 yards

Epsom G.C.
(03727) 21666
Longdown Lane, Epsom
(18) 5725 yards

Farnham G.C.
(02518) 2109
The Sands, Farnham
(18) 6313 yards

Fernfell G. & C.C.
(0483) 276626
Barhatch Lane, Cranleigh
(18) 5236 yards

Foxhills G.C.
(093287) 2050
Stonehill Road, Ottershaw
(18) 6658 yards
(18) 6406 yards

**Gatton Manor Hotel
& G.C.**
(030679) 555
Ockley, Dorking
(18) 6902 yards

Guildford G.C.
(0483) 63941
High Path Road, Merrow,
Guildford
(18) 6080 yards

Hankley Common G.C.
(025125) 2493
Tilford, Farnham
(18) 6403 yards

Hindhead G.C.
(042873) 4614
Churt Road, Hindhead
(18) 6357 yards

Hoebridge G.C.
(0483) 722611
Old Woking Road,
Old Woking
(18) 6587 yards

Kingswood G.C.
(0737) 832188
Sandy Lane, Kingswood
(18) 6821 yards

Laleham G.C.
(09328) 564211
Laleham Reach, Chertsey
(18) 6203 yards

Leatherhead G.C.
(037284) 3966
Kingston Road, Leatherhead
(18) 6069 yards

Limpsfield Chart G.C.
(088388) 2106
Limpsfield, Oxted
(9) 5718 yards

Moore Place G.C.
(0372) 63533
Portsmouth Road, Esher
(9) 3512 yards

New Zealand G.C.
(09323) 45049
Woodham Lane, Woodham,
Weybridge
(18) 6012 yards

North Downs G.C.
(088385) 2057
Northdown Road,
Woldingham
(18) 5787 yards

Puttenham G.C.
(0483) 810498
Puttenham
(18) 5367 yards

R.A.C. Country Club
(0372) 276311
Woodcote Park, Epsom
(18) 6672 yards
(18) 5520 yards

Redhill & Reigate G.C.
(0737) 240777
Pendleton Road, Redhill
(18) 5193 yards

Reigate Heath G.C.
(0737) 242610
Reigate Heath, Reigate
(9) 5554 yards

St George's Hill G.C.
(0932) 847758
St George's Hill, Weybridge
(18) 6492 yards
(9) 4562 yards

Sandown Park G.C.
(0372) 63340
Moor Lane, Esher
(9) 5658 yards

Shillinglee Park G.C.
(0428) 53237
Chiddingfold, Godalming
(9) 2500 yards

Silvermere G.C.
(0932) 67275
Redhill Road, Cobham
(18) 6333 yards

Tandridge G.C.
(0883) 712733
Oxted
(18) 6260 yards

Tyrell's Wood G.C.
(0372) 376025
Tyrell's Wood, Leatherhead
(18) 6219 yards

Walton Heath G.C.
(073781) 2380
Tadworth
(18) 6813 yards (Old)
(18) 6659 yards (New)

Wentworth G.C.
(0344) 82201
Virginia Water
(18) 6945 yards (West)
(18) 6176 yards (East)
(18) 6979 yards (Edinburgh)

West Byfleet G.C.
(09323) 43433
Sheerwater Road,
West Byfleet
(18) 6211 yards

West Hill G.C.
(04867) 4365
Bagshot Road, Brookwood
(18) 6307 yards

West Surrey G.C.
(04868) 21275
Enton Green, Godalming
(18) 6247 yards

Windlemere G.C.
(09905) 8727
Windlesham Road,
West End,
Woking
(9) 5346 yards

Woking G.C.
(0483) 760053
Pond Road, Hook Heath,
Woking
(18) 6322 yards

Worplesdon G.C.
(04867) 2277
Heath House Road, Woking
(18) 6422 yards

TYNE AND WEAR

Backworth G.C.
(091) 2681048
Backworth, Shiremoor
(9) 5930 yards

Boldon G.C.
(091) 536 5360
Dip Lane, East Boldon
(18) 6319 yards

City of Newcastle G.C.
(091) 2851775
Three Mile Bridge, Gosforth
(18) 6508 yards

Garesfield G.C.
(0207) 561278
Chopwell
(18) 6610 yards

Gosforth G.C.
(091) 285 3495
Broadway East, Gosforth
(18) 6030 yards

Gosforth Park G.C.
(091) 236 4480
High Gosforth Park,
Gosforth
(18) 6200 yards

Heworth G.C.
(0632) 692137
Heworth, Gateshead
(18) 6442 yards

Hobson Municipal G.C.
(0207) 70941
Hobson, Burnopfield
(18) 6502 yards

Houghton-le-Spring G.C.
(091) 584 1198
Copt Hill,
Houghton-le-Spring
(18) 6248 yards

Newcastle United G.C.
(091) 286 9998
Ponteland Road, Cowgate,
Newcastle
(18) 6498 yards

Northumberland G.C.
(091) 236 2498
High Gosforth Park,
Newcastle
(18) 6629 yards

Ponteland G.C.
(0661) 22689
Bell Villas, Ponteland,
Newcastle
(18) 6512 yards

Ravensworth G.C.
(091) 487 2843
Wrekenton, Gateshead
(18) 5872 yards

Ryton G.C.
(091) 413 3737
Clara Vale, Ryton
(18) 6034 yards

South Shields G.C.
(091) 456 8942
Cleadon Hills, South Shields
(18) 6264 yards

Tynemouth G.C.
(091) 257 4578
Spital Dean, Tynemouth,
North Shields
(18) 6351 yards

Tyneside G.C.
(091) 413 2742
Westfield Lane, Ryton
(18) 6055 yards

Wallsend G.C.
(091) 262 8989
Bigges Main, Wallsend
(18) 6601 yards

Washington G.C.
(091) 417 8346
Cellar Road, Washington
(18) 6604 yards

Wearside G.C.
(091) 534 2518
Coxgreen, Sunderland
(18) 6204 yards

Westerhope G.C.
(091) 286 9125
Westerhope, Newcastle
(18) 6468 yards

Whickham G.C.
(091) 488 7309
Hollinside Park, Newcastle
(18) 6129 yards

Whitburn G.C.
(091) 529 4210
Lizard Lane, South Shields
(18) 6035 yards

Whitley Bay G.C.
(091) 252 0180
Claremount Road,
Whitley Bay
(18) 6712 yards

WARWICKSHIRE

Atherstone G.C.
(08277) 714579
The Outwoods, Atherstone
(18) 6239 yards

Kenilworth G.C.
(0926) 58517
Crew Lane, Kenilworth
(18) 6408 yards

Leamington & Country G.C.
(0926) 28014
Whitnash, Leamington Spa
(18) 6430 yards

Newbold Comyn G.C.
(0926) 421157
Newbold Terrace East,
Leamington Spa
(18) 6430 yards

Nuneaton G.C.
(0203) 347810
Whitestone, Nuneaton
(18) 6368 yards

Purley Chase G.C.
(0203) 395 348
Ridge Lane, Nuneaton
(18) 6604 yards

Rugby G.C.
(0788) 75134
Clifton Road, Rugby
(18) 5457 yards

Stratford-upon-Avon G.C.
(0789) 205749
Tiddington Road,
Stratford
(18) 6309 yards

Warwick G.C.
(0926) 494316
The Racecourse, Warwick
(9) 5364 yards

Welcombe Hotel & G.C.
(0789) 295252
Warwick Road,
Stratford-upon-Avon
(18) 6202 yards

WEST MIDLANDS

The Belfry
(0675) 470301
Lichfield Road, Wishaw,
Sutton Coldfield
(18) 6975 yards (Brabazon)
(18) 6127 yards (Derby)

Bloxwich G.C.
(0922) 405724
Stafford Road, Bloxwich
(18) 6286 yards

Boldmere G.C.
(021) 354 3379
Monmouth Drive,
Sutton Coldfield
(18) 4463 yards

Brand Hall G.C.
(021) 552 2195
Heron Road, Oldbury,
Warley
(18) 5813 yards

Calderfields G.C.
(0922) 32243
Aldridge Road, Walsall
(18) 6636 yards

City of Coventry G.C.
(0203) 85032
Brandon Lane, Coventry
(18) 6530 yards

Cocks Moor Woods G.C.
(021) 444 3584
Alcester Road South, Kings
Heath, Birmingham
(18) 5888 yards

Copt Heath G.C.
(05645) 2650
Warwick Road, Knowle,
Solihull
(18) 6504 yards

Coventry G.C.
(0203) 414152
Finham Park, Coventry
(18) 6613 yards

Dartmouth G.C.
(021) 588 2131
Vale Street, West Bromwich
(9) 6060 yards

Druids Heath G.C.
(0922) 55595
Stonnall Road, Aldridge
(18) 6914 yards

Dudley G.C.
(0384) 53719
Turners Hill, Dudley
(18) 5715 yards

Edgbaston G.C.
(021) 454 1736
Church Road, Edgbaston
(18) 6118 yards

Enville G.C.
(0384) 872074
Highgate Common,
Stourbridge
(18) 6541 yards

Forest of Arden G. & C.C.
(0676) 22118
Maxstone Lane, Meriden,
Coventry
(18) 6867 yards

Fulford Heath G.C.
(0564) 822806
Tanners Green Lane, Wythall
(18) 6256 yards

Gay Hill G.C.
(021) 430 8544
Alcester Road, Hollywood,
Birmingham
(18) 6532 yards

Grange G.C.
(0203) 451465
Copeswood, Coventry
(9) 6002 yards

Great Barr G.C.
(021) 357 1232
Chapel Lane, Birmingham
(18) 6545 yards

Hagley C.C.
(0562) 883701
Wassell Grove, Stourbridge
(18) 6353 yards

Halesowen G.C.
(021) 501 3606
The Leasowes, Halesowen
(18) 5673 yards

Handsworth G.C.
(021) 554 0599
Sunningdale Close,
Handsworth,
Birmingham
(18) 6297 yards

Harborne G.C.
(021) 427 1728
Tennal Road, Harborne,
Birmingham
(18) 6240 yards

Hatchford Brook G.C.
(021) 743 9821
Coventry Road, Sheldon,
Birmingham
(18) 6164 yards

Hearsall G.C.
(0203) 713470
Beechwood Avenue,
Coventry
(18) 5951 yards

Hill Top G.C.
(021) 554 4463
Park Lane, Handsworth,
Birmingham
(18) 6200 yards

Himley Hall G.C.
(0902) 895207
Himley Hall Park, Dudley
(9) 3090 yards

Kings Norton G.C.
(0564) 826706
Brockhill Lane, Weatheroak,
Alvechurch
(18) 6754 yards
(9) 3290 yards

Ladbrook Park G.C.
(05644) 2264
Poolhead Lane,
Tanworth-in-Arden, Solihull
(18) 6407 yards

Lickey Hills G.C.
(021) 453 3159
Rednal, Birmingham
(18) 6010 yards

Little Aston G.C.
(021) 353 2066
Streetly, Sutton Coldfield
(18) 6724 yards

Maxstone Park G.C.
(0203) 64915
Castle Lane, Coleshill,
Birmingham
(18) 6437 yards

Moor Hall G.C.
(021) 308 6130
Moor Hall Park,
Sutton Coldfield
(18) 6249 yards

Moseley G.C.
(021) 444 4957
Springfield Road,
Kings Heath,
Birmingham
(18) 6227 yards

North Warwickshire G.C.
(0676) 22259
Hampton Lane, Meriden,
Coventry
(9) 6362 yards

**North Worcestershire
G.C.**
(021) 475 1047
Northfield, Birmingham
(18) 5919 yards

Olton G.C.
(021) 705 7296
Mirfield Road, Solihull
(18) 6229 yards

Oxley Park G.C.
(0902) 25445
Bushbury, Wolverhampton
(18) 6153 yards

Penn G.C.
(0902) 341142
Penn Common,
Wolverhampton
(18) 6449 yards

Pype Hayes G.C.
(021) 351 1014
Walmley, Sutton Coldfield
(18) 5811 yards

Robin Hood G.C.
(021) 706 0061
St Bernards Road, Solihull
(18) 6609 yards

Sandwell Park G.C.
(021) 553 4637
Birmingham Road,
West Bromwich
(18) 6470 yards

Shirley G.C.
(021) 744 6001
Stratford Road, Solihull
(18) 6445 yards

South Staffordshire G.C.
(0902) 751065
Danescourt Road, Tettenhall,
Wolverhampton
(18) 6538 yards

Stourbridge G.C.
(0384) 395566
Pedmore, Stourbridge
(18) 6178 yards

Sutton Coldfield G.C.
(021) 353 9633
Thornhill Road,
Sutton Coldfield
(18) 6541 yards

Walmley G.C.
(021) 373 0029
Wylde Green,
Sutton Coldfield
(18) 6340 yards

Walsall G.C.
(0922) 613512
The Broadway, Walsall
(18) 6232 yards

Warley G.C.
(021) 429 2440
Lightwood Hill, Warley
(9) 5212 yards

WEST SUSSEX

Bognor Regis G.C.
(0243) 821929
Downview Road, Felpham,
Bognor
Regis
(18) 6238 yards

Copthorne G.C.
(0342) 712508
Borers Arms Road,
Copthorne
(18) 6505 yards

Cottesmore G.C.
(0293) 28256
Buchan Hill, Crawley
(18) 6097 yards (North)
(18) 5321 yards (South)

Cowdray Park G.C.
(073081) 3599
Midhurst
(18) 6212 yards

Effingham Park G.C.
(0342) 716528
Copthorne
(9) 1749 yards

Goodwood G.C.
(0243) 774968
Goodwood, Chichester
(18) 6370 yards

Ham Manor G.C.
(0903) 783288
Angmering
(18) 6216 yards

Haywards Heath G.C.
(0444) 414457
High Beech Lane, Haywards
Heath
(18) 6202 yards

Hill Barn G.C.
(0903) 37301
Hill Barn Lane, Worthing
(18) 6224 yards

Ifield G. & C.C.
(0293) 20222
Rusper Road, Ifield, Crawley
(18) 6289 yards

Littlehampton G.C.
(0903) 717170
Rope Walk, Littlehampton
(18) 6202 yards

Mannings Heath G.C.
(0403) 210228
Goldings Lane,
Mannings Heath
(18) 6402 yards

Selsey G.C.
(0243) 602203
Golf Links Lane, Selsey
(9) 5932 yards

Tilgate Forest G.C.
(0293) 30103
Titmus Drive, Tilgate,
Crawley
(18) 6359 yards

West Chiltington G.C.
(07983) 3574
Broadford Road,
West Chiltington
(18) 5969 yards

West Sussex G.C.
(07982) 2563
Pulborough
(18) 6156 yards

Worthing G.C.
(0903) 60801
Links Road, Worthing
(18) 6519 yards (Lower)
(18) 5243 yards (Upper)

WEST YORKSHIRE

Alwoodley G.C.
(0532) 681680
Wigton Lane, Alwoodley,
Leeds
(18) 6686 yards

Baildon G.C.
(0274) 595162
Baildon, Shipley
(18) 6085 yards

Ben Rhydding G.C.
(0943) 608759
Ben Rhydding, Ilkley
(9) 4711 yards

Bingley St Ives G.C.
(0274) 562506
Harden, Bingley
(18) 6480 yards

Bradford G.C.
(0943) 75570
Hawksworth Lane, Guisley
(18) 6259 yards

Bradford Moor G.C.
(0274) 638313
Pollard Lane, Bradford
(9) 5854 yards

Bradley Park G.C.
(0484) 539988
Bradley Road, Huddersfield
(18) 6100 yards

Branshaw G.C.
(0535) 43235
Oakworth, Keighley
(18) 5790 yards

City of Wakefield G.C.
(0924) 360282
Luspet Park, Wakefield
(18) 6405 yards

Clayton G.C.
(0724) 880047
Thornton View Road,
Clayton,
Bradford
(9) 5527 yards

**Cleckheaton & District
G.C.**
(0274) 877851
Bradford Road, Cleckheaton
(18) 5994 yards

Crosland Heath G.C.
(0484) 653262
Crosland Heath,
Huddersfield
(18) 5962 yards

Dewsbury District G.C.
(0924) 492399
Sands Lane, Mirfield
(18) 6226 yards

East Bierley G.C.
(0274) 681023
South View Road, Bierley,
Bradford
(9) 4692 yards

Elland G.C.
(0422) 372505
Leach Lane, Elland
(9) 5526 yards

Fulneck G.C.
(0532) 565191
Pudsey
(9) 5432 yards

Garforth G.C.
(0532) 863308
Long Lane, Garforth, Leeds
(18) 6327 yards

Gott's Park G.C.
(0532) 638232
Armley Ridge Road, Leeds
(18) 4449 yards

Halifax G.C.
(0422) 244171
Union Lane, Ogden, Halifax
(18) 6038 yards

Halifax Bradley Hall G.C.
(0422) 70231
Holywell Green, Halifax
(18) 6213 yards

Hanging Heaton G.C.
(0924) 461729
Bennett Lane, Dewsbury
(9) 5874 yards

Headingley G.C.
(0532) 679573
Back Church Lane, Adel,
Leeds
(18) 6238 yards

Headley G.C.
(0274) 833481
Thornton, Bradford
(9) 4918 yards

Horsforth G.C.
(0532) 585200
Horsforth, Leeds
(18) 6293 yards

Howley Hall G.C.
(0924) 478417
Scotchman Lane, Morley,
Leeds
(18) 6209 yards

Huddersfield G.C.
(0484) 426203
Fixby Hall, Huddersfield
(18) 6424 yards

Ilkley G.C.
(0943) 600214
Myddleton, Ilkley
(18) 6249 yards

Keighley G.C.
(0535) 604778
Howden Park, Keighley
(18) 6139 yards

Leeds G.C.
(0532) 658775
Elmete Lane, Roundhay,
Leeds
(18) 6097 yards

Lightcliffe G.C.
(0422) 202459
Knowle Top Road, Lightcliffe
(9) 5888 yards

Longley Park G.C.
(0484) 422304
Maple Street, Huddersfield
(9) 5269 yards

Low Laithes G.C.
(0924) 274667
Flushdyke, Ossett
(18) 6440 yards

Marsden G.C.
(0484) 844253
Hemplow, Marsden
(9) 5702 yards

Meltham G.C.
(0484) 850227
Meltham, Huddersfield
(18) 6145 yards

Middleton Park G.C.
(0532) 700449
Middleton Park, Leeds
(18) 5233 yards

Moor Allerton G.C.
(0532) 661154
Coal Road, Wike, Leeds
(9) 3242 yards
(9) 3138 yards
(9) 3441 yards

Moortown G.C.
(0532) 686521
Harrogate Road, Leeds
(18) 6544 yards

Mount Skip G.C.
(0422) 842896
Wadsworth, Hebden Bridge
(9) 5114 yards

Normanton G.C.
(0924) 220134
Syndale Road, Normanton
(9) 5284 yards

Northcliffe G.C.
(0274) 596731
High Bank Lane
(18) 6093 yards

Otley G.C.
(0943) 463403
West Busk Lane, Otley
(18) 6225 yards

Outlane G.C.
(0422) 74762
Outlane, Huddersfield
(18) 5590 yards

Painthorpe G.C.
(0924) 255083
Crigglestone, Wakefield
(9) 4108 yards

Phoenix Park G.C.
(0274) 667178
Phoenix Park, Thornbury
(9) 4982 yards

Pontefract & District G.C.
(0977) 792115
Park Lane, Pontefract
(18) 6227 yards

Queensbury G.C.
(0274) 882155
Brighouse Road, Queensbury
(9) 5102 yards

Rawdon G.C.
(0532) 506040
Rawdon, Leeds
(9) 5964 yards

Riddlesden G.C.
(0535) 602148
Riddleston, Keighley
(18) 4247 yards

Roundhay G.C.
(0532) 661686
Park Lane, Leeds
(9) 5166 yards

Sand Moor G.C.
(0532) 683925
Alwoodley Lane, Leeds
(18) 6429 yards

Scarcroft G.C.
(0532) 892311
Skye Lane, Leeds
(18) 6426 yards

Shipley G.C.
(0274) 568652
Cottingley Bridge, Bingley
(18) 6203 yards

Silsden G.C.
(0535) 52998
Silsden, Keighley
(14) 4780 yards

South Bradford G.C.
(0274) 676911
Odsal, Bradford
(9) 6004 yards

South Leeds G.C.
(0532) 771676
Gipsy Lane, Leeds
(18) 5835 yards

Temple Newsam G.C.
(0532) 645624
Temple Newsam Road, Leeds
(18) 6448 yards
(18) 6029 yards

Wakefield G.C.
(0924) 255380
Sandal, Wakefield
(18) 6626 yards

West Bowling G.C.
(0274) 393207
Rooley Lane, Bradford
(18) 5756 yards

West Bradford G.C.
(0274) 542767
Haworth Road, Bradford
(18) 5752 yards

West End G.C.
(0422) 363293
Highroad Well, Halifax
(18) 6003 yards

Wetherby G.C.
(0937) 62527
Linton Lane, Wetherby
(18) 6244 yards

Whitwood G.C.
(0997) 558596
Whitwood, Castleford
(9) 6176 yards

Woodhall Hills G.C.
(0532) 554594
Calverley, Rudsey
(18) 6102 yards

Woodsome Hall G.C.
(0484) 602971
Fenay Bridge, Huddersfield
(18) 6068 yards

WILTSHIRE

Bremhill Park G.C.
(0793) 782946
Shrivenham, Swindon
(18) 6040 yards

Brinkworth G.C.
(066641) 277
Brinkworth,
Chippenham
(18) 6086 yards

Broome Manor G.C.
(0793) 532403
Pipers Way, Swindon
(18) 6359 yards
(9) 5610 yards

Chippenham G.C.
(0249) 652040
Malmesbury Road,
Chippenham
(18) 5540 yards

High Post G.C.
(0722) 73356
Great Durnford, Salisbury
(18) 6267 yards

Kingsdown G.C.
(0225) 73219
Kingsdown, Corsham
(18) 6445 yards

Marlborough G.C.
(0672) 52147
The Common, Marlborough
(18) 6440 yards

North Wilts G.C.
(038068) 627
Bishops Cannings, Devizes
(18) 6450 yards

R.A.F. Upavon G.C.
(0980) 630787
R.A.F. Upavon, Pewsey
(9) 5597 yards

Salisbury & South Wilts G.C.
(0722) 742645
Netherhampton, Salisbury
(18) 6189 yards
(9) 4848 yards

Swindon G.C.
(067284) 287
Ogbourne St George,
Marlborough
(18) 6226 yards

Tidworth Garrison G.C.
(0980) 42321
Bulford Road, Tidworth
(18) 5990 yards

West Wilts G.C.
(0985) 212110
Elm Hill, Warminster
(18) 5701 yards

Little Aston

SCOTLAND

BORDERS

Duns G.C.
(0361) 82717
Hardens Road, Duns
(9) 5826 yards

Eyemouth G.C.
(08907) 50551
Gunsgreen Road, Eyemouth
(9) 5446 yards

Galashiels G.C.
(0896) 3724
Ladhope Recreation Ground
Galashiels
(18) 5309 yards

Hawick G.C.
(0450) 72293
Vertish Hill, Hawick
(18) 5929 yards

Innerliethen G.C.
(0896) 830951
Innerliethen Water
(9) 5820 yards

Jedburgh G.C.
(0835) 63587
Dunion Road, Jedburgh
(9) 5520 yards

Kelso G.C.
(0573) 23009
Racecourse Road, Kelso
(18) 6066 yards

Lauder G.C.
(05782) 409
Galashiels Road, Lauder
(9) 6002 yards

Melrose G.C.
(089682) 2855
Dingleton, Melrose
(9) 5464 yards

Minto G.C.
(0450) 72267
Minto Village, Denholm,
Hawick
(18) 5460 yards

Peebles G.C.
(0721) 20153
Kirkland Street, Peebles
(18) 6137 yards

St Boswells G.C.
(0835) 22359
St Boswells
(9) 5054 yards

Selkirk G.C.
(0750) 20621
The Hill, Selkirk
(9) 5560 yards

West Linton G.C.
(0968) 60256
West Linton
(18) 5835 yards

CENTRAL

Aberfoyle G.C.
(087 72) 441
Braval, Aberfoyle, Stirling
(18) 5205 yards

Alloa G.C.
(0259) 722745
Schawpark, Sauchie, Alloa
(18) 6230 yards

Alva G.C.
(0259) 60431
Beauclerc Street, Alva
(9) 4574 yards

Bonnybridge G.C.
(0324) 812645
Larbert Road, Bonnybridge
(9) 6058 yards

Braehead G.C.
(0259) 722078
Cambus, Alloa
(18) 6013 yards

Bridge of Allan G.C.
(0786) 832332
Sunnylaw, Bridge of Allan
(9) 4932 yards

Buchanan Castle G.C.
(0360) 60307
Drymen
(18) 6032 yards

Callander G.C.
(0877) 30090
Aveland Road, Callander
(18) 5125 yards

Dollar G.C.
(02594) 2400
Brewlands House, Dollar
(18) 5144 yards

Dunblane New G.C.
(0786) 823711
Perth Road, Dunblane
(18) 5878 yards

Falkirk G.C.
(0324) 611061
Stirling Road, Falkirk
(18) 6090 yards

Falkirk Tryst G.C.
(0324) 562091
Burnhead Road, Larbert
(18) 6053 yards

Glenbervie G.C.
(0324) 562605
Stirling Road, Larbert
(18) 6452 yards

Grangemouth G.C.
(0324) 711500
Polmont, Falkirk
(18) 6339 yards

Muckhart G.C.
(025981) 423
Dramburn Road, Muckhart,
Dollar
(18) 6115 yards

Polmont G.C.
(0324) 711277
Maddison, Falkirk
(9) 6088 yards

Stirling G.C.
(0786) 64098
Queens Road, Stirling
(18) 6409 yards

Tillicoultry G.C.
(0259) 50741
Alva Road, Tillicoultry
(9) 5256 yards

Tulliallan G.C.
(0259) 30897
Alloa Road, Kincardine,
Alloa
(18) 5982 yards

DUMFRIES & GALLOWAY

Castle Douglas G.C.
(0556) 2801
Abercromby Road,
Castle Douglas
(9) 5408 yards

Colvend G.C.
(055663) 398
Sandyhills, Dalbeattie
(9) 4208 yards

Dumfries & County G.C.
(0387) 62045
Edinburgh Road, Dumfries
(18) 5914 yards

Dumfries & Galloway G.C.
(0387) 63848
Laurieston Avenue, Dumfries
(18) 5782 yards

Kirkcudbright G.C.
(0557) 30542
Stirling Crescent,
Kirkcudbright
(18) 5598 yards

Langholm G.C.
(0541) 80429
Langholm
(9) 2872 yards

Lochmaben G.C.
(038781) 0552
Castlehill Gate, Lochmaben
(9) 5338 yards

Lockerbie G.C.
(05762) 2165
Currie Road, Lockerbie
(18) 5228 yards

Moffatt G.C.
(06833) 20020
Coateshill, Moffatt
(18) 5218 yards

Newton Stewart G.C.
(0671) 2172
Newton Stewart
(9) 5512 yards

Portpatrick (Dunskey) G.C.
(077681) 273
Portpatrick, Stranraer
(18) 5644 yards

Powfoot G.C.
(04612) 2866
Cummertrees, Annan
(18) 6283 yards

Sanquhar G.C.
(0659) 50577
Old Barr Road, Sanquhar
(9) 5144 yards

Southerness G.C.
(038788) 677
Southerness
(18) 6554 yards

Stranraer G.C.
(0776) 87245
Creachmore, Stranraer
(18) 6300 yards

Thornhill G.C.
(0848) 30546
Blacknest, Thornhill
(18) 6011 yards

Wigtown & Bladnoch G.C.
(09884) 3354
Wigtown
(9) 5462 yards

Wigtownshire County G.C.
(05813) 420
Mains of Park, Glenluce
(9) 5826 yards

FIFE

Aberdour G.C.
(0383) 860353
Seaside Place, Aberdour
(18) 5469 yards

Anstruther G.C.
(0333) 312055
Anstruther
(9) 4504 yards

Auchterderran G.C.
(0592) 721579
Woodend Road, Cardenden
(9) 5250 yards

Balbirnie Park G.C.
(0592) 752006
Balbirnie Park, Markinch,
Glenrothes
(18) 6444 yards

Ballingry G.C.
(0592) 860086
Crosshill, Lochgelly
(9) 6244 yards

Burntisland Golf House Club
(0592) 874093
Dodhead, Burntisland
(18) 5871 yards

Canmore G.C.
(0383) 726098
Venturefair Avenue,
Dunfermline
(18) 5474 yards

Crail Golfing Society
(0333) 50278
Balcomie Clubhouse,
Fifeness,
Crail
(18) 5720 yards

Cupar G.C.
(0334) 53549
Cupar
(9) 5074 yards

Dunfermline G.C.
(0383) 723534
Pitfirrane, Crossford,
Dunfermline
(18) 6271 yards

Dunnikier Park G.C.
(0592) 267462
Dunnikier Way, Kirkcaldy
(18) 6601 yards

Glenrothes G.C.
(0592) 758686
Golf Course Road,
Glenrothes
(18) 6444 yards

Golf House Club (Elie)
(0333) 330301
Elie, Leven
(18) 6241 yards

Kinghorn G.C.
(0592) 890345
Macduff Crescent, Kinghorn
(18) 5269 yards

Kirkcaldy G.C.
(0592) 203258
Balwearie Road, Kirkcaldy
(18) 6007 yards

Ladybank G.C.
(0337) 30814
Annsmuir, Ladybank
(18) 6617 yards

Leslie G.C.
Leslie 741449
Balsillie Laws, Leslie
(9) 4686 yards

Leven Links
(0333) 23509
Links Road, Leven
(18) 6434 yards

Leven Municipal
(0333) 27057
Leven Links
(18) 5403 yards

Lochgelly G.C.
(0592) 780174
Cartmore Road, Lochgelly
(18) 5491 yards

Lundin Links
(0333) 320202
Golf Road, Lundin Links
(18) 6377 yards

Lundin Ladies G.C.
(0333) 320022
Woodiela Road,
Lundin Links
(9) 4730 yards

Pitreavie G.C.
(0383) 722591
Queensferry Road,
Dunfermline
(18) 6086 yards

St Andrews
(0334) 75757
St Andrews
(18) 6933 yards (Old)
(18) 6604 yards (New)
(18) 6284 yards (Jubilee)
(18) 5971 yards (Eden)

St Michaels G.C.
(033483) 365
Leuchars
(9) 5510 yards

Saline G.C.
(0383) 852591
Kineddar Hill, Saline
(9) 5302 yards

Scotscraig G.C.
(0382) 730880
Golf Road, Tayport
(18) 6486 yards

Thornton G.C.
(0592) 771111
Station Road, Thornton
(18) 6177 yards

GRAMPIAN

Aboyne G.C.
(03398) 86328
Formaston Park, Aboyne
(18) 5330 yards

Auchinblae G.C.
Auchinblae
(9) 4748 yards

Auchmill G.C.
(0224) 642121
Auchmill, Aberdeen
(9) 5500 yards

Ballater G.C.
(03397) 55567
Ballater
(18) 6106 yards

Balnagesk G.C.
(0224) 876407
St. Fittick's Road, Aberdeen
(18) 5975 yards

Banchory G.C.
(03302) 2365
Kinneskie, Banchory
(18) 5271 yards

Braemar G.C.
(033083) 618
Cluniebank, Braemar
(18) 5011 yards

Buckpool G.C.
(0542) 32236
Barhill Road, Buckie
(18) 6257 yards

Cruden Bay G.C.
(0779) 812285
Aulton Road, Cruden Bay
(18) 6401 yards (Championship)
(9) 4710 yards (St. Olaf)

Cullen G.C.
(0542) 40685
The Links, Cullen
(18) 4610 yards

Deeside G.C.
(0224) 867697
Bieldside, Aberdeen
(18) 5972 yards

Duff House Royal G.C.
(02612) 2062
Barnyards, Banff
(18) 6161 yards

Dufftown G.C.
(0340) 20325
Dufftown
(9) 4556 yards

Elgin G.C.
(0343) 542338
Birnie Road, Elgin
(18) 6401 yards

Fraserburgh G.C.
(0346) 28287
Philarth, Fraserburgh
(18) 6217 yards

Hazelhead G.C.
(0224) 317336
Hazelhead Park, Aberdeen
(18) 6595 yards
(9) 5205 yards

Huntly G.C.
(0466) 2643
Cooper Park, Huntly
(18) 5399 yards

Inverallochy G.C.
(03465) 2324
Inverlallochy, Fraserburgh
(18) 5137 yards

Inverurie G.C.
(0467) 24080
Blackhall Road, Inverurie
(18) 5703 yards

Keith G.C.
(05422) 2469
Fife Park, Keith
(18) 5745 yards

Kings Links
(0224) 632269
Kings Links, Aberdeen
(18) 6520 yards

Kintore G.C.
(0467) 32631
Kintore, Inverurie
(9) 5240 yards

McDonald G.C.
(0358) 20576
Hospital Road, Ellon
(18) 5986 yards

Moray G.C.
(034381) 2018
Stotfield Road, Lossiemouth
(18) 6258 yards (New)
(18) 6643 yards (Old)

Murcar G.C.
(0224) 704370
Bridge of Don, Aberdeen
(18) 6240 yards

Newburgh-on-Ythan G.C.
(03586) 389
Millend, Newburgh
(9) 6404 yards

Old Meldrum G.C.
(06512) 2212
Old Meldrum
(9) 5252 yards

Peterhead G.C.
(0779) 72149
Craigewan Links, Peterhead
(18) 6070 yards

Royal Aberdeen G.C.
(0224) 702221
Balgownie, Bridge of Don, Aberdeen
(18) 6372 yards
(18) 4003 yards

Royal Tarlair G.C.
(0261) 32897
Buchan Street, Macduff
(18) 5866 yards

Spey Bay G.C.
(0343) 820424
Spey Bay, Fochabers
(18) 6059 yards

Stonehaven G.C.
(0569) 62124
Cowie, Stonehaven
(18) 5103 yards

Strathiene G.C.
(0542) 31798
Buckie
(18) 5957 yards

Tarland G.C.
(033981) 413
Tarland, Aboyne
(9) 5812 yards

Torphine G.C.
(033982) 493
Golf Road, Torphine
(9) 2330 yards

Turriff G.C.
(0888) 62745
Rosehall, Turriff
(18) 6105 yards

Westhill G.C.
(0224) 740159
Westhill, Skene
(18) 5866 yards

HIGHLAND

Abernethy G.C.
(047982) 637
Nethybridge
(9) 2484 yards

Alness G.C.
(0349) 883877
Ardross Road, Alness
(9) 4718 yards

Boat-of-Garten G.C.
(047983) 282
Boat-of-Garten
(18) 5720 yards

Bonar Bridge G.C.
(054982) 248
Bonar Bridge
(9) 4616 yards

Muirfield

Brora G.C.
(0408) 21475
Golf Road, Brora
(18) 6110 yards

Carrbridge G.C.
(047986) 674
Carrbridge
(9) 5250 yards

Forres G.C.
(0309) 72949
Muiryshade, Forres
(18) 6141 yards

Fort Augustus G.C.
(0320) 6460
Markethill, Fort Augustus
(9) 5454 yards

**Fortrose & Rosemarkie
G.C.**
(0381) 20529
Ness Road East, Fortrose
(18) 5964 yards

Fort William G.C.
(0397) 4464
North Road, Fort William
(18) 5640 yards

Gairloch G.C.
(0445) 2407
Gairloch
(9) 4186 yards

**Garmouth & Kingston
G.C.**
(034387) 388
Garmouth Road, Fochabers
(18) 5649 yards

Golspie G.C.
(04083) 3266
Ferry Road, Golspie
(18) 5763 yards

Grantown-on-Spey G.C.
(0479) 2667
Golf Course Road,
Grantown-on-Spey
(18) 5672 yards

Hopeman G.C.
(0348) 830578
Hopeman
(18) 5439 yards

Invergordon G.C.
(0349) 852116
Cromlet Drive, Invergordon
(9) 6028 yards

Inverness G.C.
(0463) 239882
Culcabock Road, Inverness
(18) 6226 yards

Kingussie G.C.
(0540) 661600
Bynack Road, Kingussie
(18) 5466 yards

Lybster G.C.
(05932) 359
Main Street, Lybster
(9) 3770 yards

Muir of Ord G.C.
(0463) 870825
Great Northern Road, Muir
of Ord
(18) 5022 yards

Nairn G.C.
(0667) 53208
Seabank Road, Nairn
(18) 6452 yards

Nairn Dunbar G.C.
(0667) 52741
Lochloy Road, Nairn
(18) 6431 yards

Newtonmore G.C.
(05403) 328
Golf Course Road,
Newtonmore
(18) 5890 yards

Orkney G.C.
(0856) 2457
Grainbank, Kirkwall, Orkney
(18) 5406 yards

Reay G.C.
(084781) 288
Reay, Thurso
(18) 5876 yards

Royal Dornoch G.C.
(0862) 810902
Golf Road, Dornoch
(18) 6577 yards
(9) 2485 yards

Sconser G.C.
(0478) 2364
Sconser, Isle of Skye
(9) 4796 yards

Shetland G.C.
(059584) 369
Dale, Shetland
(18) 5791 yards

Stornoway G.C.
(0851) 2240
Lady Lever Park, Stornoway,
Isle of Lewis
(18) 5119 yards

Strathpeffer Spa G.C.
(0997) 21219
Strathpeffer
(18) 4813 yards

Stromness G.C.
(0856) 850772
Ness, Stromness, Orkney
(18) 4665 yards

Tain G.C.
(0862) 2314
Tain
(18) 6222 yards

Tarbat G.C.
(086287) 519
Portmahomack
(9) 4656 yards

Thurso G.C.
(0847) 63807
Newlands of Geise, Thurso
(18) 5818 yards

Torvean G.C.
(0463) 237543
Glenurquart Road, Inverness
(18) 4308 yards

Wick G.C.
(0955) 2726
Reiss, Wick
(18) 5976 yards

LOTHIAN

Baberton G.C.
(031) 453 4911
Juniper Green, Edinburgh
(18) 6098 yards

Bathgate G.C.
(0506) 630505
Edinburgh Road, Bathgate
(18) 6326 yards

Braids United G.C.
(031) 447 6666
Braids Hill Approach,
Edinburgh
(18) 5731 yards (No. 1)
(18) 4832 yards (no. 2)

Broomieknowe G.C.
(031) 663 9317
Golf Course Road,
Bonnyrigg
(18) 6046 yards

Bruntsfield Links Golfing Society
(031) 336 1479
Barnton Avenue, Edinburgh
(18) 6407 yards

Craigmillar Park G.C.
(031) 667 2837
Observatory Road,
Edinburgh
(18) 5846 yards

Dalmahoy Hotel G. & C.C.
(031) 449 3975
Dalmahoy, Kirknewton
(18) 6664 yards (East)
(18) 5212 yards (West)

Deer Park G. & C.C.
(0506) 38843
Livingston
(18) 6636 yards

Duddingston G.C.
(031) 661 7688
Duddingston Road,
Edinburgh
(18) 6647 yards

Dunbar G.C.
(0368) 62317
East Links, Dunbar
(18) 6426 yards

Dundas Park G.C.
(031) 331 3090
South Queensferry
(9) 6026 yards

East Links G.C.
(0620) 2340
East Links, North Berwick
(18) 6079 yards

Gifford G.C.
(062081) 267
Station Road, Gifford
(9) 6138 yards

Glencorse G.C.
(0968) 77189
Milton Bridge, Penicuik
(18) 5205 yards

Greenburn G.C.
(0501) 70292
Bridge Street, Fauldhouse
(18) 6210 yards

Gullane G.C.
(0620) 842255
Gullane
(18) 6479 yards (No. 1)
(18) 6127 yards (No. 2)
(18) 5035 yards (No. 3)

Honourable Company of Edinburgh Golfers (Muirfield)
(0620) 842123
Muirfield, Gullane
(18) 6941 yards

Kilspindie G.C.
(0875) 358
Aberlady
(18) 5410 yards

Kingsknowe G.C.
(031) 441 1145
Lanark Road, Edinburgh
(18) 5979 yards

Linlithgow G.C.
(0506) 842585
Braehead, Linlithgow
(18) 5858 yards

Longniddry G.C.
(0875) 52141
Links Road, Longniddry
(18) 6210 yards

Lothianburn G.C
(031) 445 2288
Biggar Road, Edinburgh
(18) 5671 yards

Luffness New G.C.
(0620) 843336
Aberlady
(18) 6085 yards

Merchants of Edinburgh G.C.
(031) 447 1219
Craighill Gardens, Edinburgh
(18) 4889 yards

Mortonhall G.C.
(031) 447 6974
Braid Road, Edinburgh
(18) 6557 yards

Murrayfield G.C.
(031) 337 3478
Murrayfield Road,
Edinburgh
(18) 5727 yards

Muirfield (see Hon. Co. of Edinburgh Golfers)

Musselburgh G.C.
(031) 665 2005
Monktonhall, Musselburgh
(18) 6623 yards

Newbattle G.C.
(031) 663 2123
Abbey Road, Dalkeith
(18) 6012 yards

North Berwick G.C.
(0620) 2135
West Links, Beach Road,
North Berwick
(18) 6298 yards

Prestonfield G.C.
(031) 667 9665
Piestfield Road North,
Edinburgh
(18) 6216 yards

Ratho Park G.C.
(031) 333 1752
Ratho, Newbridge
(18) 6028 yards

Royal Burgess Golfing Society
(031) 339 2075
Whitehouse Road, Barton,
Edinburgh
(18) 6604 yards

Royal Musselburgh G.C.
(0875) 810276
Prestongrange House,
Prestonpans
(18) 6204 yards

Silverknowes G.C.
(031) 336 5359
Silverknowes, Parkway,
Edinburgh
(18) 6210 yards

Swanston G.C.
(031) 445 2239
Swanston Road, Edinburgh
(18) 5024 yards

Torphin Hill G.C.
(031) 441 1100
Torphin Road, Colinton,
Edinburgh
(18) 5030 yards

Turnhouse G.C.
(031) 339 7701
Turnhouse Road, Edinburgh
(18) 6171 yards

Uphall G.C.
(0506) 856404
Uphall
(18) 5567 yards

West Lothian G.C.
(0506) 826030
Airngath Hill, Linlithgow
(18) 6629 yards

Winterfield G.C.
(0368) 62564
North Road, Dunbar
(18) 5053 yards

STRATHCLYDE

Airdrie G.C.
(0236) 62195
Rochsoles, Airdrie
(18) 6004 yards

Alexandra Park Municipal G.C.
(041) 556 3711
Alexandra Parade, Glasgow
(9) 4562 yards

Annanhill G.C.
(0563) 21644
Irvine Road, Kilmarnock
(18) 6269 yards

Ardeer G.C.
(0294) 64035
Greenhead, Stevenston
(18) 6630 yards

Ayr Belleisle G.C.
(0292) 41258
Belleisle Park, Ayr
(18) 6540 yards (Belleisle)
(18) 5244 yards (Seafield)

Ayr Dalmilling G.C.
(0292) 263893
Westwood Avenue, Ayr
(18) 5401 yards

Ballochmyle G.C.
(0290) 50469
Ballochmyle, Mauchline
(18) 5952 yards

Balmore G.C.
(041) 332 0392
Balmore, Torrance
(18) 5735 yards

Barshaw G.C.
(041) 884 2533
Barshaw Park, Paisley
(18) 5703 yards

Bearsden G.C.
(041) 942 2351
Thorn Road, Bearsden,
Glasgow
(9) 5977 yards

Beith G.C.
(05055) 2011
Bigholm, Beith
(9) 5488 yards

Bellshill G.C.
(0698) 745124
Orbiston, Bellshill
(18) 6607 yards

Biggar G.C.
(0899) 20618
Broughton Road, Biggar
(18) 5256 yards

Bishopbriggs G.C.
(041) 772 1810
Brackenbrae Road,
Bishopbriggs,
Glasgow
(18) 6041 yards

Blairbeth G.C.
(041) 634 3355
Rutherglen, Glasgow
(18) 5448 yards

Blairmore & Strone G.C.
(036984) 217
Blairmore, Argyll
(9) 4224 yards

Bonnyton G.C.
(03553) 2256
Eaglesham, Glasgow
(18) 6252 yards

Bothwell Castle G.C.
(0698) 853177
Blantyre Road, Bothwell,
Glasgow
(18) 6432 yards

Brodick G.C.
(0770) 2513
Brodick, Isle of Arran
(18) 4404 yards

Bute G.C.
(0700) 83242
Kilchaltan Bay, Bute
(9) 5594 yards

Calderbraes G.C.
(0698) 813425
Roundknowe Road,
Uddingston
(9) 5186 yards

Caldwell G.C.
(050585) 616
Uplawnmoor
(18) 6102 yards

Cambuslang G.C.
(041) 641 3130
Westburn Drive,
Cambuslang,
Glasgow
(9) 6072 yards

Campsie G.C.
(0360) 310244
Crow Road, Lennoxtown,
Glasgow
(18) 5517 yards

Caprington G.C.
(0563) 23702
Ayr Road, Kilmarnock
(18) 5718 yards

Cardross G.C.
(0389) 841350
Main Road, Cardross,
Dumbarton
(18) 6466 yards

Carluke G.C.
(0555) 71070
Hallcraig, Carluke
(18) 5805 yards

Carnwath G.C.
(0555) 840251
Main Street, Carnwath
(18) 5860 yards

Carradale G.C.
(05833) 387
Carradale, Argyll
(9) 4774 yards

Cathcart Castle G.C.
(041) 638 9449
Mearns Road, Clarkston,
Glasgow
(18) 5832 yards

Cathkin Braes G.C.
(041) 634 4007
Cathkin Road, Rutherglen,
Glasgow
(18) 6266 yards

Cawder G.C.
(041) 772 7101
Cadder Road, Bishopbriggs,
Glasgow
(18) 6229 yards (Cawder)
(18) 5877 yards (Keir)

Clober G.C.
(041) 956 1685
Craigton Road, Milngavie
(18) 5068 yards

Clydebank & District G.C.
(0389) 73289
Hardgate, Clydebank
(18) 5815 yards

Clydebank Municipal G.C.
(041) 952 6372
Overtoun Road, Clydebank
(18) 5349 yards

Cochrane Castle G.C.
(0505) 20146
Craigston, Johnstone
(18) 6226 yards

Colonsay G.C.
(09512) 316
Isle of Colonsay
(18) 4775 yards

Colville Park G.C.
(0698) 63017
Jerviston Estate, Motherwell
(18) 6208 yards

Corrie G.C.
(077081) 223
Corrie, Isle of Arran
(9) 3896 yards

Cowal G.C.
(0396) 5673
Kirn, Dunoon
(18) 5820 yards

Cowglen G.C.
(041) 632 0556
Barhead Road, Glasgow
(18) 5976 yards

Crow Wood G.C.
(041) 779 1943
Muirhead, Chryston
(18) 6209 yards

Cumbernauld Municipal G.C.
(02367) 28138
Cumbernauld
(18) 6412 yards

Dougalston G.C.
(041) 956 5750
Milngavie, Glasgow
(18) 6683 yards

Douglas Park G.C.
(041) 942 2220
Hillfoot, Bearsden, Glasgow
(18) 5957 yards

Douglas Water G.C.
(0555) 2295
Douglas Water, Lanark
(9) 5832 yards

Drumpellier G.C.
(0236) 24139
Drumpellier, Coatbridge
(18) 6227 yards

Dullatur G.C.
(02367) 27847
Dullatur, Glasgow
(18) 6253 yards

Dumbarton G.C.
(0389) 32830
Broadmeadow, Dumbarton
(18) 5981 yards

Dunaverty G.C.
(No tel.)
Southend, Campbeltown,
Argyll
(18) 4597 yards

Easter Moffat G.C.
(0236) 21864
Mansion House, Plains,
Airdrie
(18) 6221 yards

East Kilbride G.C.
(03552) 47728
Chapelside Road, Nerston,
East Kilbride
(18) 6419 yards

East Renfrewshire G.C.
(03555) 258
Pilmuir, Newton Mearns,
Glasgow
(18) 6097 yards

Eastwood G.C.
(03555) 280
Muirshield, Newton Mearns,
Glasgow
(18) 5864 yards

Elderslie G.C.
(0505) 23956
Main Road, Elderslie
(18) 6004 yards

Erskine G.C.
(0505) 2302
Bishopston
(18) 6287 yards

Fereneze G.C.
(041) 881 1519
Fereneze Avenue, Barrhead,
Glasgow
(18) 5821 yards

Girvan G.C.
(0465) 4272
Golf Course Road, Girvan
(18) 5075 yards

Glasgow Gailes G.C.
(0294) 311347
Gailes, Irvine
(18) 6447 yards

Glasgow Killermont G.C.
(041) 942 2011
Killermont, Glasgow
(18) 5968 yards

Gleddoch G. & C.C.
(047554) 304
Langbank
(18) 6200 yards

Glencruitten G.C.
(0631) 62868
Glencruitten, Oban
(18) 4452 yards

Gourock G.C.
(0475) 33696
Cowal View, Gourock
(18) 6492 yards

Greenock G.C.
(0475) 20793
Forsyth Street, Greenock
(18) 5838 yards

Greenock Whinhill G.C.
(0475) 210641
Beith Road, Greenock
(18) 5454 yards

Haggs Castle G.C.
(041) 427 1157
Drumbreck Road, Glasgow
(18) 6464 yards

Hamilton G.C.
(0698) 282872
Riccarton, Ferniegair,
Hamilton
(18) 6264 yards

Hayston G.C.
(041) 775 0882
Campsie Road, Kirkintilloch,
Glasgow
(18) 6042 yards

Helensburgh G.C.
(0436) 74173
East Abercromby Street,
Helensburgh
(18) 6058 yards

Hollandbush G.C.
(0555) 893484
Lesmahagow, Coalburn
(18) 6110 yards

Innellan G.C.
(0369) 3546
Innellan, Argyll
(9) 4878 yards

Prestwick

Irvine (Bogside) G.C.
(0294) 75979
Bogside, Irvine
(18) 6450 yards

Irvine Ravenspark G.C.
(0294) 79550
Kidsneuk Road, Irvine
(18) 6496 yards

Kilbirnie Place G.C.
(050582) 683398
Largs Road, Kilbirnie
(18) 5479 yards

Kilmacolm G.C.
(050587) 2695
Porterfield, Kilmacolm
(18) 5964 yards

Kilmarnock (Barassie) G.C.
(0292) 311077
Hillhouse Road, Barassie, Troon
(18) 6473 yards

Kilsyth Lennox G.C.
(0236) 822190
Tak-Ma-Doon Road, Kilsyth, Glasgow
(9) 5944 yards

Kirkhill G.C.
(041) 641 8499
Greenlees Road, Cambuslang, Glasgow
(18) 5889 yards

Kirkintilloch G.C.
(041) 776 1256
Todhill, Campsie Road, Kirkintilloch
(18) 5269 yards

Knightswood G.C.
(041) 959 2131
Lincoln Avenue, Knightswood, Glasgow
(9) 2717 yards

Kyles of Bute G.C.
(0700) 811355
Tighnabruaich, Argyll
(9) 4758 yards

Lamlash G.C.
(07706) 296
Lamlash, Isle of Arran
(18) 4681 yards

Lanark G.C.
(0555) 3219
The Moor, Lanark
(18) 6416 yards

Landoun G.C.
(0563) 821993
Edinburgh Road, Galston
(18) 5824 yards

Largs G.C.
(0475) 672497
Irvine Road, Largs
(18) 6257 yards

Larkhall G.C.
(0698) 881113
Burnhead Road, Larkhall
(9) 6236 yards

Leadhills G.C.
(0659) 74222
Leadhills, Biggar
(9) 4062 yards

Lenzie G.C.
(041) 776 1535
Crosshill Road, Lenzie, Glasgow
(18) 5982 yards

Lethamhill G.C.
(041) 770 6220
Cumbernauld Road, Glasgow
(18) 6073 yards

Linn Park G.C.
(041) 637 5871
Simshill Road, Glasgow
(18) 4832 yards

Littlehill G.C.

(041) 772 1916
Auchinairn Road,
Bishopbriggs,
Glasgow
(18) 6199 yards

Lochranza G.C.

(077083) 273
Brodick, Isle of Arran
(9) 3580 yards

Lochwinnoch G.C.

(0505) 842153
Burnfoot Road,
Lochwinnoch
(18) 6223 yards

Machrie Hotel and G.C.

(0496) 2310
Machrie Hotel, Port Ellen,
Isle of Islay
(18) 6226 yards

Machrie Bay G.C.

(077084) 258
Machrie Bay, Isle of Arran
(9) 4246 yards

Machrihanish G.C.

(0586) 81213
Machrihanish,
Campbeltown,
Argyll
(18) 6228 yards

Maybole G.C.

Maybole 82454
Memorial Park,
Maybole
(9) 5270 yards

Millport G.C.

(0475) 530485
Golf Road, Millport,
Isle of Cumbrae
(18) 5831 yards

Milngavie G.C.

(041) 956 1619
Laigh Park, Milngavie,
Glasgow
(18) 5818 yards

Mount Ellen G.C.

(0236) 782277
Johnston House, Gartcosh,
Glasgow
(18) 5525 yards

Paisley G.C.

(041) 884 2292
Braehead, Paisley
(18) 6424 yards

Pollok G.C.

(041) 632 4351
Barrhead Road, Glasgow
(18) 6257 yards

Port Bannatyne G.C.

(0700) 2009
Port Bannatyne, Isle of Bute
(13) 4654 yards

Port Glasgow G.C.

(0475) 704181
Port Glasgow
(18) 5712 yards

Prestwick G.C.

(0292) 77404
Links Road, Prestwick
(18) 6544 yards

Prestwick St Cuthbert G.C.

(0292) 79120
East Road, Prestwick
(18) 6470 yards

Prestwick St Nicholas G.C.

(0292) 77608
Grangemuir Road, Prestwick
(18) 5926 yards

Raiston G.C.

(041) 882 1349
Raiston, Paisley
(18) 6100 yards

Ranfurly Castle G.C.

(0505) 612609
Golf Road, Bridge of Weir
(18) 6284 yards

Renfrew G.C.

(041) 886 6692
Blythswood Estate,
Inchinnan Road, Renfrew
(18) 6818 yards

Rothesay G.C.

(0700) 2244
Rothesay, Isle of Bute
(18) 5358 yards

Routenburn G.C.

(0475) 674289
Largs
(18) 5650 yards

Royal Troon G.C.

(0292) 311555
Craigend Road, Troon
(18) 6641 yards (Old)
(18) 6274 yards (Portland)

Sandyhills G.C.

(041) 778 1179
Sandyhills Road, Glasgow
(18) 6253 yards

Shiskine G.C.

(077086) 293
Blackwaterfoot, Isle of Arran
(12) 3000 yards

Shotts G.C.

(0501) 20431
Blairhead, Shotts
(18) 6125 yards

Skelmorlie G.C.

(0475) 520152
Skelmorlie
(13) 5056 yards

Strathaven G.C.

(0357) 20421
Overton Avenue,
Glasgow Road,
Strathaven
(18) 6226 yards

Strathclyde Park G.C.

(0698) 66155
Motel Hill, Hamilton
(9) 6294 yards

Tarbert G.C.

(08802) 565
Kilberry Road, Tarbert,
Argyll
(9) 4460 yards

Torrance House G.C.

(03552) 33451
Strathaven Road,
East Kilbride,
Glasgow
(18) 6640 yards

Troon Municipal G.C.

(0292) 312464
Harling Drive, Troon
(18) 6687 yards (Lochgreen)
(18) 6327 yards (Darley)
(18) 4784 yards (Fullarton)

Turnberry Hotel

(0655) 31000
Turnberry Hotel, Turnberry
(18) 6956 yards (Ailsa)
(18) 6276 yards (Arran)

Vaul G.C.

(08792) 566
Scarinish, Isle of Tiree, Argyll
(9) 6246 yards

Western Gailes G.C.

(0294) 311649
Gailes, Irvine
(18) 6614 yards

Western Isles G.C.

(0688) 2020
Tobermory, Isle of Mull
(9) 4920 yards

Westerwood Hotel & G.C.

(0236) 457171
St Andrews Drive,
Cumbernauld
(18) 6800 yards

West Kilbride G.C.

(0294) 823911
Fullerton Drive,
West Kilbride
(18) 6348 yards

Whitecraigs G.C.
(041) 639 4530
Ayr Road, Giffnock, Glasgow
(18) 6230 yards

Whiting Bay G.C.
(07707) 487
Whiting Bay, Isle of Arran
(18) 4405 yards

Williamwood G.C.
(041) 637 2715
Clarkeston Road, Netherlee,
Glasgow
(18) 5878 yards

Windyhill G.C.
(041) 942 7157
Baljaffray Road, Bearsden,
Glasgow
(18) 6254 yards

Wishaw G.C.
(0698) 372869
Cleland Road, Wishaw
(18) 6134 yards

TAYSIDE

Aberfeldy G.C.
(0887) 20203
Taybridge Road, Aberfeldy
(9) 5466 yards

Alyth G.C.
(08283) 2411
Pitcrocknie, Alyth
(18) 6226 yards

Arbroath G.C.
(0241) 72666
Elliot, Arbroath
(18) 6078 yards

Auchterarder G.C.
(07646) 2804
Auchterarder
(18) 5737 yards

Bishopshire G.C.
(0592) 860379
Kinnesswood
(9) 4360 yards

Blair Atholl G.C.
(079681) 274
Blair Atholl
(9) 5710 yards

Blairgowrie G.C.
(0250) 3116
Rosemount, Blairgowrie
(18) 6592 yards (Rosemount)
(18) 6865 yards (Lansdowne)
(9) 4614 yards (Wee)

Brechin G.C.
(03562) 2383
Trinity, Brechin
(18) 5267 yards

Caird Park G.C.
(0382) 44003
Mains Loan, Dundee
(18) 6303 yards

Camperdown (Municipal) G.C.
(0382) 68340
Camperdown Park, Dundee
(18) 6561 yards

Carnoustie
(0241) 53789
Links Parade, Carnoustie
(18) 6931 yards (Championship)
(18) 5935 yards (Burnside)
(18) 6445 yards (Buddon Links)

Comrie G.C.
(0764) 70544
Polinard, Comrie
(9) 5966 yards

Craigie Hill G.C.
(0738) 22644
Cherrybank, Perth
(18) 5379 yards

Crieff G.C.
(0764) 2909
(18) 6363 yards (Ferntower)
(9) 4772 yards (Dornock)

Dalmunzie Hotel G.C.
(025085) 224
Spittal of Glenshee,
Blairgowrie
(9) 4458 yards

Downfield G.C.
(0382) 825595
Turnberry Avenue, Dundee
(18) 6899 yards

Dunkeld & Birnam G.C.
(03502) 524
Fungarth, Dunkeld
(9) 5264 yards

Dunning G.C.
(076484) 398
Rollo Park, Dunning
(9) 4836 yards

Edzell G.C.
(03564) 7283
High Street, Edzell, Brechin
(18) 6299 yards

Forfar G.C.
(0307) 63773
Cunninghill, Arbroath Road,
Forfar
(18) 6255 yards

Glenalmond G.C.
(073888) 270
Trinity College, Glenalmond
(9) 5812 yards

Gleneagles Hotel
(0764) 63543
Gleneagles Hotel,
Auchterarder
(18) 6452 yards (King's)
(18) 5964 yards (Queen's)

Green Hotel G.C.
(0577) 63467
Green Hotel, Kinross
(18) 6339 yards

Killin G.C.
(05672) 312
Killin
(9) 5016 yards

King James VI G.C.
(0738) 32460
Moncrieffe Island, Perth
(18) 6037 yards

Kirriemuir G.C.
(0575) 73317
23 Bank Street, Kirriemuir,
Angus
(18) 5591 yards

Letham Grange G. & C.C.
(0241) 89373
Letham Grange, Colliston,
Arbroath
(18) 6290 yards

Milnathort G.C.
(0577) 64069
South Street, Milnathort
(9) 5918 yards

Monifieth Golf Links
(0382) 533300
Ferry Road, Monifieth
(18) 6657 yards (Medal)
(18) 5123 yards (Ashludie)

Montrose Links
(0674) 72634
Trail Drive, Montrose
(18) 6451 yards (Medal)
(18) 4815 yards (Broomfield)

Murrayshall G.C.
(0738) 52784
Murrayshall, New Scone
(18) 6416 yards

Muthill G.C.
(0764) 3319
Peat Road, Muthill, Crieff
(9) 4742 yards

Panmure G.C.
(0241) 53120
Burnside Road, Barry
(18) 6302 yards

Pitlochry G.C.
(0796) 2792
Golf Course Road, Pitlochry
(18) 5811 yards

St Fillans G.C.
(076485) 312
St Fillans
(9) 5268 yards

Taymouth Castle G.C.
(08873) 228
Kenmore, Aberfeldy
(18) 6066 yards

WALES

CLWYD

Abergele & Pensarn G.C.
(0745) 824034
Tan-y-Goppa Road, Abergele
(18) 6500 yards

Denbigh G.C.
(074571) 4159
Henllan Road, Denbigh
(18) 5650 yards

Flint G.C.
(03526) 2186
Cornist Park, Flint
(9) 5829 yards

Hawarden G.C.
(0244) 531447
Groomsdale Lane, Hawarden
(9) 5735 yards

Holywell G.C.
(0352) 710040
Brynford, Holywell
(9) 6484 yards

Mold G.C.
(0352) 740318
Pantmywyn, Nr. Mold
(18) 5521 yards

Old Colwyn G.C.
(0492) 515581
Old Colwyn, Colwyn Bay
(9) 5268 yards

Old Padeswood G.C.
(0244) 547401
Station Road, Padeswood,
Mold
(18) 6728 yards

**Padeswood & Buckley
G.C.**
(0244) 543636
Station Lane, Padeswood
(18) 5746 yards

Prestatyn G.C.
(07456) 88353
Marine Road East, Prestatyn
(18) 6714 yards

Rhuddlan G.C.
(0745) 590675
Rhuddlan, Rhyl
(18) 6038 yards

Rhyl G.C.
(0745) 53171
Coast Road, Rhyl
(9) 6153 yards

Ruthin-Pwllglas G.C.
(08242) 4658
Ruthin-Pwllglas, Ruthin
(9) 5306 yards

St Melyd G.C.
(07456) 4405
Melyden Road, Prestatyn
(9) 5805 yards

Vale of Llangollen G.C.
(0978) 860050
Holyhead Road, Llangollen
(18) 6617 yards

Wrexham G.C.
(0978) 364268
Holt Road, Wrexham
(18) 6038 yards

DYFED

Aberystwyth G.C.
(0970) 615104
Bryn-y-Mor, Aberystwyth
(18) 5868 yards

Ashburnham G.C.
(05546) 2269
Cliff Terrace, Burry Port
(18) 6916 yards

Borth and Ynyslas G.C.
(097081) 202
Borth
(18) 6094 yards

Cardigan G.C.
(0239) 612035
Gwbert-on-Sea
(18) 6207 yards

Carmarthen G.C.
(0267) 214
Blaenycoed Road,
Carmarthen
(18) 6212 yards

Cilgywn G.C.
(0570) 45286
Llangybi
(9) 5318 yards

Glynhir G.C.
(0269) 850571
Glynhir Road, Llandybie,
Nr. Ammanford
(18) 6090 yards

Haverfordwest G.C.
(0437) 68409
Arnolds Down,
Haverfordwest
(18) 5945 yards

Milford Haven G.C.
(06462) 2521
Milford Haven
(18) 6235 yards

Newport (Pembs) G.C.
(0239) 820244
Newport
(9) 6178 yards

St David's City G.C.
(0437) 720403
Whitesands Bay, St Davids
(9) 5695 yards

**South Pembrokeshire
G.C.**
(0646) 682035
Defensible Barracks,
Pembroke Dock
(9) 5804 yards

Tenby G.C.
(0834) 2978
The Burrows, Tenby
(18) 6232 yards

GWENT

Blackwood G.C.
(0495) 223152
Cwmgelli, Blackwood
(9) 5304 yards

Caerleon G.C.
(0633) 420342
Caerleon, Newport
(9) 6184 yards

Greenmeadow G.C.
(06333) 626262
Treherbert Road, Cwmbran
(9) 6128 yards

Llanwern G.C.
(0633) 415233
Tennyson Avenue, Llanwern
(18) 6202 yards
(9) 5674 yards

Monmouth G.C.
(0600) 2212
Leasebrook Lane, Monmouth
(9) 5434 yards

Monmouthshire G.C.
(0873) 2606
Llanfoist, Abergavenny
(18) 6045 yards

Newport G.C.
(0633) 892643
Great Oak, Rogerstone,
Newport
(18) 6370 yards

Pontnewydd G.C.
(0633) 32170
West Pontnewydd, Cwmbran
(10) 5321 yards

Pontypool G.C.
(04955) 3655
Trevethyn, Pontypool
(18) 6070 yards

Royal Porthcawl

Rolls of Monmouth G.C.
(0600) 5353
The Hendre, Monmouth
(18) 6723 yards

St Mellons G.C.
(0633) 680401
St Mellons, Nr. Cardiff
(18) 6225 yards

St Pierre G. & C.C.
(0291) 625261
St Pierre Park, Chepstow
(18) 6700 yards (Old)
(18) 5762 yards (New)

Tredegar Park G.C.
(0633) 894433
Bassaleg Road, Newport
(18) 6044 yards

Tredegar and Rhymney G.C.
(0685) 894433
Rhymney
(9) 5564 yards

West Monmouthshire G.C.
(0495) 310233
Pond Road, Nantyglo
(18) 6097 yards

GWYNEDD

Aberdovey G.C.
(065472) 493
Aberdovey
(18) 6445 yards

Abersoch G.C.
(075881) 2622
Pwllheli, Abersoch
(9) 5722 yards

Bala G.C.
(0678) 520359
Penlan, Bala
(10) 4934 yards

Betws-y-Coed G.C.
(06902) 556
Betws-y-Coed
(9) 5030 yards

Caernarfon G.C.
(0286) 2642
Llanfaglan, Caernarfon
(18) 5859 yards

Caernarvonshire G.C.
(0492) 592423
Conway
(18) 6901 yards

Criccieth G.C.
(076671) 2154
Ednyfed Hill, Criccieth
(18) 5755 yards

Dolgellau G.C.
(0341) 422603
Pencefn Road, Dolgellau
(9) 4662 yards

Ffestiniog G.C.
(0766) 831829
Blaenau Ffestiniog
(9) 4536 yards

Llandudno (Maesdu) G.C.
(0492) 76450
Hospital Road, Llandudno
(18) 6513 yards

Llanfairfechan G.C.
(0248) 680144
Llanfairfechan
(9) 6238 yards

Nefyn and District G.C.
(0758) 720966
Morfa Nefyn
(18) 6294 yards

North Wales G.C.
(0492) 75325
Bryniau Road, West Shore,
Llandudno
(18) 6132 yards

Penmaenmawr G.C.
(0492) 622085
Conway Old Road,
Penmaenmawr
(9) 5031 yards

Portmadog G.C.
(0766) 513828
Morfa Bychan, Portmadog
(18) 5728 yards

Pwllheli G.C.
(0758) 612520
Golf Road, Pwllheli
(18) 6110 yards

Royal St David's G.C.
(0766) 780361
Harlech
(18) 6495 yards

St Deiniol G.C.
(0248) 353098
Bangor
(18) 5545 yards

ISLE OF ANGLESEY

Anglesey G.C.
(0407) 810219
Rhosneigr
(18) 6204 yards

Baron Hill G.C.
(0248) 810231
Beaumaris
(9) 5564 yards

Bull Bay G.C.
(0407) 830960
Almwch
(18) 6160 yards

Holyhead G.C.
(0407) 2022
Trearddur Bay, Holyhead
(18) 6090 yards

MID GLAMORGAN

Aberdare G.C.
(0685) 878735
Abernant, Aberdare
(18) 5875 yards

Bargoed G.C.
(0443) 830143
Hoelddu, Bargoed
(18) 6012 yards

Bryn Meadows G. & C.C.
(0495) 221905
The Bryn, Nr. Hengoed
(18) 5963 yards

Caerphilly G.C.
(0222) 863441
Mountain Road, Caerphilly
(14) 6063 yards

Castell Heights G.C.
(0222) 861128
Caerphilly
(9) 5376 yards

Creigiau G.C.
(0222) 890263
Creigiau
(18) 5736 yards

Llantrisant and Pontyclun G.C.
(0443) 228169
Talbot Green, Llantrisant
(12) 5712 yards

Maesteg G.C.
(0656) 732037
Mount Pleasant, Maesteg
(18) 5845 yards

Merthyr Tydfil G.C.
(0685) 3063
Cilsanws Mountain,
Cefn Coed,
Merthyr Tydfil
(9) 5794 yards

Morlais Castle G.C.
(0685) 2822
Pant Dowlais,
Merthyr Tydfil
(9) 6356 yards

Mountain Ash G.C.
(0443) 472265
Cefnpennar
(18) 5535 yards

Mountain Lakes G.C.
(0222) 861128
Caerphilly
(18) 6815 yards

Pontypridd G.C.
(0443) 402359
Tygwyn Road,
Pontypridd
(18) 5650 yards

Pyle and Kenfig G.C.
(065671) 3093
Kenfig
(18) 6655 yards

Rhondda G.C.
(0443) 433204
Pontygwaith, Rhondda
(18) 6428 yards

Royal Porthcawl G.C.
(065671) 2251
Porthcawl
(18) 6691 yards

Southerndown G.C.
(0656) 880476
Ewenny, Bridgend
(18) 6615 yards

Whitehall G.C.
(0443) 740245
Nelson, Treharris
(9) 5750 yards

POWYS

Brecon G.C.
(0874) 2004
Llanfaes, Brecon
(9) 5218 yards

Builth Wells G.C.
(0982) 553296
Builth Wells
(9) 5458 yards

Cradoc G.C.
(0874) 3658
Penoyre Park, Cradoc
(18) 6318 yards

Llandrindod Wells G.C.
(0597) 2059
Llandrindod Wells
(18) 5759 yards

Machynlleth G.C.
(0654) 2000
Machynlleth
(9) 5734 yards

St Giles G.C.
(0686) 25844
Pool Road, Newtown
(9) 5864 yards

St Idloes G.C.
(05512) 2205
Penrhalt, Llanidloes
(9) 5210 yards

Welshpool G.C.
(0938) 3377
Golfa Hill, Welshpool
(18) 5708 yards

SOUTH GLAMORGAN

Brynhill G.C.
(0446) 733660
Port Road, Barry
(18) 6000 yards

Cardiff G.C.
(0222) 754772
Sherborne Avenue, Cyncoed,
Cardiff
(18) 6015 yards

Dinas Powis G.C.
(0222) 512727
Old High Walls, Dinas Powis
(18) 5377 yards

Glamorganshire G.C.
(0222) 701185
Lavernock Road, Penarth
(18) 6150 yards

Llanishen G.C.
(0222) 752205
Cwm-Lisvane, Cardiff
(18) 5296 yards

Radyr G.C.
(0222) 842408
Drysgol Road, Radyr
(18) 6031 yards

Wenvoe Castle G.C.
(0222) 594371
Wenvoe Castle, Cardiff
(18) 6411 yards

Whitchurch G.C.
(0222) 614660
Pantmawr Road,
Whitchurch,
Cardiff
(18) 6245 yards

WEST GLAMORGAN

Clyne G.C.
(0792) 401989
Owls Lodge Lane,
Mayals, Swansea
(18) 6312 yards

Fairwood Park G. & C.C.
(0792) 203648
Upper Killay, Swansea
(18) 6606 yards

Glynneath G.C.
(0639) 720679
Pontneathvaughan
(9) 5742 yards

Inco G.C.
(0792) 844216
Clydach, Swansea
(18) 5976 yards

Langland Bay G.C.
(0792) 66023
Langland Bay, Swansea
(18) 5812 yards

Morriston G.C.
(0792) 796528
Claremont Road, Morriston,
Swansea
(18) 5722 yards

Neath G.C.
(0639) 643615
Cadoxton, Neath
(18) 6460 yards

Palleg G.C.
(0639) 842524
Lower Cwmtwrch, Swansea
(9) 3209 yards

Pennard G.C.
(044128) 3131
Southgate Road, Southgate
(18) 6266 yards

Pontardawe G.C.
(0792) 863118
Cefn Llan, Pontardawe
(18) 6061 yards

Swansea Bay G.C.
(0792) 812198
Jersey Marine, Neath
(18) 6302 yards

Royal St David's

NORTHERN IRELAND

CO. ANTRIM

Ballycastle G.C.
(026) 5762536
Ballycastle
(18) 5902 yards

Ballyclare G.C.
(09603) 22051
Springvale Road, Ballyclare
(9) 6708 yards

Ballymena G.C.
(026) 6861487
Raceview Road, Ballymena
(18) 5168 yards

Bushfoot G.C.
(026) 5731317
Portballintrae, Bushmills
(9) 5572 yards

Cairndhu G.C.
(0574) 83324
Coast Road, Ballygally, Larne
(18) 6112 yards

Carrickfergus G.C.
(09603) 63713
North Road, Carrickfergus
(18) 5789 yards

Cushendall G.C.
(026) 6771318
Shore Road, Cushendall
(9) 4678 yards

Dunmurry G.C.
(0232) 621402
Dunmurry Lane, Dunmurry,
Belfast
(18) 5832 yards

Greenisland G.C.
(0232) 862236
Upper Road, Greenisland
(9) 5951 yards

Larne G.C.
(09603) 72043
Ferris Bay, Islandmagee,
Larne
(9) 6114 yards

Lisburn G.C.
(08462) 77216
Eglantine Road, Lisburn
(18) 6255 yards

Massereene G.C.
(08494) 62096
Lough Road, Antrim
(18) 6554 yards

Royal Portrush G.C.
(0265) 822311
Bushmills Road, Portrush
(18) 6810 yards (Dunluce)
(18) 6259 yards (Valley)

Whitehead G.C.
(09603) 72792
McCrae's Brae, Whitehead
(18) 6412 yards

CO. ARMAGH

County Armagh G.C.
(0861) 522501
Newry Road, Armagh
(18) 6184 yards

**Craigavon Golf &
Ski Centre**
(07622) 6606
Silverwood, Lurgan
(18) 6496 yards

Lurgan G.C.
(0762) 322087
Lurgan
(18) 6380 yards

Portadown G.C.
(0762) 335356
Carrickblacker, Portadown
(18) 6119 yards

Tandragee G.C.
(0762) 840727
Tandragee, Craigavon
(18) 6084 yards

BELFAST

Balmoral G.C.
(0232) 381514
Lisburn Road, Belfast
(18) 6250 yards

Belvoir Park G.C.
(0232) 491693
Newtown, Breda, Belfast
(18) 6476 yards

Cliftonville G.C.
(0232) 744158
Westland Road, Belfast
(9) 6240 yards

Fortwilliam G.C.
(0232) 771770
Downview Avenue, Belfast
(18) 5642 yards

The Knock G.C.
(02318) 3825
Summerfield, Dundonald,
Belfast
(18) 6292 yards

Malone G.C.
(0232) 612695
Upper Malone Road,
Dunmurry
(18) 6433 yards

Ormeau G.C.
(0232) 641069
Ravenhill Road, Belfast
(9) 5306 yards

Shandon Park G.C.
(0232) 797859
Shandon Park, Belfast
(18) 6252 yards

CO. DOWN

Ardglass G.C.
(0396) 841219
Castle Place, Ardglass
(18) 6500 yards

Banbridge G.C.
(08206) 22342
Huntly Road, Banbridge
(12) 5879 yards

Bangor G.C.
(0247) 270922
Broadway, Bangor
(18) 6450 yards

Carnalea G.C.
(0247) 270368
Carnalea
(18) 5513 yards

Clandeboye G.C.
(0247) 271767
Conlig, Newtownards
(18) 6650 yards (Dufferin)
(18) 5634 yards (Ava)

Donaghadee G.C.
(0237) 883624
Warren Road, Donaghadee
(18) 6099 yards

Downpatrick G.C.
(0396) 2152
Saul Road, Downpatrick
(18) 6196 yards

Helen's Bay G.C.
(0247) 852601
Helen's Bay, Bangor
(9) 5638 yards

Holywood G.C.
(02317) 2138
Nuns Walk, Demesne Road,
Holywood
(18) 5885 yards

Kilkeel G.C.
(069) 3762296
Mourne Park, Ballyardle
(9) 6000 yards

Kirkistown Castle G.C.
(02477) 71233
Cloughey, Newtownards
(18) 6157 yards

Mahee Island G.C.
(0238) 541234
Comber, Belfast
(9) 5580 yards

Royal Belfast G.C.
(0232) 428165
Holywood, Craigavad
(18) 6205 yards

Royal County Down G.C.
(03967) 23314
Newcastle
(18) 6692 yards
(18) 4100 yards

Scrabo G.C.
(0247) 812355
Scrabo Road,
Newtownards
(18) 6000 yards

The Spa G.C.
(0238) 562365
Grove Road, Ballynahinch
(9) 5770 yards

Warrenpoint G.C.
(06937) 73695
Lower Dromore Road,
Warrenpoint
(18) 6215 yards

CO. FERMANAGH

Enniskillen G.C.
(0365) 25250
Enniskillen
(18) 5476 yards

CO. LONDON-DERRY

Castlerock G.C.
(0265) 848314
Circular Road, Castlerock
(18) 6694 yards

City of Derry G.C.
(0504) 46369
Victoria Road, Londonderry
(18) 6362 yards (Prehen)
(9) 4708 yards (Dunhugh)

Kilrea G.C.
(026) 653 397
Drumagarner Road, Kilrea
(9) 4326 yards

Moyola Park G.C.
(0648) 68830
Shanemullagh, Castledawson
(18) 6517 yards

Portstewart G.C.
(026) 5832015
Strand Road, Portstewart
(18) 6784 yards (Strand)
(18) 4733 yards (Town)

CO. TYRONE

Dungannon G.C.
(08687) 22098
Mullaghmore, Dungannon
(18) 5914 yards

Fintona G.C.
(0662) 841480
Fintona
(9) 6250 yards

Killymoon G.C.
(06487) 62254
Killymoon, Cookstown
(18) 6000 yards

Newtownstewart G.C.
(06626) 61466
Golf Course Road,
Newtownstewart
(18) 6100 yards

Omagh G.C.
(0662) 3160
Dublin Road, Omagh
(18) 5800 yards

Strabane G.C.
(0504) 882271
Ballycolman, Strabane
(18) 6100 yards

Royal County Down

IRELAND

CO. CARLOW

Borris G.C.
(0503) 73143
Borris
(9) 6026 yards

Carlow G.C.
(0503) 31695
Carlow
(18) 6347 yards

CO. CAVAN

Belturbet G.C.
(049) 22287
Belturbet
(9) 5180 yards

Blacklion G.C.
(0017) 53024
Toam, Blacklion
(9) 6000 yards

County Cavan G.C.
(049) 31283
Drumelis
(18) 6037 yards

Virginia G.C.
(049) 44103
Virginia
(9) 4520 yards

CO. CLARE

Dromoland Castle G.C.
(061) 71144
Newmarket-on-Fergus
(9) 6098 yards

Ennis G.C.
(065) 24074
Drumbiggle Road, Ennis
(18) 5714 yards

Kilkee G.C.
(Kilkee) 48
East End, Kilkee
(9) 6058 yards

Kilrush G.C.
(Kilrush) 138
Parknamoney, Kilrush
(9) 5478 yards

Lahinch G.C.
(065) 81003
Lahinch
(18) 6515 yards (Championship)
(18) 5450 yards (Castle)

Shannon G.C.
(061) 61020
Shannon Airport
(18) 6480 yards

Spanish Point G.C.
(065) 84198
Miltow, Malbay
(9) 6248 yards

CO. CORK

Bandon G.C.
(023) 41111
Castlebernard, Bandon
(18) 6101 yards

Bantry G.C.
(027) 50579
Donemark, Bantry
(9) 6436 yards

Charleville G.C.
(063) 257
Charleville
(18) 6380 yards

Cobh G.C.
(021) 811372
Ballywilliam, Cobh
(9) 4800 yards

Cork G.C.
(021) 353451
Little Island
(18) 6600 yards

Doneraile G.C.
(022) 24137
Doneraile
(9) 5528 yards

Douglas G.C.
(021) 291086
Douglas
(18) 5651 yards

Dunmore G.C.
(023) 33352
Clonakilty, Dunmore
(9) 4180 yards

East Cork G.C.
(021) 631687
Gortacrue, Midleton
(18) 5602 yards

Fermoy G.C.
(025) 31472
Fermoy
(18) 5884 yards

Glengarriff G.C.
(027) 63150
Glengarriff
(9) 4328 yards

Kanturk G.C.
(029) 50181
Fairy Hill, Kanturk
(9) 5918 yards

Kinsale G.C.
(021) 772197
Ringnanean, Belgooly, Kinsale
(9) 5580 yards

Macroom G.C.
(026) 41072
Lackaduve, Macroom
(9) 5850 yards

Mallow G.C.
(022) 22465
Balleyellis, Mallow
(18) 6559 yards

Mitchelstown G.C.
(025) 24072
Gurrane, Mitchelstown
(9) 5550 yards

Monkstown G.C.
(021) 841225
Parkgarriffe, Monkstown
(18) 6000 yards

Muskerry G.C.
(021) 85297
Carrigrohane
(18) 6350 yards

Skibbereen G.C.
(028) 21227
Skibbereen
(9) 5890 yards

Youghal G.C.
(024) 2787
Knockaverry, Youghal
(18) 6206 yards

CO. DONEGAL

Ballybofey & Stranorlar G.C.
(074) 31093
Ballybofey
(18) 5913 yards

Ballyliffin G.C.
(077) 74417
Ballyliffin, Clonmany
(18) 6611 yards

Bundoran G.C.
(072) 41302
Great Northern Hotel, Bundoran
(18) 6328 yards

Donegal G.C.
(073) 34054
Murvagh, Donegal
(18) 6842 yards

Dunfanaghy G.C.
(074) 36238
Dunfanaghy
(18) 5572 yards

Greencastle G.C.
(077) 81013
Greencastle
(9) 2693 yards

Gweedore G.C.
(075) 31140
Derrybeg, Letterkenny
(9) 6234 yards

Letterkenny G.C.
(074) 21150
Barnhill, Letterkenny
(18) 6299 yards

Nairn & Portnoo G.C.
(075) 45107
Nairn & Portnoo
(18) 5950 yards

North West G.C.
(077) 61027
Lisfannon, Fahan
(18) 5895 yards

Otway G.C.
(074) 58319
Saltpans, Rathmullen
(9) 4134 yards

Portsalon G.C.
(074) 59102
Portsalon
(18) 5949 yards

Rosapenna G.C.
(074) 55301
Rosapenna
(18) 6254 yards

CO. DUBLIN

Balbriggan G.C.
(01) 412173
Blackhall, Balbriggan
(9) 5952 yards

Ballinascorney G.C.
(01) 512516
Ballinascorney
(18) 5500 yards

Beaverstown G.C.
(01) 436439
Beaverstown, Donabate
(18) 6000 yards

Beech Park G.C.
(01) 580522
Johnstown, Rathcoole
(18) 5600 yards

Corballis G.C.
(01) 450583
Donabate
(18) 4898 yards

Carrickmines G.C.
(01) 895 676
Carrickmines, Dublin
(9) 6044 yards

Castle G.C.
(01) 904207
Rathfarnham, Dublin
(18) 6240 yards

Clontarf G.C.
(01) 315085
Malahide Road, Dublin
(18) 5608 yards

Deerpark G.C.
(01) 322624
Deerpark Hotel, Howth
(18) 6647 yards

Donabate G.C.
(01) 436059
Balcarrick, Donabate
(18) 6187 yards

Dublin Sport G.C.
(01) 895418
Kilternan, Dublin
(18) 5413 yards

Dun Laoghaire G.C.
(01) 801055
Eglinton Park,
Dun Laoghaire,
Dublin
(18) 5950 yards

Edmonstown G.C.
(01) 931082
Rathfarnham, Dublin
(18) 6177 yards

Elm Park G.C.
(01) 693014
Donnybrook, Dublin
(18) 5485 yards

Forrest Little G.C.
(01) 401183
Cloghran
(18) 6400 yards

Foxrock G.C.
(01) 895668
Foxrock, Torquay Road,
Dublin
(9) 5699 metres

Grange G.C.
(01) 932832
Whitechurch, Rathfarnham,
Dublin
(18) 5517 yards

Hermitage G.C.
(01) 264549
Lucan
(18) 6000 yards

Howth G.C.
(01) 323055
Carrickbrae Road, Sutton,
Dublin
(18) 6168 yards

The Island G.C.
(01) 436205
Corballis, Donabate
(18) 6320 yards

Killiney G.C.
(01) 851983
Killiney
(9) 6201 yards

Lucan G.C.
(01) 280246
Lucan
(9) 6287 yards

Malahide G.C.
(01) 450248
Coast Road, Malahide
(9) 5568 yards

Milltown G.C.
(01) 976090
Lower Churchtown Road,
Dublin
(18) 6275 yards

Newlands G.C.
(01) 593157
Clondalkin, Dublin
(18) 6184 yards

Portmarnock G.C.
(01) 323082
Portmarnock
(18) 7103 yards

Rathfarnham G.C.
(01) 931201
Newtown, Dublin
(9) 6250 yards

Royal Dublin G.C.
(01) 336477
Bull Island, Dollymount,
Dublin
(18) 6858 yards

Rush G.C.
(01) 437548
Rush
(9) 5655 yards

St Anne's G.C.
(01) 336471
Bull Island, Dublin
(9) 6104 yards

Skerries G.C.
(01) 491204
Skerries
(18) 6300 yards

Slade Valley G.C.
(01) 582207
Lynch Park, Brittas
(18) 5800 yards

Woodbrook G.C.
(01) 824799
Bray
(18) 6541 yards

CO. GALWAY

Athenry G.C.
(091) 94466
Derrydonnell, Oranmore
(9) 5448 yards

Ballinasloe G.C.

(0905) 42126
Ballinasloe
(18) 5844 yards

Connemara G.C.

(095) 21153
Ballyconneely, Nr. Clifden
(18) 7100 yards

Galway G.C.

(091) 22169
Blackrock, Salthill
(18) 6193 yards

Gort G.C.

(091) 31336
Gort
(9) 5688 yards

Loughrea G.C.

(091) 41049
Loughrea
(9) 5798 yards

Mount Bellew G.C.

(0905) 79259
Mount Bellow
(9) 5564 yards

Oughterard G.C.

(091) 82131
Gurteeva, Oughterard
(9) 6356 yards

Portumna G.C.

(0509) 41059
Portumna
(9) 5776 yards

Tuam G.C.

(093) 24354
Barnacurragh, Tuam
(18) 6321 yards

CO. KERRY

Ballybunion G.C.

(068) 27146
Ballybunion
(18) 6529 yards (Old)
(18) 6477 yards (New)

Ceann Sibeal G.C.

(066) 51657
Ballyferriter, Tralee
(9) 6222 yards

Dooks G.C.

(066) 68205
Glenbeigh, Dooks
(18) 5850 yards

Kenmare G.C.

(064) 41291
Kenmare
(9) 5900 yards

**Killarney Golf
& Fishing Club**

(064) 31034
Mahony's Point, Killarney
(18) 6677 yards (Mahony's Point)
(18) 6798 yards (Killeen)

Parknasilla G.C.

(064) 45122
Parknasilla
(9) 5000 yards

Tralee G.C.

(066) 36379
West Barrow, Ardfert
(18) 6900 yards

Waterville G.C.

(0667) 4102
Waterville
(18) 7146 yards

CO. KILDARE

Athy G.C.

(0607) 31727
Geraldine, Athy
(9) 6158 yards

Bodenstown G.C.

(045) 97096
Bodenstown, Sallins
(18) 7031 yards

Cill Dara G.C.

(045) 21433
Cilldara, Kildare Town
(9) 6196 yards

Clongowes G.C.

(045) 68202
Clongowes Wood,
College Naas
(9) 5743 yards

Curragh G.C.

(045) 41238
Curragh
(18) 6565 yards

Naas G.C.

(045) 97509
Kerdiffstown, Naas
(9) 6233 yards

CO. KILKENNY

Callan G.C.

(056) 25136
Geraldine, Callan
(9) 5844 yards

Castlecomer G.C.

(056) 41139
Castlecomer
(9) 6985 yards

Kilkenny G.C.

(056) 22125
Glendine, Kilkenny
(18) 6374 yards

CO. LAOIS

Abbey Leix G.C.

(0502) 31450
Abbey Leix, Portlaoise
(9) 5680 yards

Heath G.C.

(0502) 46622
Portlaoise
(18) 6247 yards

Mountrath G.C.

(0502) 32558
Mountrath
(9) 5492 yards

Portarlington G.C.

(0502) 23115
Garryhinch, Portarlington
(9) 5700 yards

Rathdowney G.C.

(0505) 46170
Rathdowney
(9) 5416 yards

CO. LEITRIM

Ballinamore G.C.

(078) 44346
Ballinamore
(9) 5680 yards

Carrick-on-Shannon G.C.

(078) 20157
Carrick-on-Shannon
(9) 5922 yards

CO. LIMERICK

Adare Manor G.C.

(061) 86204
Adare
(9) 5430 yards

Castleroy G.C.

(061) 335753
Castleroy
(18) 6089 yards

Limerick G.C.

(061) 44083
Ballyclough, Limerick
(18) 5767 yards

Newcastle West G.C.

(069) 62015
Newcastle West
(9) 5482 yards

CO. LONGFORD

Co. Longford G.C.

(043) 46310
Dublin Road, Longford
(18) 6028 yards

CO. LOUTH

Ardee G.C.

(041) 53227
Town Parks, Ardee
(18) 5833 yards

County Louth G.C.

(041) 22329
Baltray, Drogheda
(18) 6728 yards

Ballybunion (Old Course)

Dundalk G.C.

(042) 21731
Blackrock, Dundalk
(18) 6740 yards

Greenore G.C.

(042) 73212
Greenore
(18) 6150 yards

CO. MAYO

Achill Island G.C.

(098) 43202
Keel, Achill Island
(9) 5420 yards

Ballina G.C.

(096) 21050
Mosgrove, Shanaghy, Ballina
(9) 5182 yards

Ballinrobe G.C.

(092) 41659
Ballinrobe
(9) 2895 yards

Ballyhaunis G.C.

(0907) 30014
Coolnaha, Ballyhaunis
(9) 5852 yards

Belmullet G.C.

(097) 81093
Belmullet, Balhina
(9) 5714 yards

Castlebar G.C.

(094) 21649
Rocklands, Castlebar
(18) 6109 yards

Claremorris G.C.

(094) 71527
Claremorris
(9) 5898 yards

Mulrany G.C.

(098) 36185
Mulrany, Westport
(9) 6380 yards

Swinford G.C.

(094) 51378
Swinford
(9) 5230 yards

Westport G.C.

(098) 25113
Carrowholly, Westport
(18) 6950 yards

CO. MEATH

Headfort G.C.

(046) 40148
Kells
(18) 6393 yards

Laytown & Bettystown G.C.

(041) 27534
Bettystown, Drogheda
(18) 6254 yards

Royal Tara G.C.

(046) 25244
Bellinter, Navan
(18) 6343 yards

Trim G.C.

(046) 31463
Newtownmoynagh, Trim
(9) 6266 yards

CO. MONAGHAN

Clones G.C.

(Scotshouse) 17
Hiton Park, Clone
(9) 550 yards

Nuremore G.C.
(042) 61438
Nuremore, Carrickmacross
(9) 6032 yards

Rossmore G.C.
(047) 81316
Rossmore Park, Monaghan
(9) 5859 yards

CO. OFFALY

Birr G.C.
(0509) 20082
The Glenns, Birr
(18) 6216 yards

Edenberry G.C.
(0405) 31072
Boherbree, Edenberry
(9) 5791 yards

Tullamore G.C.
(0506) 21439
Brookfield, Tullamore
(18) 6314 yards

CO. ROS-COMMON

Athlone G.C.
(0902) 2073
Hodson Bay, Athlone
(18) 6000 yards

Ballaghaderreen G.C.
(No tel.)
Ballaghaderreen
(9) 5686 yards

Boyle G.C.
(079) 62594
Roscommon Road, Boyle
(9) 5728 yards

Castlerea G.C.
(0907) 20068
Clonalis, Castlerea
(9) 5466 yards

Roscommon G.C.
(0903) 6382
Mote Park, Roscommon
(9) 6215 yards

CO. SLIGO

Ballymote G.C.
(071) 3460
Ballymote
(9) 5032 yards

County Sligo G.C.
(071) 77186
Rosses Point
(18) 6600 yards

Enniscrone G.C.
(096) 36297
Enniscrone
(18) 6511 yards

Strandhill G.C.
(071) 68188
Strandhill
(18) 5523 yards

CO. TIPPERARY

Cahir Park G.C.
(062) 41474
Kilcommon, Cahir
(9) 6262 yards

Carrick-on-Suir G.C.
(051) 40047
Garravoone, Garrick-on-Suir
(9) 5948 yards

Clonmel G.C.
(052) 21138
Lyreanearle, Clonmel
(18) 6330 yards

Nenagh G.C.
(067) 31476
Beechwood, Nenagh
(18) 5911 yards

Roscrea G.C.
(0505) 21130
Roscrea
(9) 6059 yards

Thurles G.C.
(0504) 21983
Thurles
(18) 6230 yards

Tipperary G.C.
(062) 51119
Rathanny, Tipperary
(9) 6074 yards

CO. WATERFORD

Dungarvon G.C.
(058) 41605
Ballinacourty, Dungarvan
(9) 6282 yards

Lismore G.C.
(058) 54026
Lismore
(9) 5460 yards

Tramore G.C.
(051) 81247
Tramore
(18) 6408 yards

Waterford G.C.
(051) 74182
Newrath, Waterford
(18) 6237 yards

CO. WESTMEATH

Moate G.C.
(0902) 31271
Moate
(9) 5348 yards

Mullingar G.C.
(044) 48629
Belvedere, Mullingar
(18) 6370 yards

CO. WEXFORD

Courtown G.C.
(055) 25166
Courtown Harbour, Gorey
(18) 6398 yards

Enniscorthy G.C.
(055) 33191
Knockmarshall, Enniscorthy
(9) 6220 yards

New Ross G.C.
(051) 21433
Tinneranny, New Ross
(9) 6102 yards

Rosslare G.C.
(053) 32113
Strand, Rosslare
(18) 6485 yards

Wexford G.C.
(053) 42238
Mulgannon, Wexford
(9) 6038 yards

CO. WICKLOW

Arklow G.C.
(0402) 32401
Arklow
(18) 5770 yards

Baltinglass G.C.
(0508) 81350
Baltinglass
(9) 6070 yards

Blainroe G.C.
(0404) 68168
Blainroe
(18) 6681 yards

Bray G.C.
(01) 862484
Ravenswell Road, Bray
(9) 6250 yards

Coollattin G.C.
(055) 29125
Coollattin, Shillelagh
(9) 5966 yards

Delgany G.C.
(0404) 874536
Delgany
(18) 5249 yards

Greystones G.C.
(01) 876624
Greystones
(18) 5900 yards

Wicklow G.C.
(0404) 67379
Dunbar Road, Wicklow
(9) 5536 yards

Woodenbridge G.C.
(0402) 5202
Arklow
(9) 6104 yards